LA LUCHA

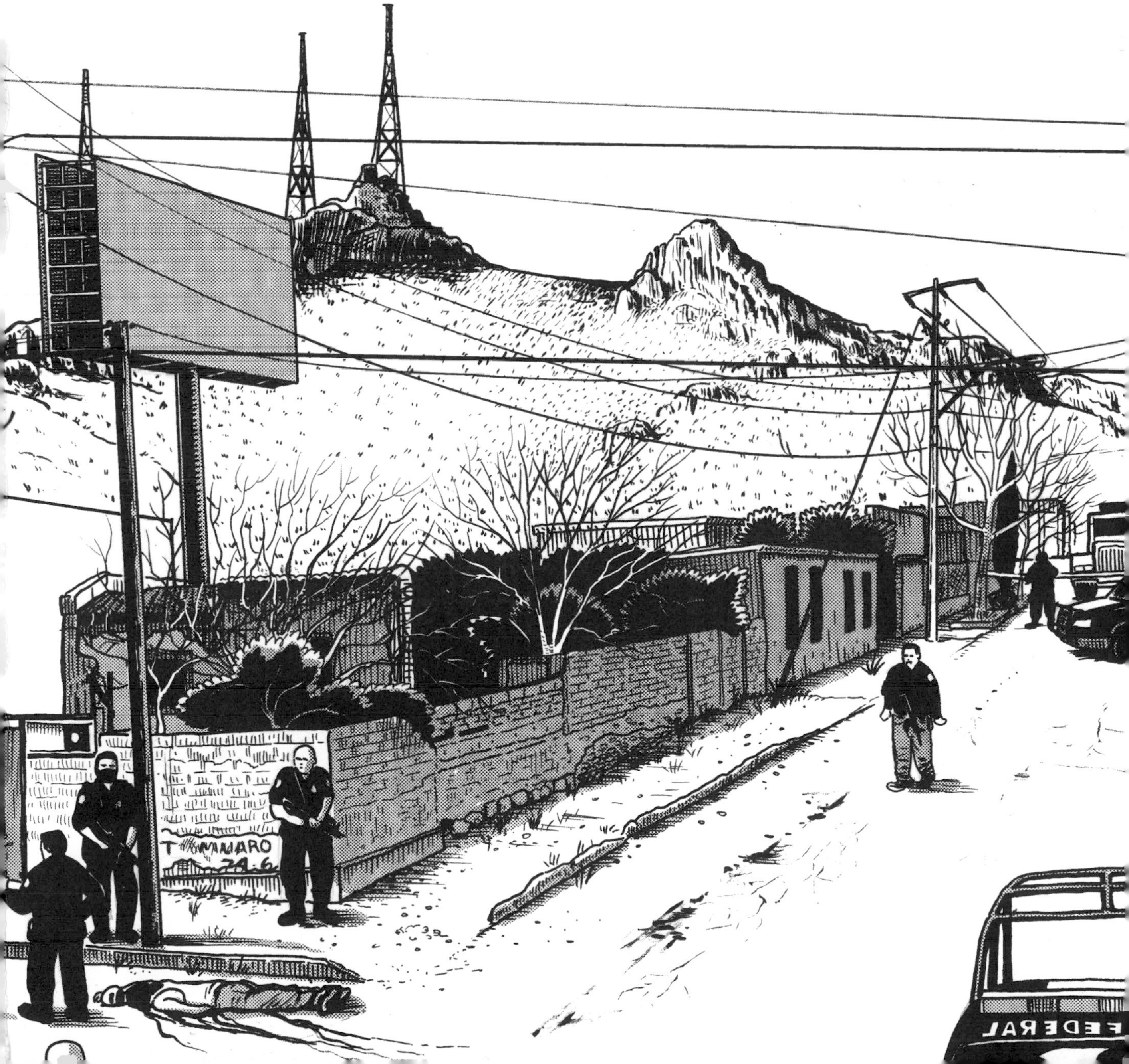

LA LUCHA

THE STORY OF LUCHA CASTRO
AND HUMAN RIGHTS IN MEXICO

JON SACK AND ADAM SHAPIRO

THE FRONT LINE DEFENDERS BOOK SERIES

FIRST PUBLISHED BY VERSO 2015
TEXT AND ARTWORK © JON SACK 2015
EDITED BY ADAM SHAPIRO
PREFACE © LUCHA CASTRO 2015
"A LETTER TO MY MOTHER" © LUIS JESÚS CASTRO 2015

1 3 5 7 9 10 8 6 4 2

VERSO
UK: 6 MEARD STREET, LONDON W1F 0EG
US: 20 JAY STREET, SUITE 1010, BROOKLYN, NY 11201
WWW.VERSOBOOKS.COM

VERSO IS THE IMPRINT OF NEW LEFT BOOKS

ISBN-13: 978-1-78168-801-4 (PB)
EISBN-13: 978-1-78168-802-1 (US)
EISBN-13: 978-1-78168-803-8 (UK)

BRITISH LIBRARY CATALOGUING IN PUBLICATION DATA
A CATALOGUE RECORD FOR THIS BOOK IS AVAILABLE FROM THE BRITISH
LIBRARY

LIBRARY OF CONGRESS CATALOGING-IN-PUBLICATION DATA
A CATALOG RECORD FOR THIS BOOK IS AVAILABLE FROM THE LIBRARY OF
CONGRESS

TYPESET MATERIAL AND DESIGN BY SEAN FORD, BROOKLYN, NY
PRINTED IN THE US BY MAPLE PRESS

CONTENTS

PREFACE BY LUCHA CASTRO   VII

A LETTER TO MY MOTHER BY LUIS JESÚS CASTRO   XIII

PROLOGUE   1

LUCHA AND GABINO   7

ALMA   27

MARISELA   31

NORMA   51

EMILIA   55

JOSEFINA   58

EPILOGUE   85

ABOUT LUCHA CASTRO   89

ABOUT FRONT LINE DEFENDERS   91

ABOUT THE CREATORS   94

ACKNOWLEDGMENTS   95

PREFACE

Seeing the way forward can be difficult when you receive death threat phone calls and the organisation you belong to, the Center for the Human Rights of Women—Centro de Derechos Humanos de las Mujeres—is under constant attack. When the highest court in the Americas, the Inter-American Court of Human Rights, decides to place you on its small and select list of beneficiaries of precautionary measures because your life is in danger; and when your close friends have been killed just for defending human rights. When you think about Marisela Escobedo, murdered in front of the Government Palace in Chihuahua for demanding justice; of Ismael Solorio and Manuela Solis, killed for defending the environment; or of Bety Cariño, murdered for defending indigenous communities and others.

Our voices are sometimes lost or silenced. The strength in our legs sometimes falters, and fear can paralyze us.

I would like to share a family story with you. Three years ago, I said goodbye to my son Luis Jesús. He was returning to the USA to finish his last year of college, and when we parted we hugged very tightly and we both promised to take care of ourselves, and, before leaving, I performed the ritual I always perform when one of my children goes away. I go to my prayer corner and I give them my blessing, which is the last image that they have of their home before leaving.

My son came back in from the doorway and I could see the fear in his eyes when he said, "I'm sure the military will not do anything to you, but to mess you up they could torture or kill me." And in a firm voice he told me, "Without being paranoid, let's make a plan until I am safe," and we invented a secret code so we could communicate by phone during the long four-hour journey by road to cross the border.

When my son left, I couldn't hold back the tears. How far had I taken my family down this human rights road?

This anecdote and many others that could fill a book are what make my work as a human rights defender painful. The risk I have placed my family under, the price I pay, is very high. My three daughters, my son, and my five grandchildren live far away from me. For security reasons I live apart from them, and not a day goes by without a longing seizing me, when I think that I will not be there when my grandchildren take their first steps or when they say their first word or have their birthday parties. To my grandchildren I am a stranger who visits each year to show them love for a few days and whom they hardly remember. Then I leave again with my soul shattered. I live in exile in my own country, fighting against the ghosts of homesickness. That's why I became a writer of tales and stories, sent to them to be read before bedtime, so that I could be in some way close to their lives.

I thank my family for understanding. My dear life companion, Luis, a wise, loving and kind man who lives and lets live. My daughters and son: Larissa, Liliana, Laura and Luis Jesús, the loveliest experiences of my life. My grandchildren: Sophia, Ana, Santiago, Juan Pablo and Eliza Sophia, whom I think about when I am immersed in the most terrible loneliness and fear. Just remembering them brings back my composure, and their presence gives me butterflies.

Whenever the danger escalates, the phone starts ringing. "Mum what are you doing there, come here, we can take care of you," and I tell them, fire fighters love their profession, they do not want to get burned, but when there is a fire they go out to fight it. The same goes for doctors, when there is a risk of an epidemic, they face the disease. In Chihuahua there is an epidemic of human rights violations. That's why I'm here.

In my organization, we started by defending human rights in gender-based crimes, that is to say femicide, traffick-

ing, domestic violence and sexual violence. Then the invisible victims of the war on drugs came knocking on our doors: mothers, daughters, sisters of the tortured, the forcibly disappeared, and human rights defenders under threat. In all modesty, we became the front line of Chihuahua.

Human rights defenders have always faced up to political and economic powers. However, there is now a new player that has increased the risks: namely organized crime working hand in hand with the police and military to implement mega-projects, with no qualms about threatening, torturing or murdering activists.

In the place where I work, there are areas where organized crime has supplanted the state with the complicity of the authorities, and where women and girls are the most vulnerable. I am talking about women from villages who are forced to coexist with criminal groups, and with the police and mili-

tary. Women walk in terror under the menacing gaze of men who are ready to fire their weapons, who would raid their homes or take their children as the spoils of war. In the logic of this armed conflict, it has become difficult to distinguish members of organized criminal gangs from the police, to the point that it is impossible to discern the perpetrators of attacks.

My life story is no greater than that of many readers. My walk between light and shadow as a human rights defender has deep, deep roots in the legacy left by my mother, grandmother, sisters, and other women in history with whom I share the dream of freedom.

I began to develop the ideals that drive my life when I was little ... well, I still am, but I mean little in age, not height. My schoolmates and I always wanted to know what was happening behind a huge wall that the nuns used to isolate us from the world and preserve our ignorance, which they called "innocence."

We organized ourselves so that we could discover what was happening outside the institutional limits that the nuns placed on us to control us and raise us as "respectable" girls. What followed was one of my first acts of rebellion, which I did not yet recognize as the defense of human rights. This is what we did: one of us would clasp our hands together as a platform so that another of the girls could climb up and tell us what was happening outside the walls. We called this maneuver "Operation Little Foot."

This image of solidarity and shared dreams of freedom has haunted me for life. Through this childhood game, I learned the importance of listening to and respecting the other's point of view, to wait for my turn with patience and excitement, to talk about the world from my own perspective, and also to feel good about being the "little-foot girl"—that's what we called the one girl who supported the other so she could see over the wall.

And so it was that years ago I decided to become a "little-foot girl" to many women, offering my hands, my arms, my lap, my voice, so that other women could learn that another world is possible, another world without violence.

I have held hands with hundreds of women in peaceful civil resistance to prevent evictions; I have offered my arms for hugs when suffering disrupts their lives. I have clasped my hands together as a little-foot girl so that women can climb up and reach their dreams of living a life free from violence, and have raised my voice so they can be heard.

On my way through law school as a young student, the seeds were planted in my heart, and from these seeds grew the strength and rebellion that still drives me today to long for a more just world.

At one stage in my life I was a successful entrepreneur whose business was drilling wells. However, while doing that job, a desire for a different world sprang into my heart, along with a rebellious impulse to search for alternatives in my personal life. That is to say, every day the belief grew stronger in me that I could not be part of inhumane structures that offered me a more-or-less comfortable living, as long as I forgot about those who were suffering.

I refused to cooperate further with a patriarchal and unjust system and changed the direction of my life. My search for answers to the question "What should I do in this world?" took me to a seminary in Chihuahua to study theology, and this new narrative had a profound effect on my life.

Of all the skins that I've covered my body with, the one that I feel best in is that of human rights defender. I have several simple ways to check whether the way of life I have chosen is best for me. The first is whether what I do makes me happy, and I have decided to accept that the day that ceases to be the case, I will look for another path. The second is by looking at my diary and reflecting on how I spend my life. Another way to assess my path in life is to drink from the wisdom of women in history. One in particular, the Bible story of Mary of Bethany, is my favorite because it reminds me of this commitment to myself to choose the better path.

Life is full of choices, and the defense of human rights has been my best choice. It fills my heart and I chose it by listening to my inner voice, because that is what reconciles me with my needs. I know I can be wrong, I cannot win everything, but I cannot lose it all either. I am happy to have lived by my own choice despite the risks.

In my journey as a defender, I have learned to listen to the stories of women who suffer violations of their human rights, with compassion and a reverence that compels me to respect their lives. I am convinced that it is through acts of love and justice that we can proclaim the scandal of all the unjust acts imposed on women, represented by all forms of violence, many of them hidden. By empowering women we can encourage them to rebuild their lives.

Finally, I am still here, and I would like to repeat the words of my dear friend Bety Cariño, who I once heard saying, at the last public event before she was killed, a Front Line Defenders event to which we were both invited, "We denounce human rights violations so that we do not forget, to preserve historical memory in the heads and hearts of the torturers who burn down our houses, threaten us, rape, disappear and murder our children."

—Lucha Castro,
Chihuahua, Mexico

A LETTER TO MY MOTHER

Dear Mum,

I am really happy and hugely proud that the Spanish Association for Human Rights is recognizing your career and your professional-personal achievements. I just invented that term, but it doesn't matter, that's what it is.

Because through your work over the last ten to fifteen years (first defending the constitutional right to decent housing, then seeking justice for murdered girls, and now supporting women survivors of sexual violence) I have been able to witness the fact that defending human rights is not a nine-to-five job but rather a way of life.

You have always pushed yourself forward using your genuinely selfless and hugely noble strength, passion, and empathy. A strength that I secretly fear I may never be able to understand, because all the tragicomic and horrific stories that I have heard from you and Laura, nestled and cradled in Chihuahua, have made me feel skeptical toward people in general and the way in which they often treat each other.

I am glad they are flying you to Madrid. It will give you a chance to relax, see our cousin Karla, and Larissa and her family. Aside from the prestige, applause and smiles of approval, this will serve as a way for you to rest and recover from the heavy weight that defending the rights of people brings with it.

All the sleepless nights, all the articles, books, trials, all the reading and rereading websites, the lengthy meetings and missed mealtimes, the interviews and travel, dealing with petty politicians, media questions, insults, undignified slurs and death threats.

None of these pains and torments can be compared to the harassment, beatings, rape, kidnappings of children, and murders suffered by all the women (and families) who have approached the Center for the Human Rights of Women (Centro de Derechos Humanos de las Mujeres) for help.

This has been your vocation. It is what fulfills you and makes you get up in the morning. However, while on one hand this gives me courage, it also makes me a little sad. Due to this work, I have seen you go through a metamorphosis.

The mum I remember many years ago—confident, extremely cheerful, the happiness of her children and sisters her only worries—has turned into a woman who is constantly nervous, less confrontational (in discussions),

apprehensive, slightly worn out and overly sensitive—unable to see a Bruce Willis movie without covering your eyes "because it's so violent."

But not all the changes in the revolution you have undergone in your life have been "negative." Your character has become enviable. You have skills that would be much sought after on Wall Street—getting funding in Latin America for a human rights NGO is like teaching a pig to fly.

You have developed a Che-Guevaran integrity: unshakably ethical and built around non-negotiable ideals. You have been cited in bibliographic references, featured in YouTube videos, and been the recipient of countless thanks, acknowledgments, prayers, and favors from the people you've helped.

Gradually, the mum I remember from my childhood memories has conquered her fears, her limitations, and especially, her dreams.

I remember when I was about eight or ten years old and we were traveling somewhere by plane. You had a genuine fear of flying and you were crossing yourself the whole time. Now you have more frequent flyer miles than the entire family put together. You've become not only an expert in the law, but also a pioneer, helping to restructure the archaic judicial system in our country.

You have rubbed shoulders with intellectuals, journalists, artists, and leaders; you are always connected, technologically speaking, answering emails, preparing PowerPoints and press releases, all done with that Blackberry in your hand that keeps my dad awake at night.

It sounds a bit redundant but here it is anyway: the work you do makes the world a better place to live in. And I can't think of a better reason to be alive than that.

Congratulations! And I love you.

—Luis Jesús

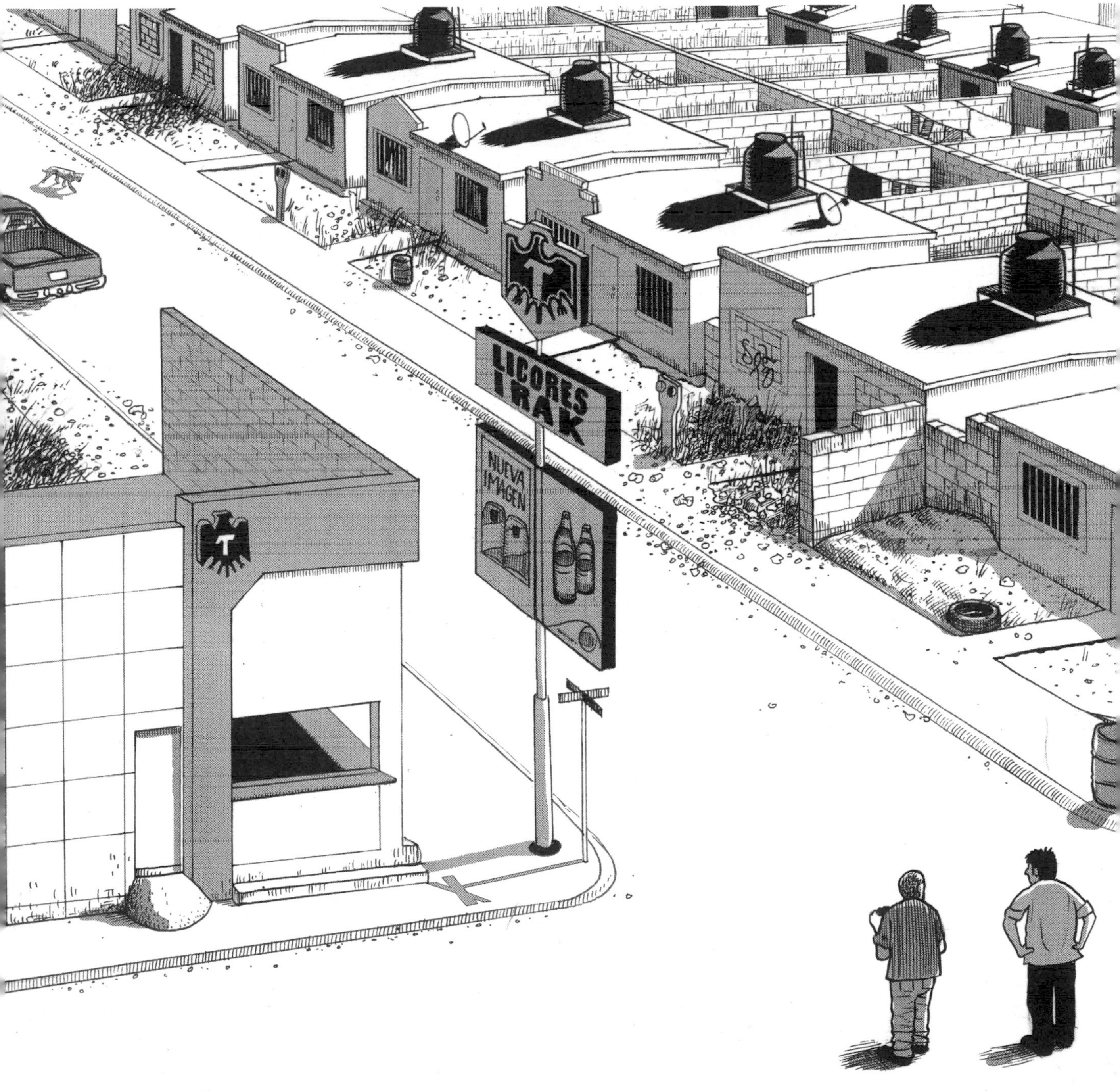
LICORES IRAK
NUEVA IMAGEN

prologue

A Conversation at the Border

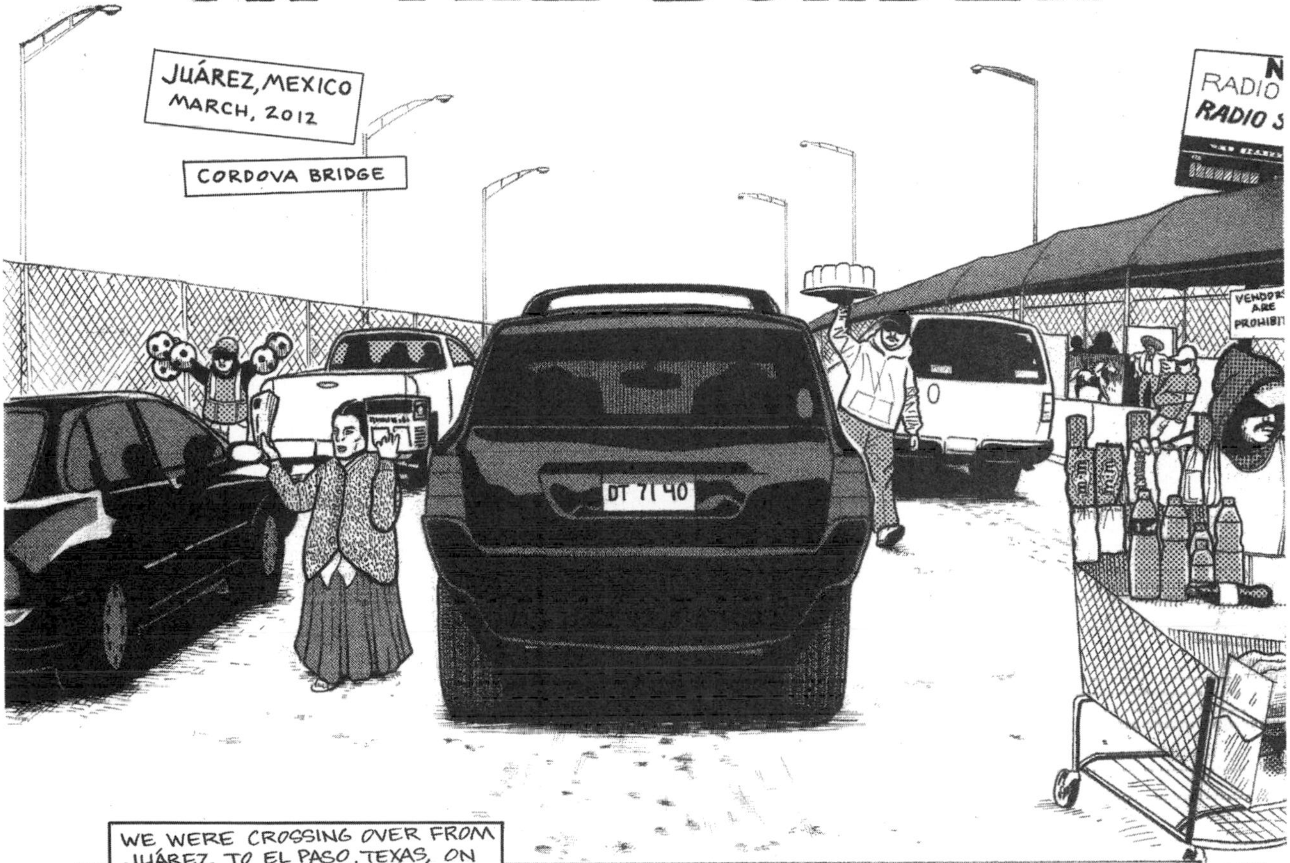
JUÁREZ, MEXICO
MARCH, 2012
CORDOVA BRIDGE

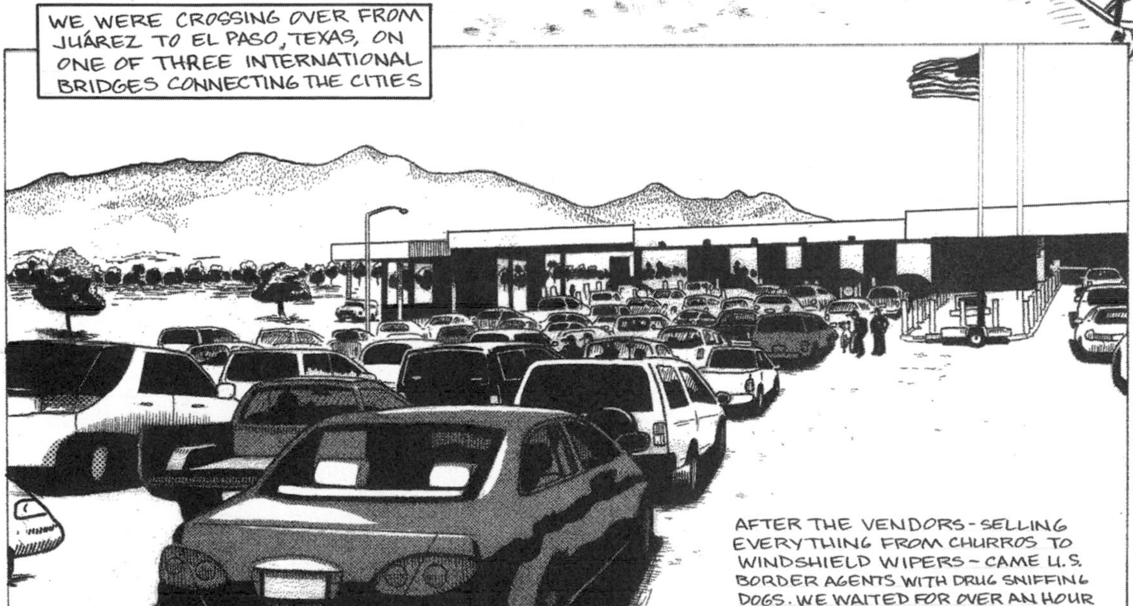
WE WERE CROSSING OVER FROM JUÁREZ TO EL PASO, TEXAS, ON ONE OF THREE INTERNATIONAL BRIDGES CONNECTING THE CITIES
AFTER THE VENDORS - SELLING EVERYTHING FROM CHURROS TO WINDSHIELD WIPERS - CAME U.S. BORDER AGENTS WITH DRUG SNIFFING DOGS. WE WAITED FOR OVER AN HOUR

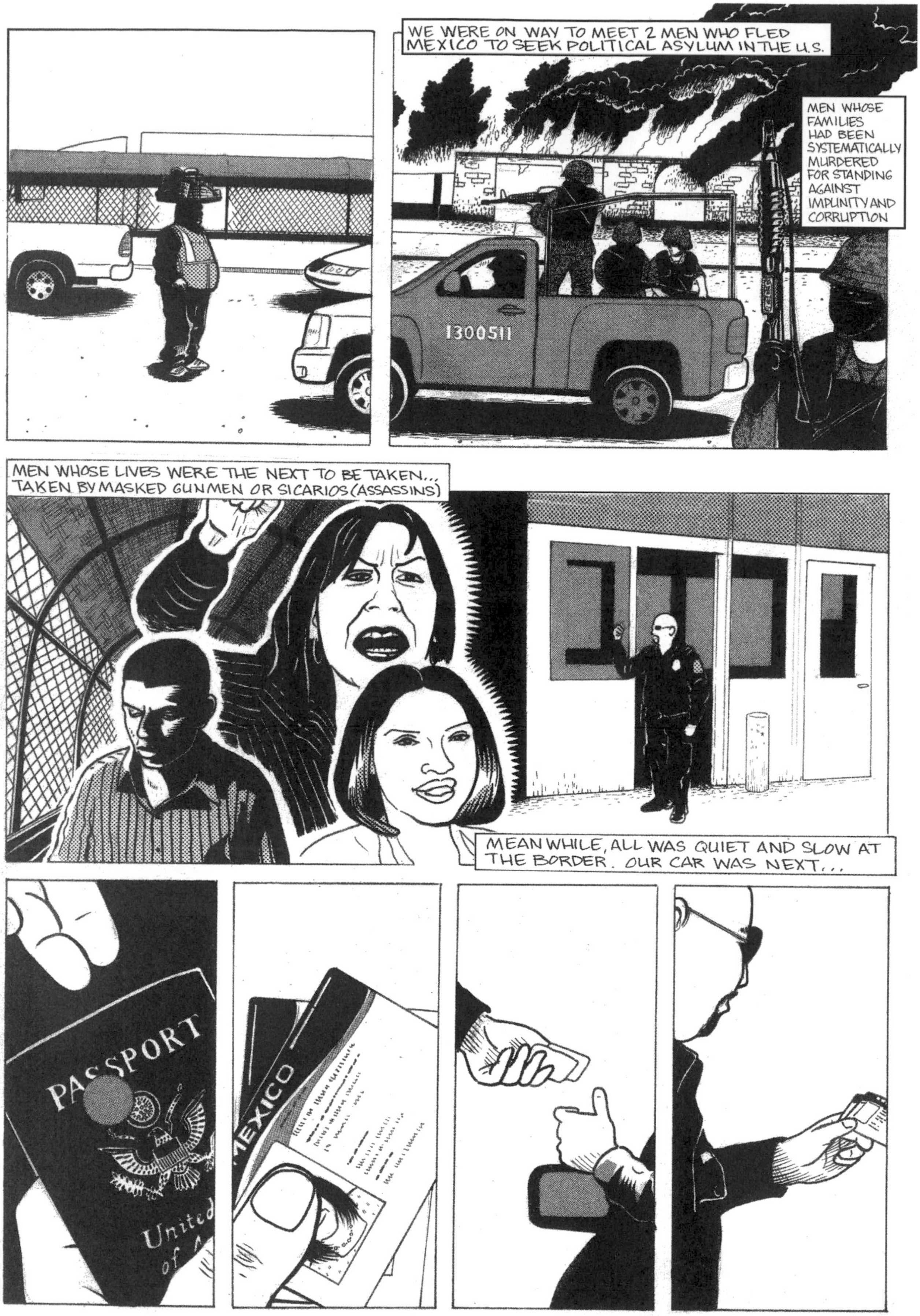
WE WERE ON WAY TO MEET 2 MEN WHO FLED MEXICO TO SEEK POLITICAL ASYLUM IN THE U.S.
MEN WHOSE FAMILIES HAD BEEN SYSTEMATICALLY MURDERED FOR STANDING AGAINST IMPUNITY AND CORRUPTION
1300511
MEN WHOSE LIVES WERE THE NEXT TO BE TAKEN... TAKEN BY MASKED GUNMEN OR SICARIOS (ASSASSINS)
MEANWHILE, ALL WAS QUIET AND SLOW AT THE BORDER. OUR CAR WAS NEXT...
PASSPORT
MEXICO

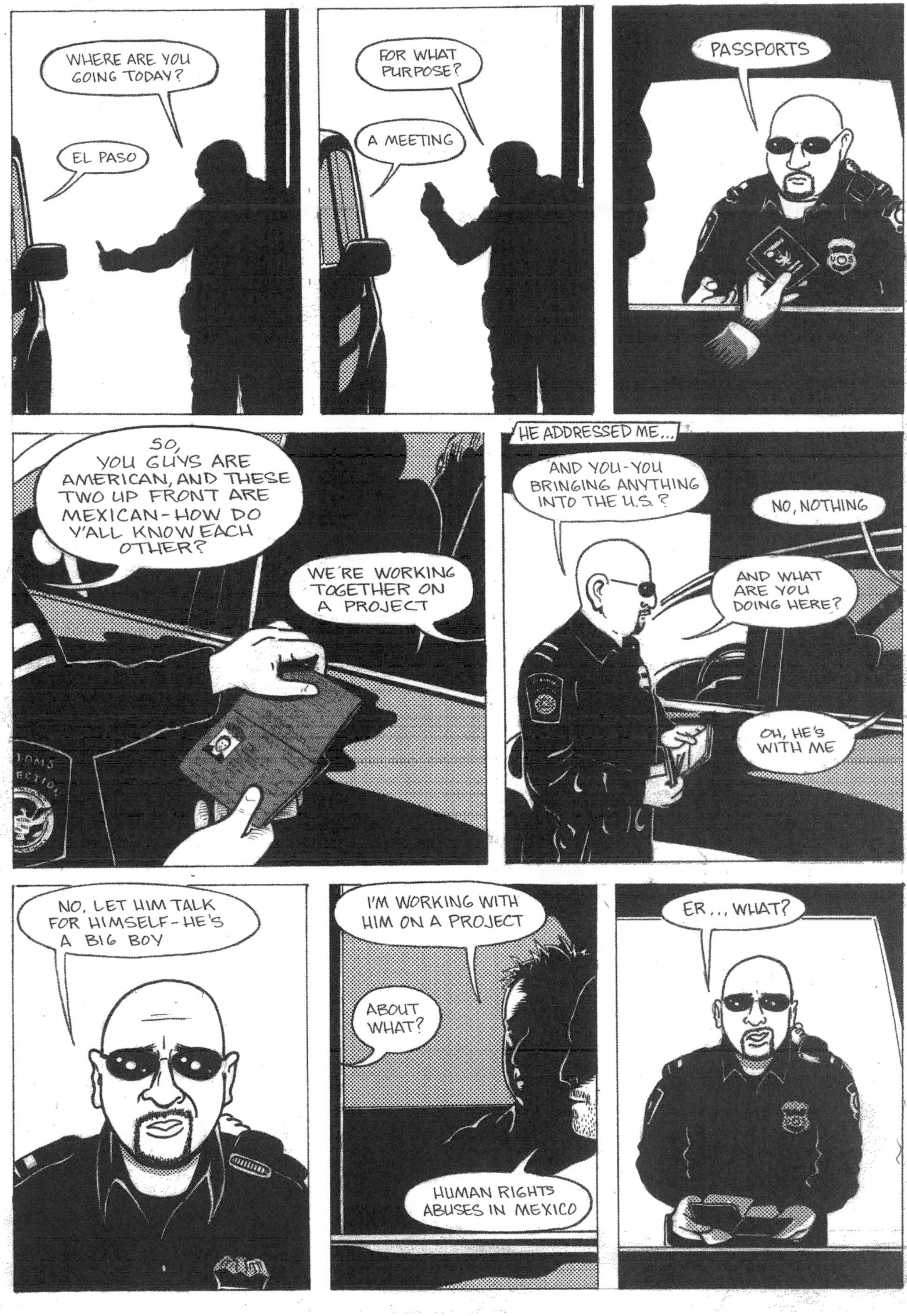
WHERE ARE YOU GOING TODAY?
EL PASO
FOR WHAT PURPOSE?
A MEETING
PASSPORTS
SO, YOU GUYS ARE AMERICAN, AND THESE TWO UP FRONT ARE MEXICAN- HOW DO Y'ALL KNOW EACH OTHER?
WE'RE WORKING TOGETHER ON A PROJECT
HE ADDRESSED ME...
AND YOU- YOU BRINGING ANYTHING INTO THE U.S.?
NO, NOTHING
AND WHAT ARE YOU DOING HERE?
OH, HE'S WITH ME
NO, LET HIM TALK FOR HIMSELF- HE'S A BIG BOY
I'M WORKING WITH HIM ON A PROJECT
ABOUT WHAT?
HUMAN RIGHTS ABUSES IN MEXICO
ER... WHAT?

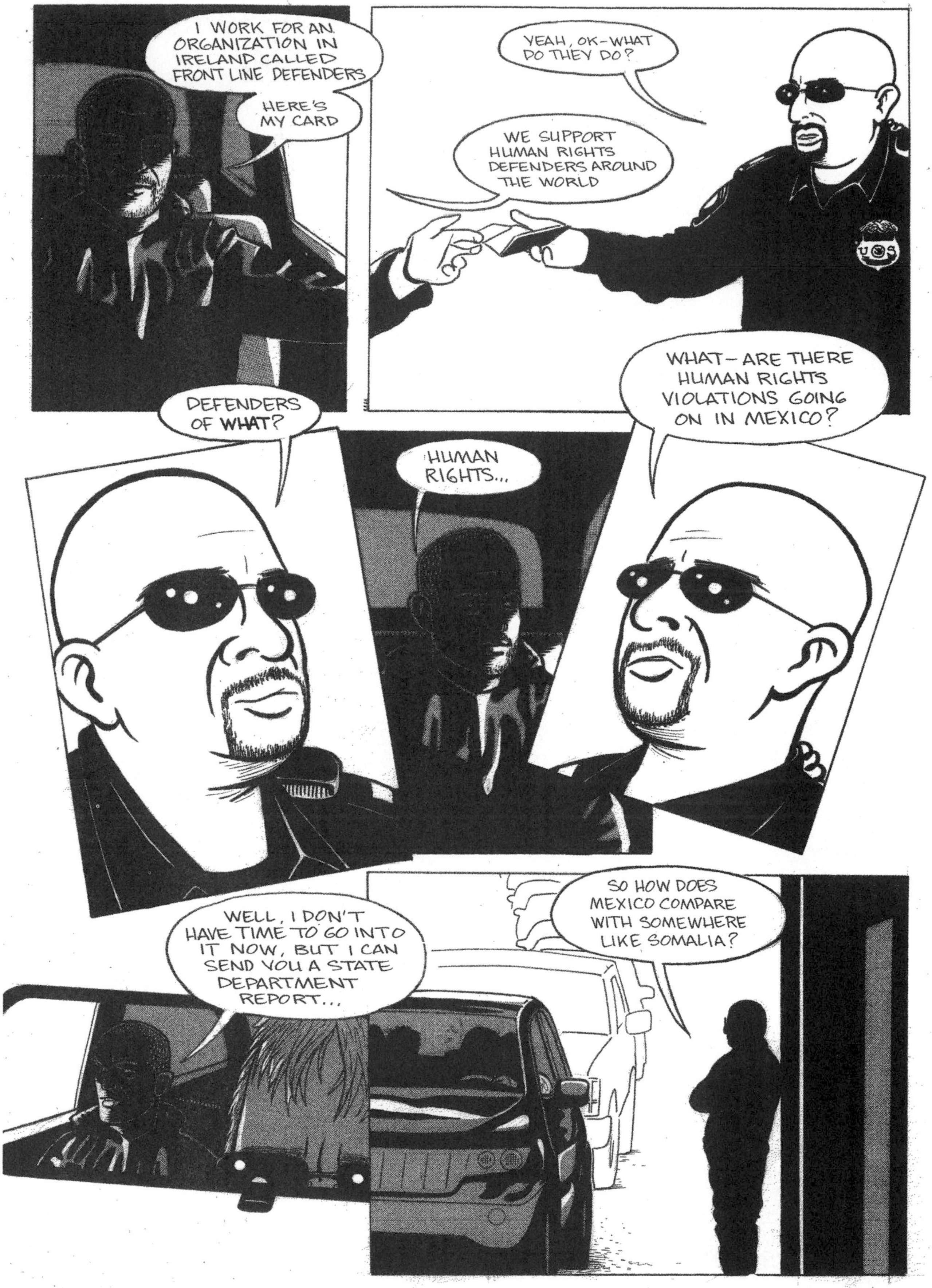
I WORK FOR AN ORGANIZATION IN IRELAND CALLED FRONT LINE DEFENDERS
HERE'S MY CARD
YEAH, OK-WHAT DO THEY DO?
WE SUPPORT HUMAN RIGHTS DEFENDERS AROUND THE WORLD
DEFENDERS OF WHAT?
HUMAN RIGHTS...
WHAT- ARE THERE HUMAN RIGHTS VIOLATIONS GOING ON IN MEXICO?
WELL, I DON'T HAVE TIME TO GO INTO IT NOW, BUT I CAN SEND YOU A STATE DEPARTMENT REPORT...
SO HOW DOES MEXICO COMPARE WITH SOMEWHERE LIKE SOMALIA?

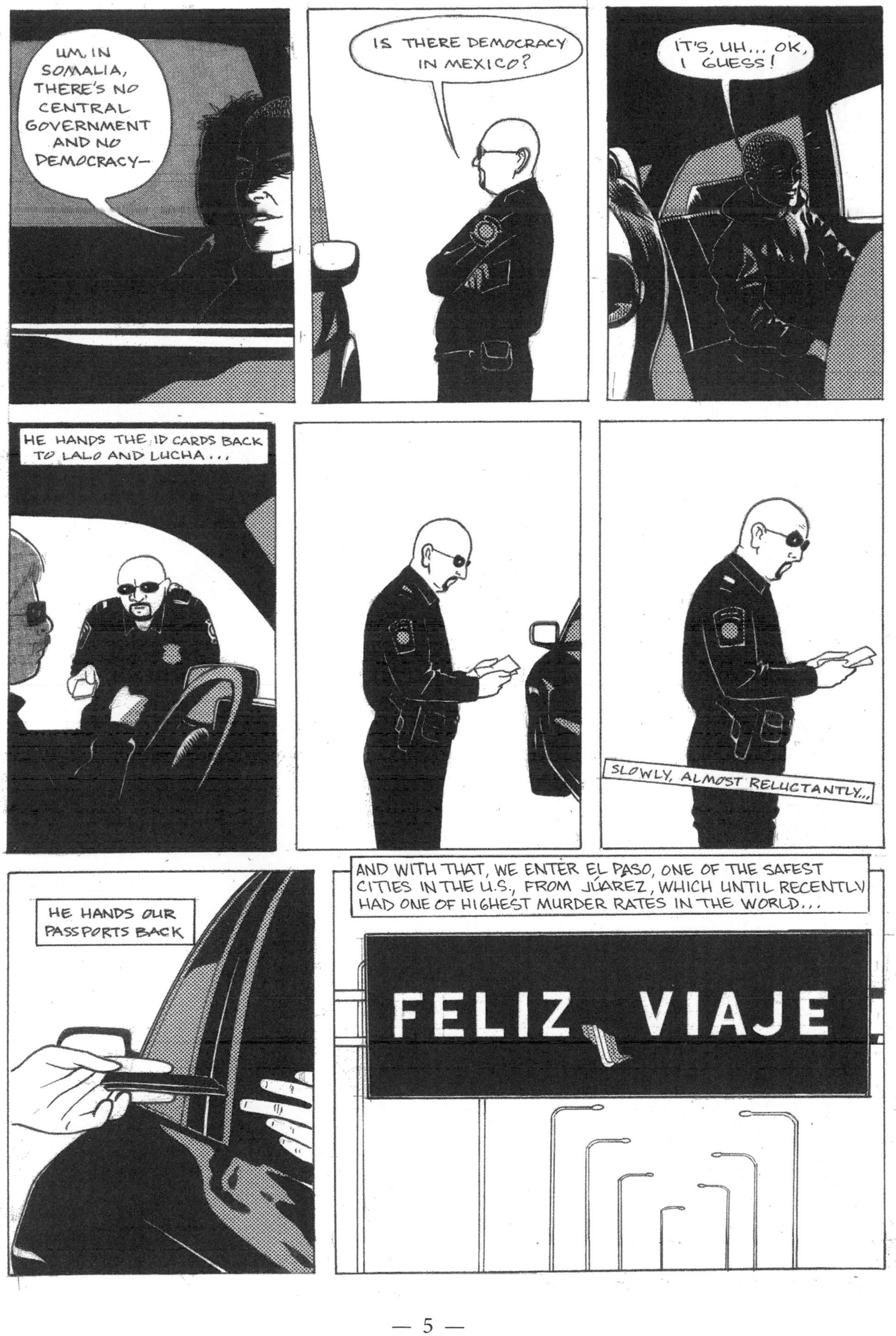
UM, IN SOMALIA, THERE'S NO CENTRAL GOVERNMENT AND NO DEMOCRACY—
IS THERE DEMOCRACY IN MEXICO?
IT'S, UH... OK, I GUESS!
HE HANDS THE ID CARDS BACK TO LALO AND LUCHA...
SLOWLY, ALMOST RELUCTANTLY...
HE HANDS OUR PASSPORTS BACK
AND WITH THAT, WE ENTER EL PASO, ONE OF THE SAFEST CITIES IN THE U.S., FROM JÚAREZ, WHICH UNTIL RECENTLY HAD ONE OF HIGHEST MURDER RATES IN THE WORLD...
FELIZ VIAJE

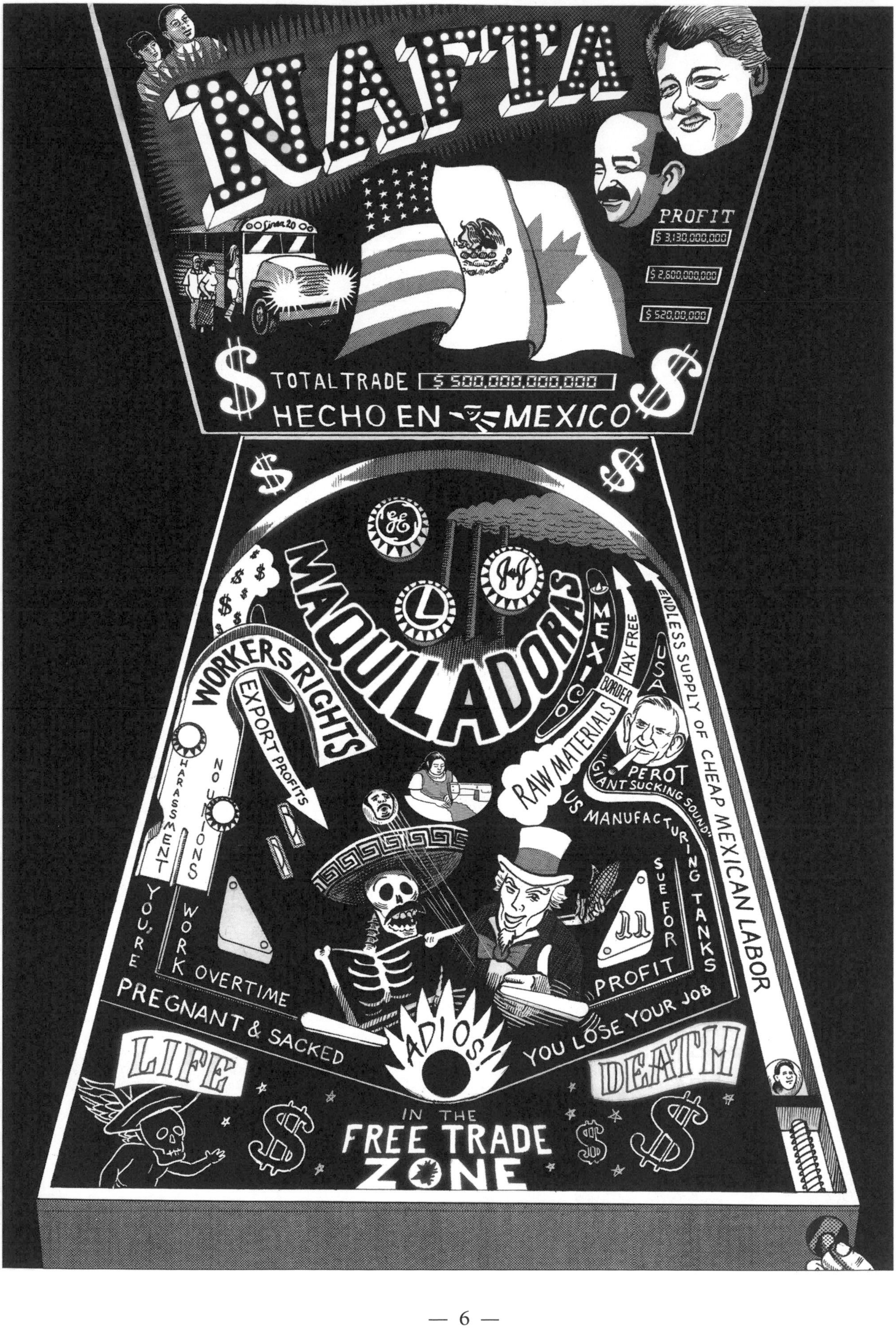
NAFTA
PROFIT
$ 3,130,000,000
$ 2,600,000,000
$ 520,00,000
TOTAL TRADE $ 500,000,000,000
HECHO EN MEXICO
MAQUILADORAS
WORKERS RIGHTS
EXPORT PROFITS
HARASSMENT
NO UNIONS
MEXICO
USA
BORDER
TAX FREE
RAW MATERIALS
ENDLESS SUPPLY OF CHEAP MEXICAN LABOR
PEROT
"GIANT SUCKING SOUND"
US MANUFACTURING
SUE FOR PROFIT
TANKS
YOU'RE
WORK
OVERTIME
PREGNANT & SACKED
ADIOS!
YOU LOSE YOUR JOB
LIFE
DEATH
IN THE
FREE TRADE
ZONE

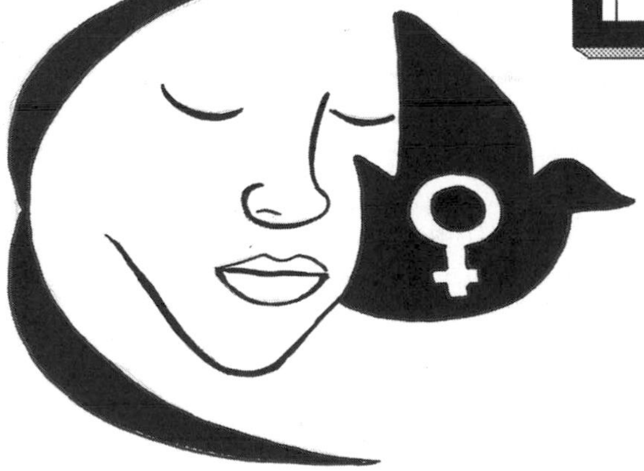

LUCHA AND GABINO

WHY JUÁREZ?

IN THE LAST DECADE, THE ENDEMIC AND SOARING VIOLENCE IN JUÁREZ HAS RECEIVED MASSIVE MEDIA ATTENTION— SO WHY FOCUS ON CIUDAD JUÁREZ AGAIN?

Two Drug Slay Rock U.S. Cons

LA UNIÓN, Mexico - Gun

town of Ciudad Juare

The Washington Post

10 killed in massacre near Mexican city of Ciudad Juarez
September 23, 2013

CIUDA EZ Mexico — A gunman burst into a

home   where people were

cele   lled 10

JENNIFER LOPEZ   MARTIN SHEEN
BORDERTOWN

LIES CORRUPTION MURDER

El Diario

Ejecutan a ot

Hallan los cuerpos en una camioneta en la Diaz Ordaz

Fueron encontrados adentro de una Lobo, color negro, con varios impactos

El Diario
25 AÑOS

Matan a fotógrafo d El Diario de Juáre

us Carlos Santiago rde la vida de era instantanea l lugar de los

The Seattle Times
April 26, 2012
MOVIE REVIEW

'Murder Capital of The World': Sober War

A review of "Murder Capital of the sobering account of drug car in Juárez, Mexico, incl

Padre e hijo son ejecutados en Chihuahua

AFTER ALL, THERE AREN'T BOMBS AND MISSILES FALLING ON PEOPLES' HOUSES...

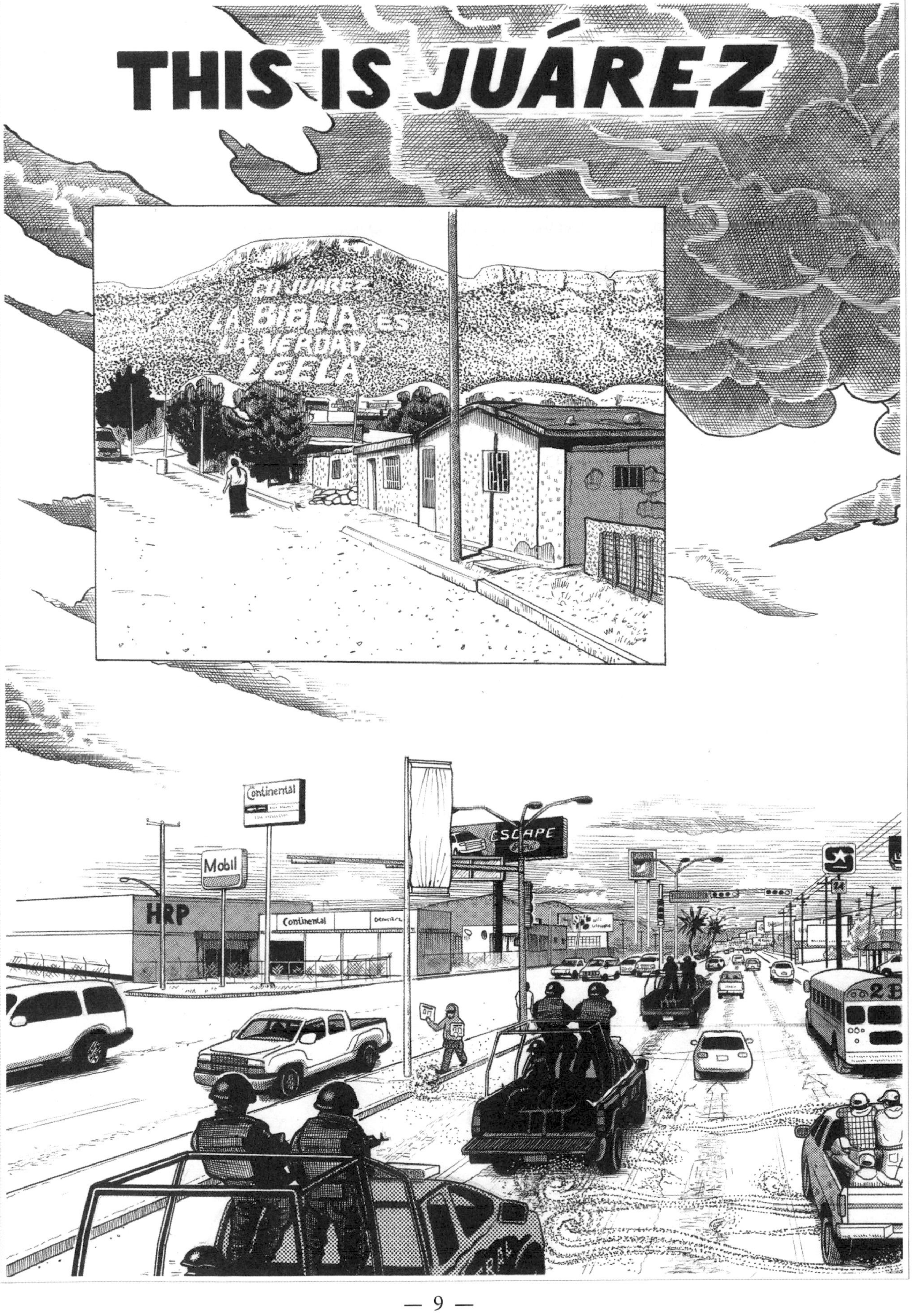
THIS IS JUÁREZ
CD JUAREZ
LA BIBLIA ES LA VERDAD LEELA
Continental
Mobil
HRP
Continental
ESCAPE

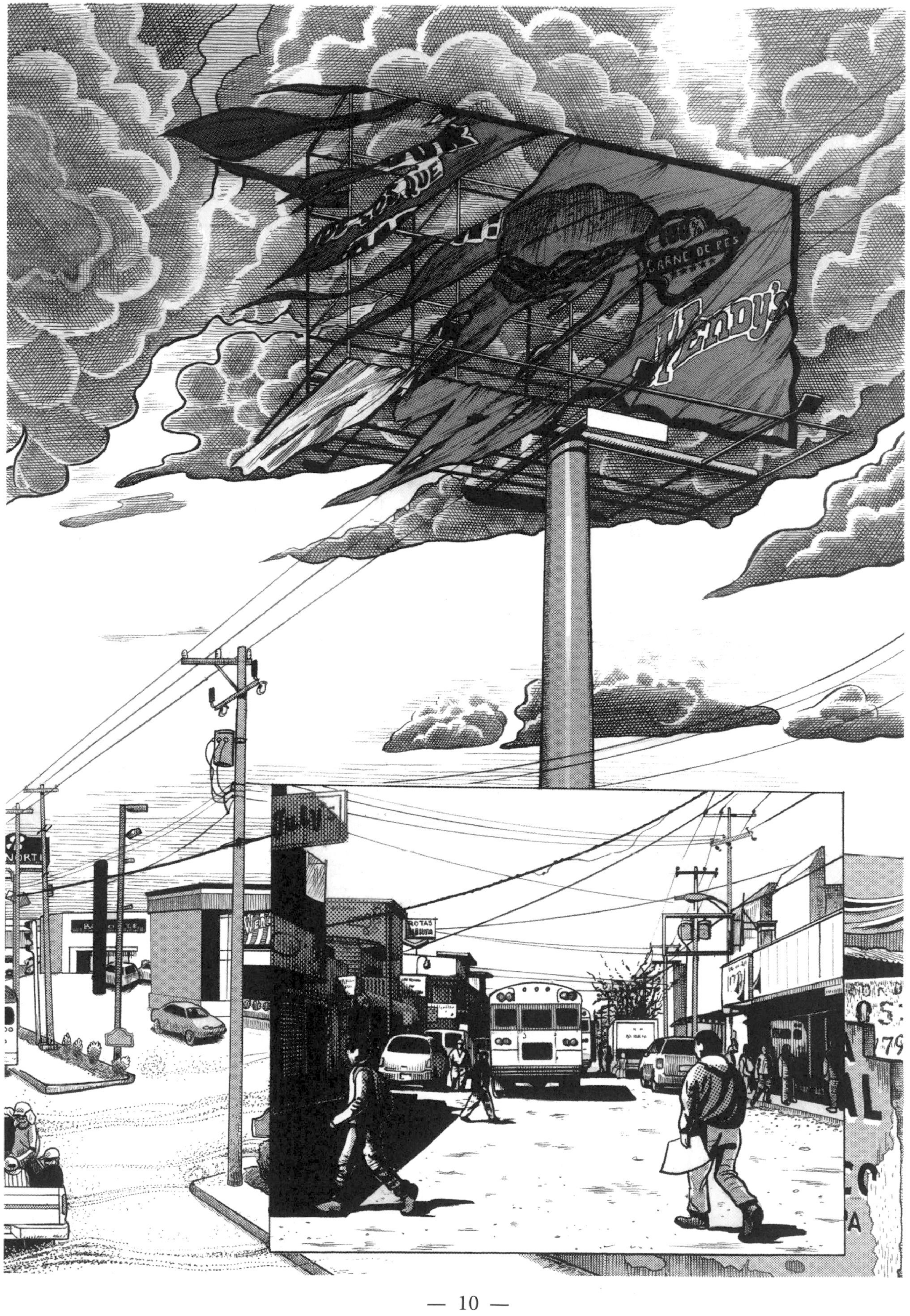
CARNE DE RES

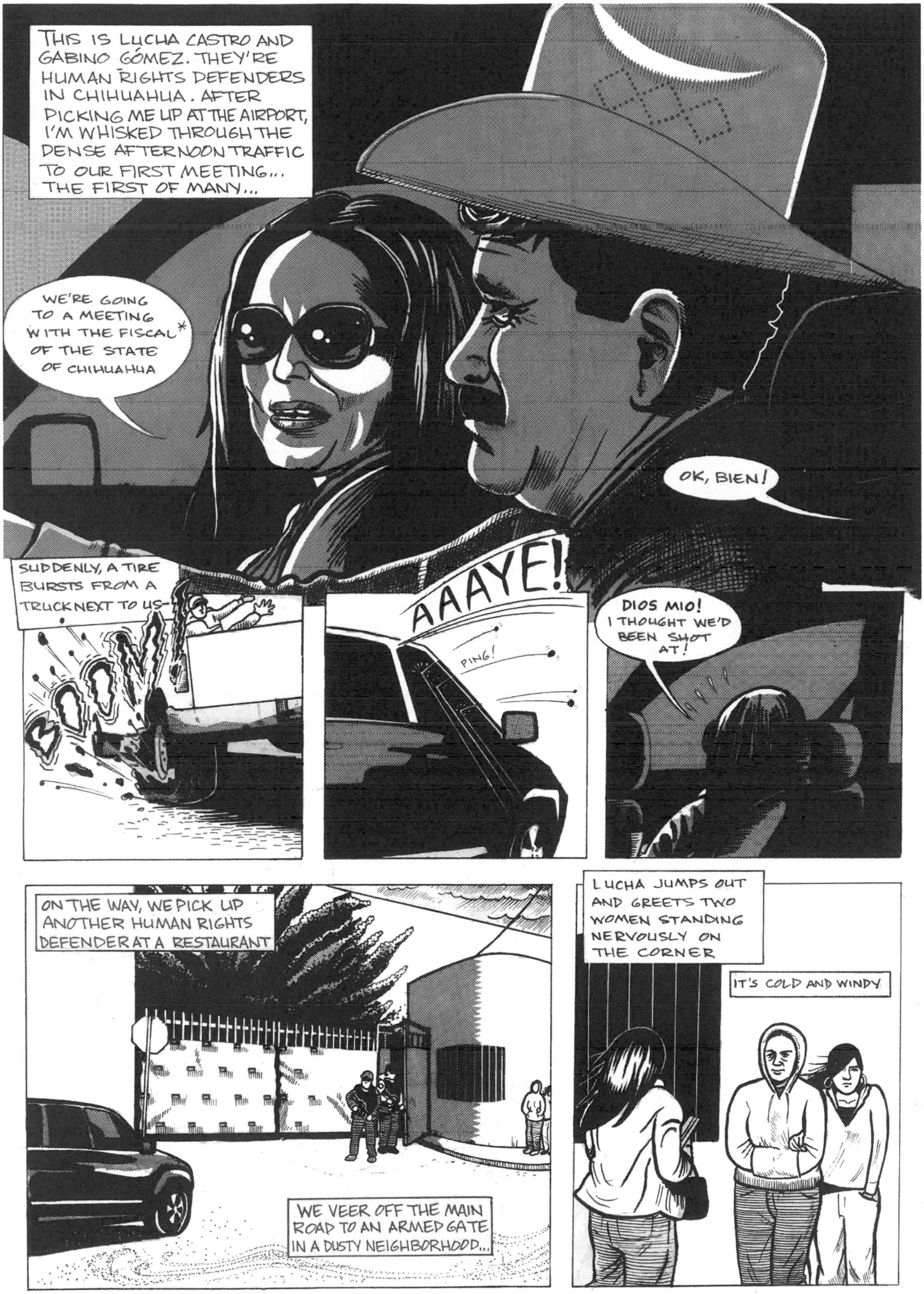
THIS IS LUCHA CASTRO AND GABINO GÓMEZ. THEY'RE HUMAN RIGHTS DEFENDERS IN CHIHUAHUA. AFTER PICKING ME UP AT THE AIRPORT, I'M WHISKED THROUGH THE DENSE AFTERNOON TRAFFIC TO OUR FIRST MEETING... THE FIRST OF MANY...
WE'RE GOING TO A MEETING WITH THE FISCAL* OF THE STATE OF CHIHUAHUA
OK, BIEN!
SUDDENLY, A TIRE BURSTS FROM A TRUCK NEXT TO US–
BOOM
AAAYE!
PING!
DIOS MIO! I THOUGHT WE'D BEEN SHOT AT!
ON THE WAY, WE PICK UP ANOTHER HUMAN RIGHTS DEFENDER AT A RESTAURANT
WE VEER OFF THE MAIN ROAD TO AN ARMED GATE IN A DUSTY NEIGHBORHOOD...
LUCHA JUMPS OUT AND GREETS TWO WOMEN STANDING NERVOUSLY ON THE CORNER
IT'S COLD AND WINDY

* ATTORNEY GENERAL

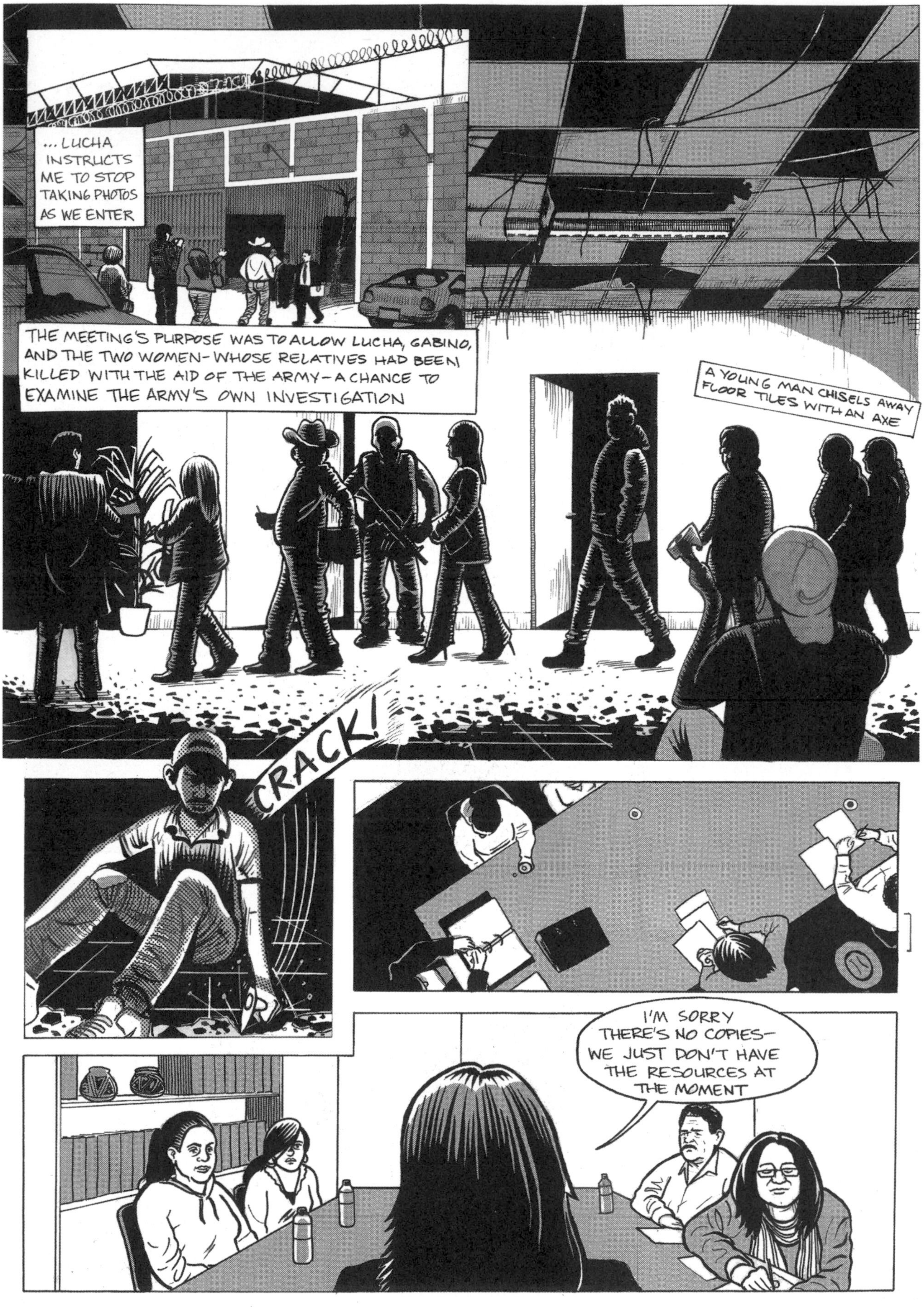
...LUCHA INSTRUCTS ME TO STOP TAKING PHOTOS AS WE ENTER
THE MEETING'S PURPOSE WAS TO ALLOW LUCHA, GABINO, AND THE TWO WOMEN- WHOSE RELATIVES HAD BEEN KILLED WITH THE AID OF THE ARMY- A CHANCE TO EXAMINE THE ARMY'S OWN INVESTIGATION
A YOUNG MAN CHISELS AWAY FLOOR TILES WITH AN AXE
CRACK!
I'M SORRY THERE'S NO COPIES- WE JUST DON'T HAVE THE RESOURCES AT THE MOMENT

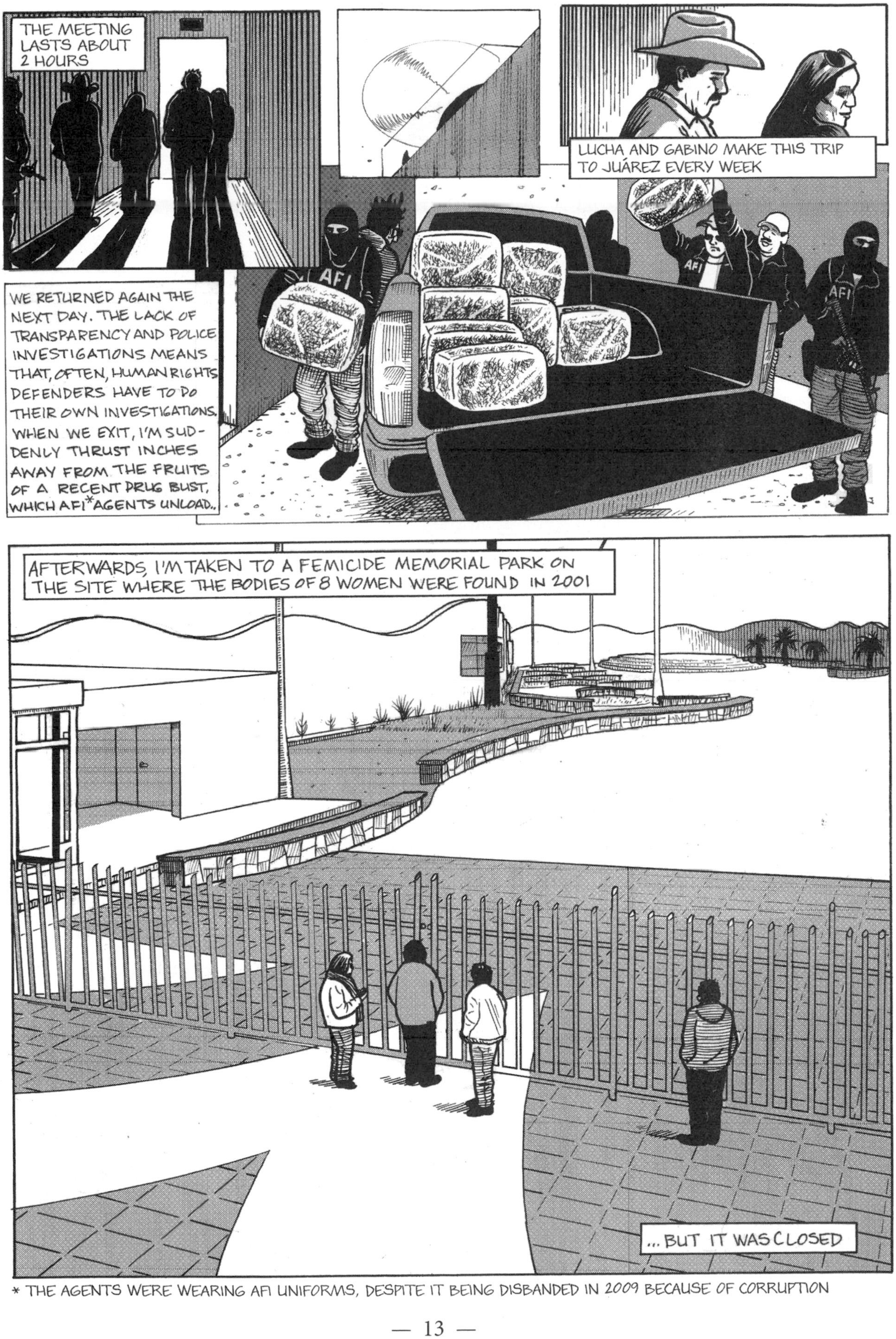
THE MEETING LASTS ABOUT 2 HOURS
LUCHA AND GABINO MAKE THIS TRIP TO JUÁREZ EVERY WEEK
WE RETURNED AGAIN THE NEXT DAY. THE LACK OF TRANSPARENCY AND POLICE INVESTIGATIONS MEANS THAT, OFTEN, HUMAN RIGHTS DEFENDERS HAVE TO DO THEIR OWN INVESTIGATIONS. WHEN WE EXIT, I'M SUDDENLY THRUST INCHES AWAY FROM THE FRUITS OF A RECENT DRUG BUST, WHICH AFI* AGENTS UNLOAD..
AFI
AFI
AFI
AFTERWARDS, I'M TAKEN TO A FEMICIDE MEMORIAL PARK ON THE SITE WHERE THE BODIES OF 8 WOMEN WERE FOUND IN 2001
... BUT IT WAS CLOSED

* THE AGENTS WERE WEARING AFI UNIFORMS, DESPITE IT BEING DISBANDED IN 2009 BECAUSE OF CORRUPTION

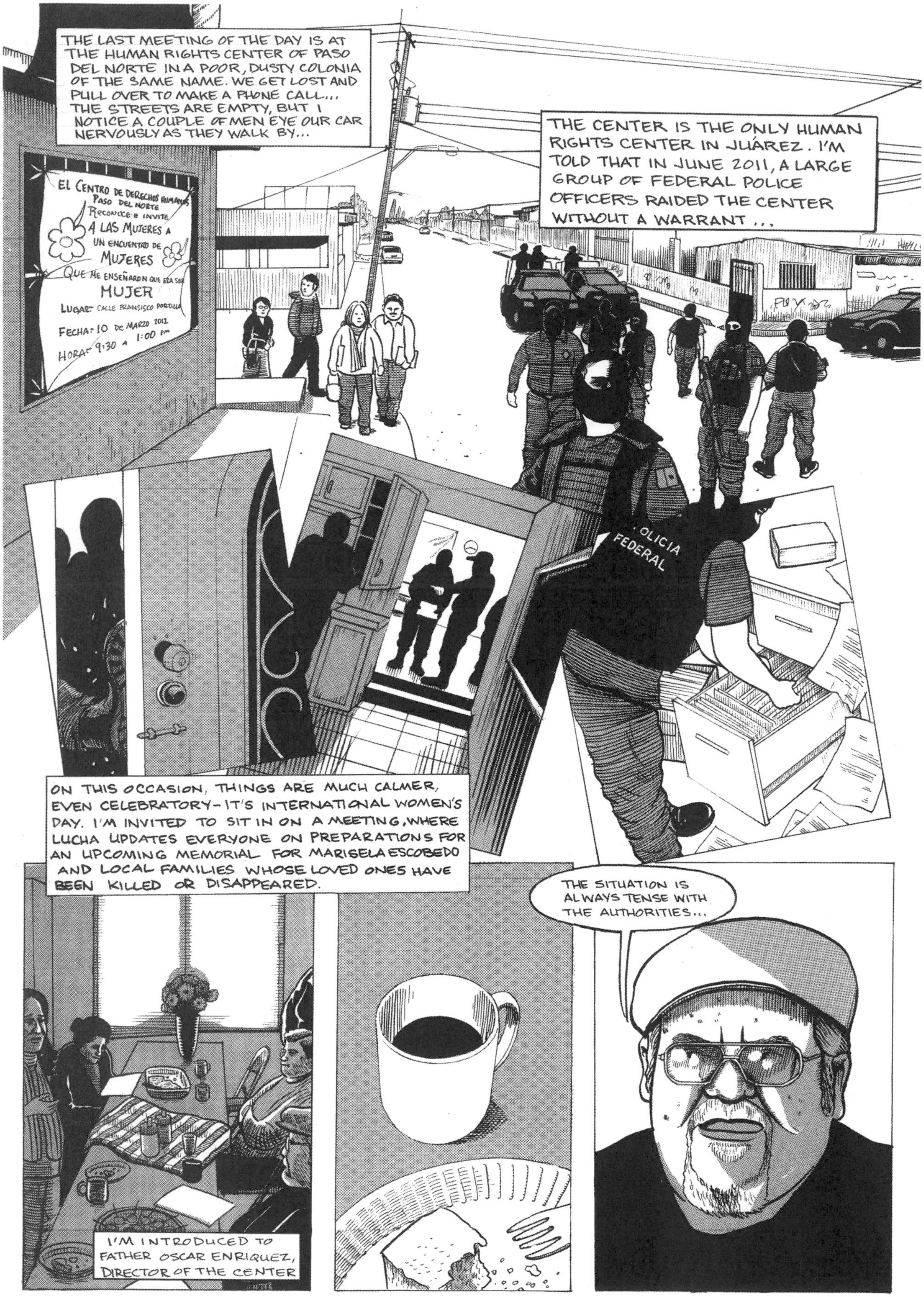
THE LAST MEETING OF THE DAY IS AT THE HUMAN RIGHTS CENTER OF PASO DEL NORTE IN A POOR, DUSTY COLONIA OF THE SAME NAME. WE GET LOST AND PULL OVER TO MAKE A PHONE CALL... THE STREETS ARE EMPTY, BUT I NOTICE A COUPLE OF MEN EYE OUR CAR NERVOUSLY AS THEY WALK BY...
EL CENTRO DE DERECHOS HUMANOS PASO DEL NORTE
Reconoce e invite
A LAS MUJERES A UN ENCUENTRO DE MUJERES
QUE ME ENSEÑARON QUE ERA SER MUJER
Lugar: Calle Fransisco Portillo
Fecha: 10 de Marzo 2012
Hora: 9:30 a 1:00 pm
THE CENTER IS THE ONLY HUMAN RIGHTS CENTER IN JUÁREZ. I'M TOLD THAT IN JUNE 2011, A LARGE GROUP OF FEDERAL POLICE OFFICERS RAIDED THE CENTER WITHOUT A WARRANT...
FEDERAL
ON THIS OCCASION, THINGS ARE MUCH CALMER, EVEN CELEBRATORY - IT'S INTERNATIONAL WOMEN'S DAY. I'M INVITED TO SIT IN ON A MEETING, WHERE LUCHA UPDATES EVERYONE ON PREPARATIONS FOR AN UPCOMING MEMORIAL FOR MARISELA ESCOBEDO AND LOCAL FAMILIES WHOSE LOVED ONES HAVE BEEN KILLED OR DISAPPEARED.
I'M INTRODUCED TO FATHER OSCAR ENRIQUEZ, DIRECTOR OF THE CENTER
THE SITUATION IS ALWAYS TENSE WITH THE AUTHORITIES...

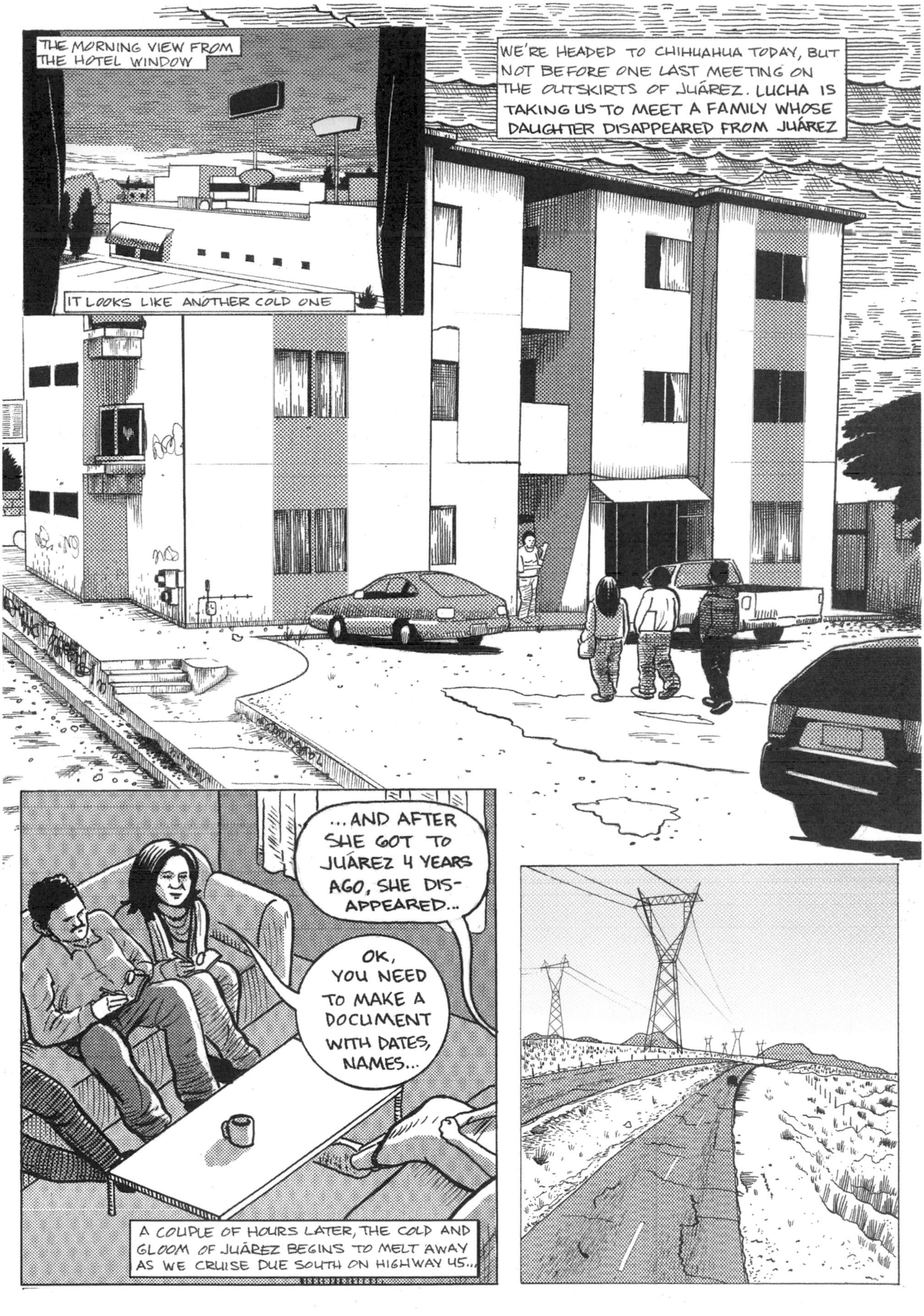
THE MORNING VIEW FROM THE HOTEL WINDOW
IT LOOKS LIKE ANOTHER COLD ONE
WE'RE HEADED TO CHIHUAHUA TODAY, BUT NOT BEFORE ONE LAST MEETING ON THE OUTSKIRTS OF JUÁREZ. LUCHA IS TAKING US TO MEET A FAMILY WHOSE DAUGHTER DISAPPEARED FROM JUÁREZ
...AND AFTER SHE GOT TO JUÁREZ 4 YEARS AGO, SHE DIS-APPEARED...
OK, YOU NEED TO MAKE A DOCUMENT WITH DATES, NAMES...
A COUPLE OF HOURS LATER, THE COLD AND GLOOM OF JUÁREZ BEGINS TO MELT AWAY AS WE CRUISE DUE SOUTH ON HIGHWAY 45...

CENTER FOR HUMAN RIGHTS FOR WOMEN

IN DOWNTOWN CHIHUAHUA

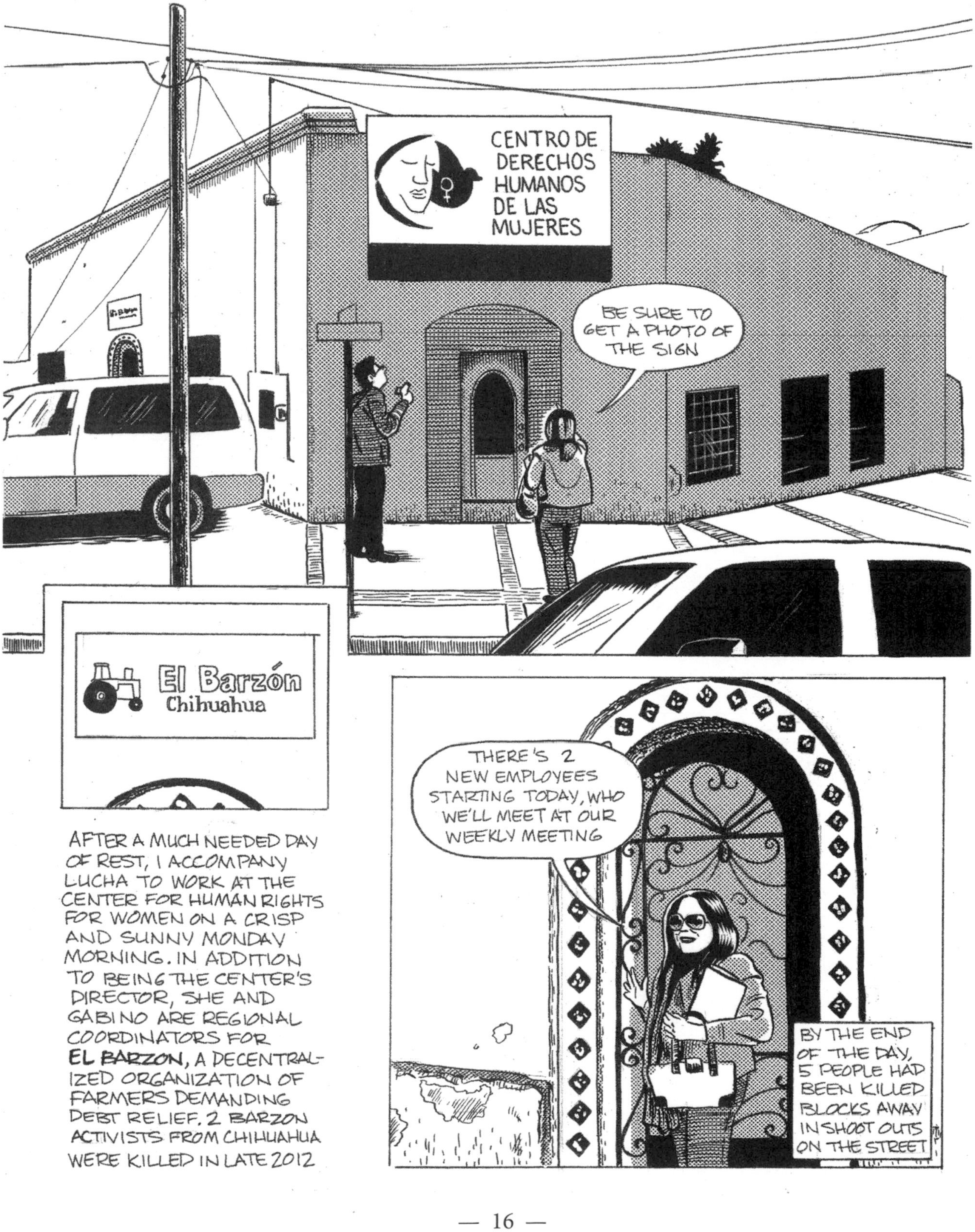
CENTRO DE DERECHOS HUMANOS DE LAS MUJERES
BE SURE TO GET A PHOTO OF THE SIGN
El Barzón Chihuahua
AFTER A MUCH NEEDED DAY OF REST, I ACCOMPANY LUCHA TO WORK AT THE CENTER FOR HUMAN RIGHTS FOR WOMEN ON A CRISP AND SUNNY MONDAY MORNING. IN ADDITION TO BEING THE CENTER'S DIRECTOR, SHE AND GABINO ARE REGIONAL COORDINATORS FOR EL BARZON, A DECENTRALIZED ORGANIZATION OF FARMERS DEMANDING DEBT RELIEF. 2 BARZON ACTIVISTS FROM CHIHUAHUA WERE KILLED IN LATE 2012
THERE'S 2 NEW EMPLOYEES STARTING TODAY, WHO WE'LL MEET AT OUR WEEKLY MEETING
BY THE END OF THE DAY, 5 PEOPLE HAD BEEN KILLED BLOCKS AWAY IN SHOOT OUTS ON THE STREET

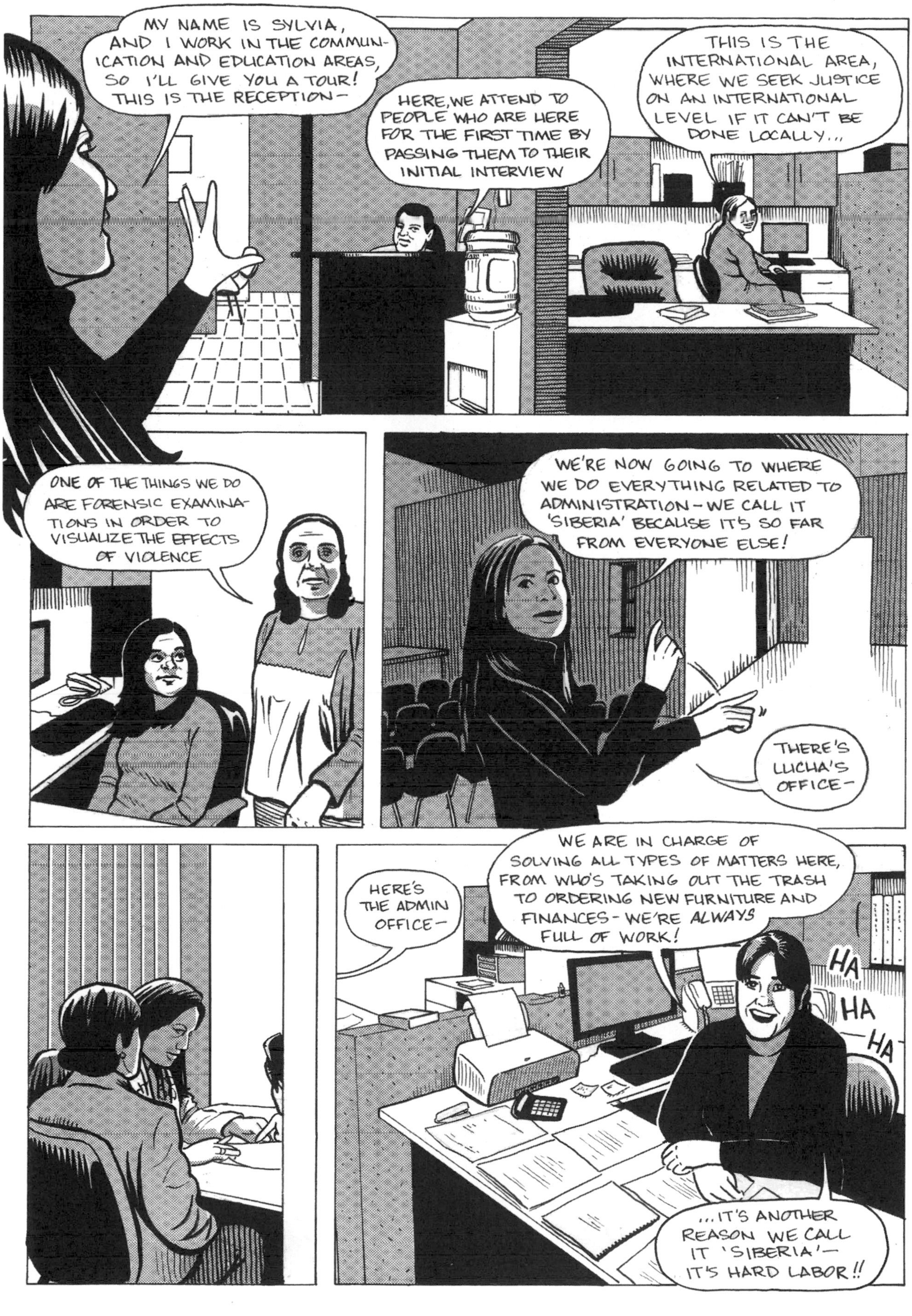
MY NAME IS SYLVIA, AND I WORK IN THE COMMUNICATION AND EDUCATION AREAS, SO I'LL GIVE YOU A TOUR! THIS IS THE RECEPTION–
HERE, WE ATTEND TO PEOPLE WHO ARE HERE FOR THE FIRST TIME BY PASSING THEM TO THEIR INITIAL INTERVIEW
THIS IS THE INTERNATIONAL AREA, WHERE WE SEEK JUSTICE ON AN INTERNATIONAL LEVEL IF IT CAN'T BE DONE LOCALLY...
ONE OF THE THINGS WE DO ARE FORENSIC EXAMINATIONS IN ORDER TO VISUALIZE THE EFFECTS OF VIOLENCE
WE'RE NOW GOING TO WHERE WE DO EVERYTHING RELATED TO ADMINISTRATION – WE CALL IT 'SIBERIA' BECAUSE IT'S SO FAR FROM EVERYONE ELSE!
THERE'S LUCHA'S OFFICE–
HERE'S THE ADMIN OFFICE–
WE ARE IN CHARGE OF SOLVING ALL TYPES OF MATTERS HERE, FROM WHO'S TAKING OUT THE TRASH TO ORDERING NEW FURNITURE AND FINANCES – WE'RE ALWAYS FULL OF WORK!
HA HA HA
...IT'S ANOTHER REASON WE CALL IT 'SIBERIA' – IT'S HARD LABOR!!

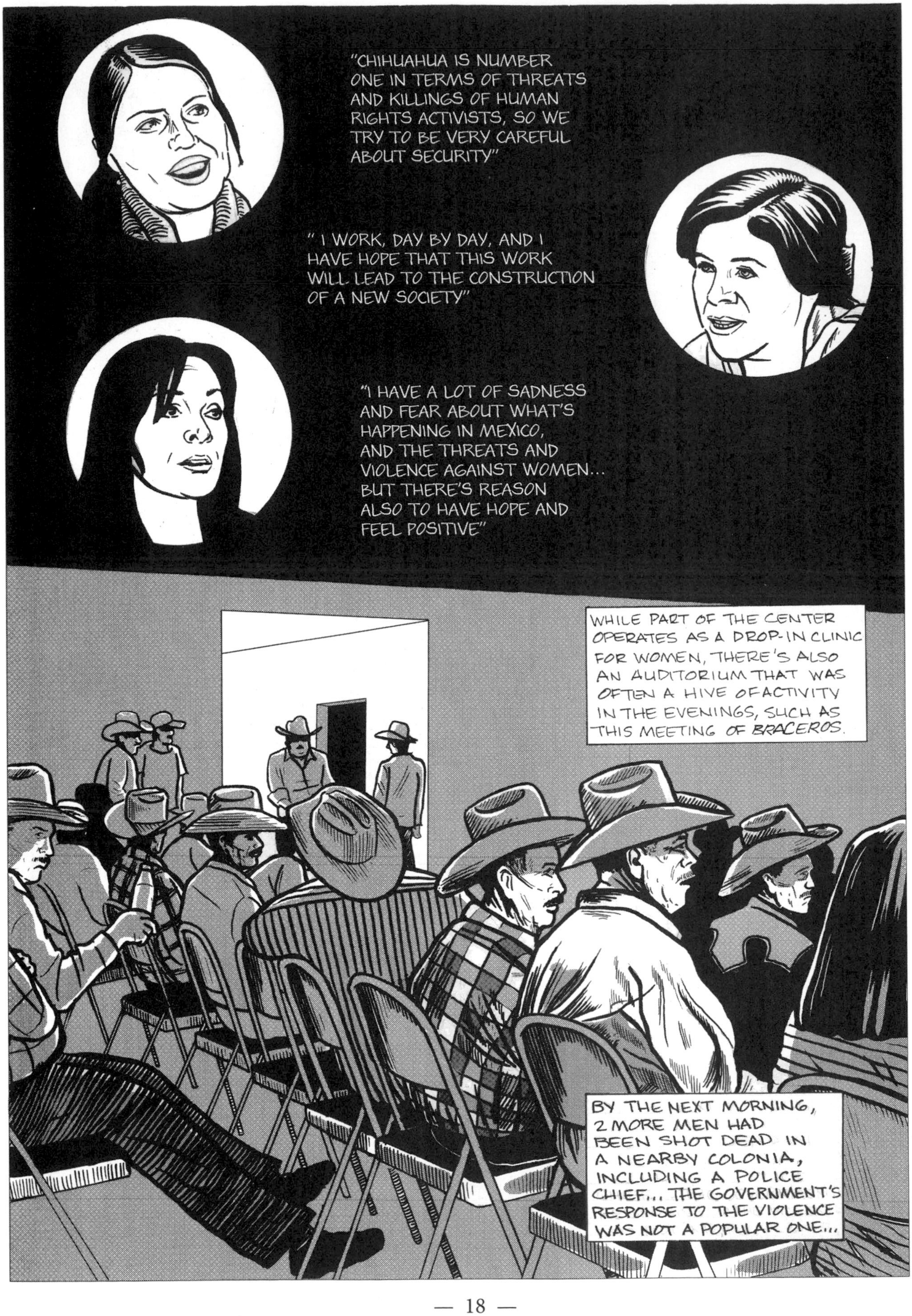
"CHIHUAHUA IS NUMBER ONE IN TERMS OF THREATS AND KILLINGS OF HUMAN RIGHTS ACTIVISTS, SO WE TRY TO BE VERY CAREFUL ABOUT SECURITY"
" I WORK, DAY BY DAY, AND I HAVE HOPE THAT THIS WORK WILL LEAD TO THE CONSTRUCTION OF A NEW SOCIETY"
"I HAVE A LOT OF SADNESS AND FEAR ABOUT WHAT'S HAPPENING IN MEXICO, AND THE THREATS AND VIOLENCE AGAINST WOMEN... BUT THERE'S REASON ALSO TO HAVE HOPE AND FEEL POSITIVE"
WHILE PART OF THE CENTER OPERATES AS A DROP-IN CLINIC FOR WOMEN, THERE'S ALSO AN AUDITORIUM THAT WAS OFTEN A HIVE OF ACTIVITY IN THE EVENINGS, SUCH AS THIS MEETING OF *BRACEROS*.
BY THE NEXT MORNING, 2 MORE MEN HAD BEEN SHOT DEAD IN A NEARBY COLONIA, INCLUDING A POLICE CHIEF... THE GOVERNMENT'S RESPONSE TO THE VIOLENCE WAS NOT A POPULAR ONE...

...THE ARMY WAS NOW PATROLLING THE STREETS...

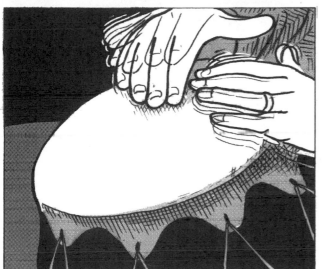

STRESS RELIEF EXERCISES ARE A REGULAR FEATURE AT THE CENTER...

THE STAFF ARE LED THROUGH A GUIDED MEDITATION...

...WHERE THEY PLACE THEIR STRESS IN AN IMAGINARY BALLOON AND RELEASE IT. BY DAYS END, 14 MORE PEOPLE HAD BEEN KILLED

SOON AFTERWARDS, THE STAFF WOULD RETURN TO THEIR WORK... WHILE SCENES LIKE THIS WERE OCCURRING AT AN ALARMING RATE JUST A FEW MINUTES AWAY...

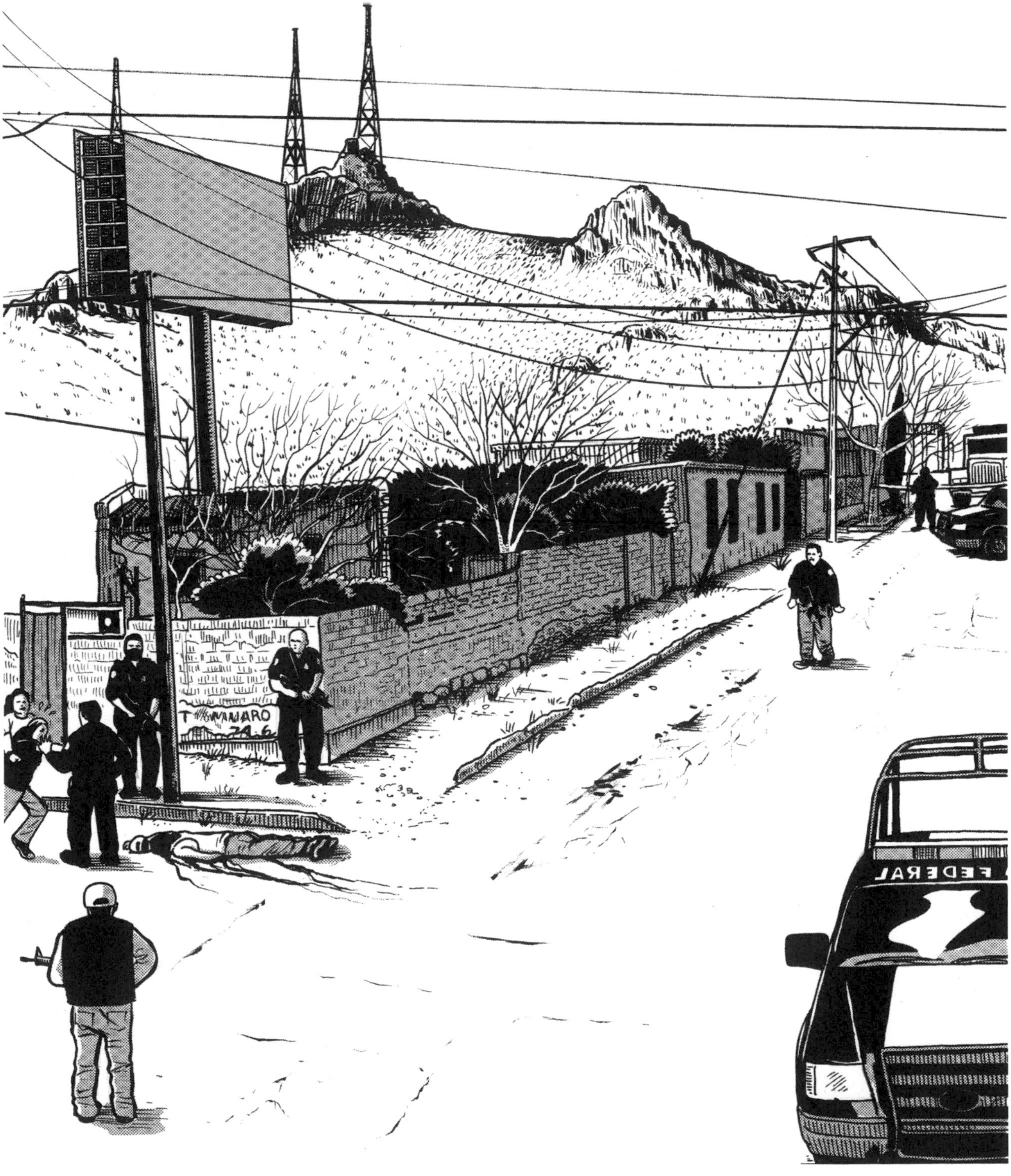
FEDERAL

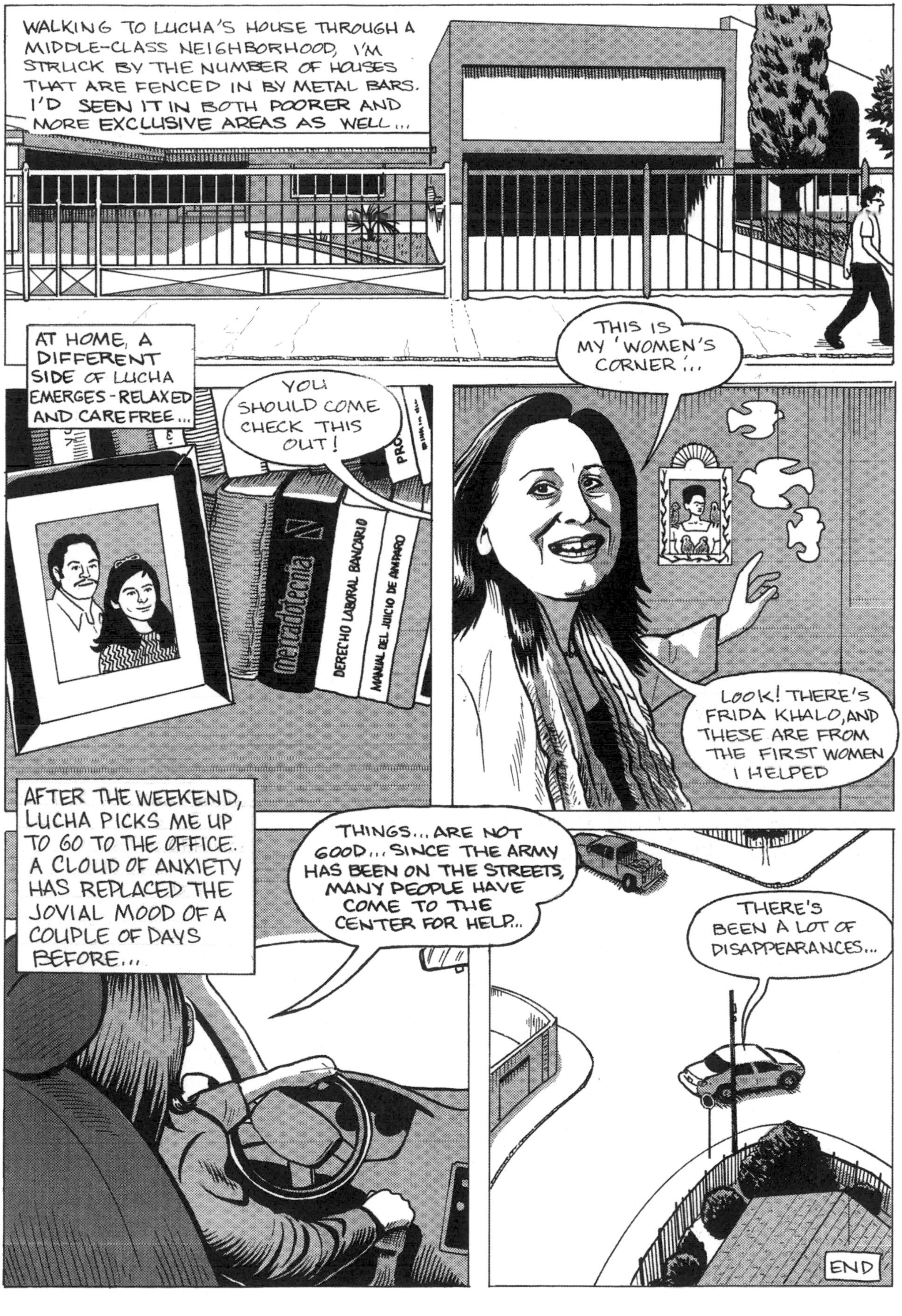
WALKING TO LUCHA'S HOUSE THROUGH A MIDDLE-CLASS NEIGHBORHOOD, I'M STRUCK BY THE NUMBER OF HOUSES THAT ARE FENCED IN BY METAL BARS. I'D SEEN IT IN BOTH POORER AND MORE EXCLUSIVE AREAS AS WELL...
AT HOME, A DIFFERENT SIDE OF LUCHA EMERGES-RELAXED AND CAREFREE...
YOU SHOULD COME CHECK THIS OUT!
DERECHO LABORAL BANCARIO
MANUAL DEL JUICIO DE AMPARO
THIS IS MY 'WOMEN'S CORNER'...
LOOK! THERE'S FRIDA KHALO, AND THESE ARE FROM THE FIRST WOMEN I HELPED
AFTER THE WEEKEND, LUCHA PICKS ME UP TO GO TO THE OFFICE. A CLOUD OF ANXIETY HAS REPLACED THE JOVIAL MOOD OF A COUPLE OF DAYS BEFORE...
THINGS... ARE NOT GOOD... SINCE THE ARMY HAS BEEN ON THE STREETS, MANY PEOPLE HAVE COME TO THE CENTER FOR HELP...
THERE'S BEEN A LOT OF DISAPPEARANCES...
END

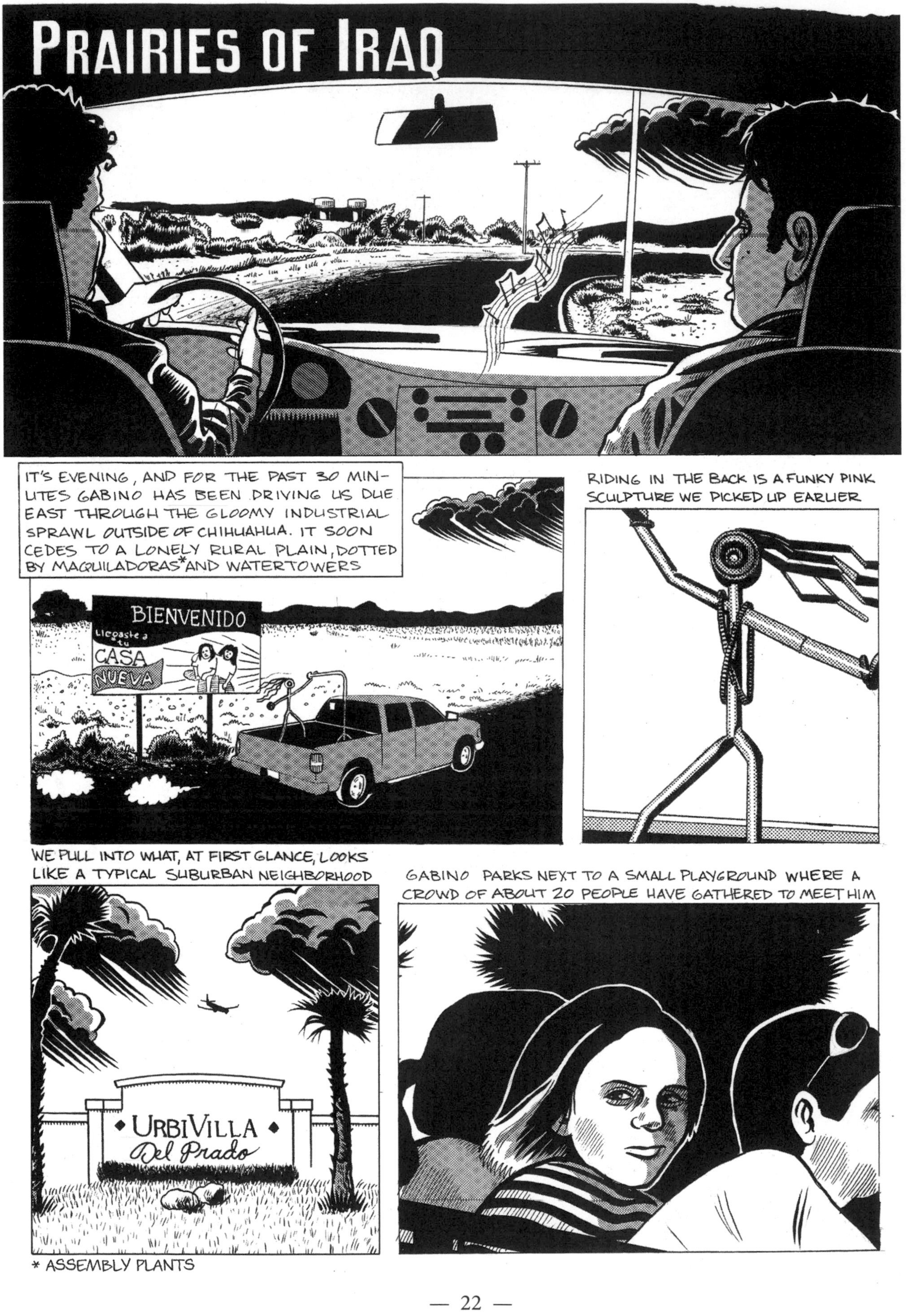
PRAIRIES OF IRAQ
IT'S EVENING, AND FOR THE PAST 30 MIN-UTES GABINO HAS BEEN DRIVING US DUE EAST THROUGH THE GLOOMY INDUSTRIAL SPRAWL OUTSIDE OF CHIHUAHUA. IT SOON CEDES TO A LONELY RURAL PLAIN, DOTTED BY MAQUILADORAS* AND WATERTOWERS
BIENVENIDO
Llegaste a tu
CASA
NUEVA
RIDING IN THE BACK IS A FUNKY PINK SCULPTURE WE PICKED UP EARLIER
WE PULL INTO WHAT, AT FIRST GLANCE, LOOKS LIKE A TYPICAL SUBURBAN NEIGHBORHOOD
URBIVILLA
Del Prado
GABINO PARKS NEXT TO A SMALL PLAYGROUND WHERE A CROWD OF ABOUT 20 PEOPLE HAVE GATHERED TO MEET HIM

* ASSEMBLY PLANTS

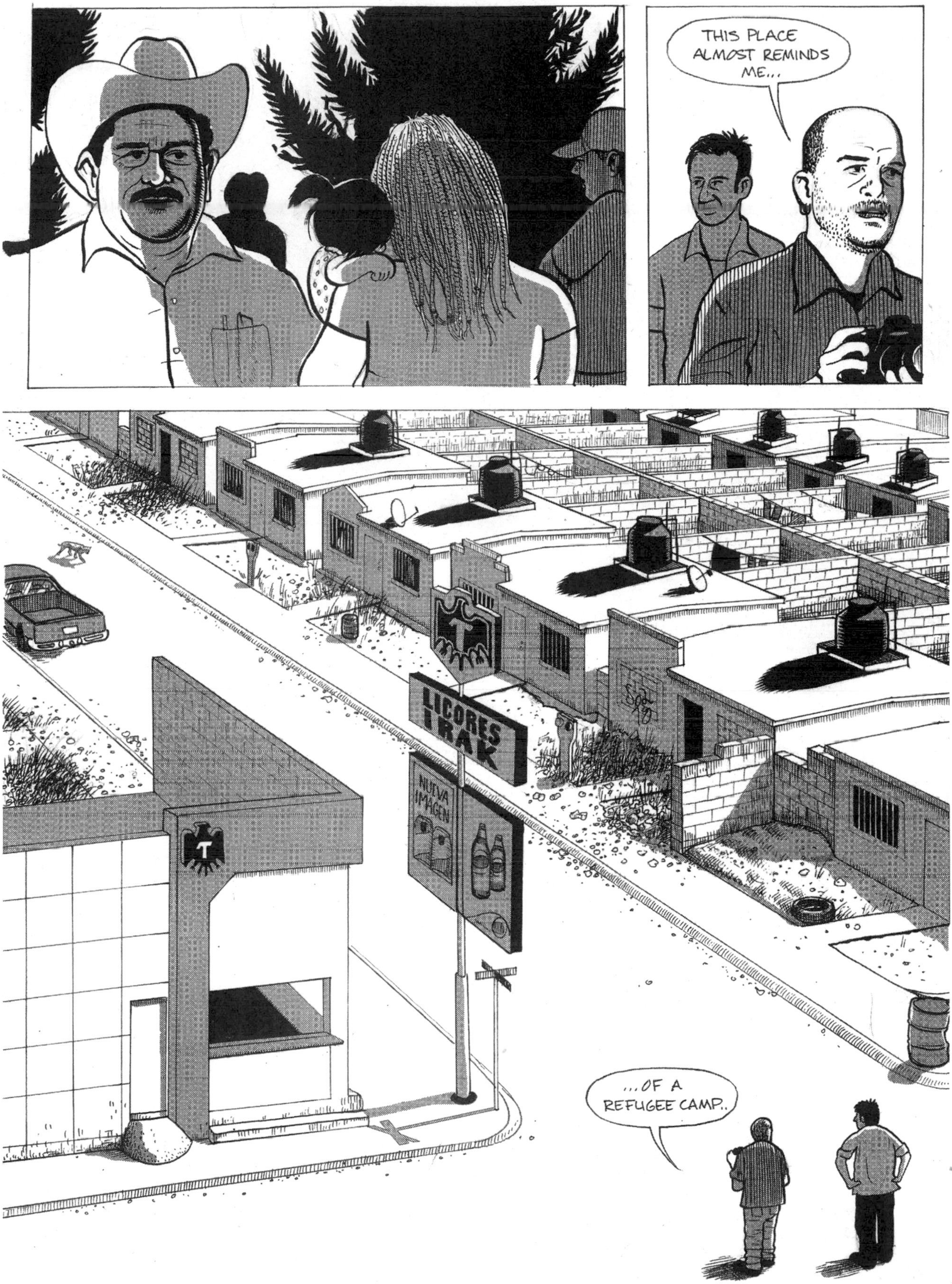
THIS PLACE ALMOST REMINDS ME...
LICORES IRAK
NUEVA IMAGEN
...OF A REFUGEE CAMP..

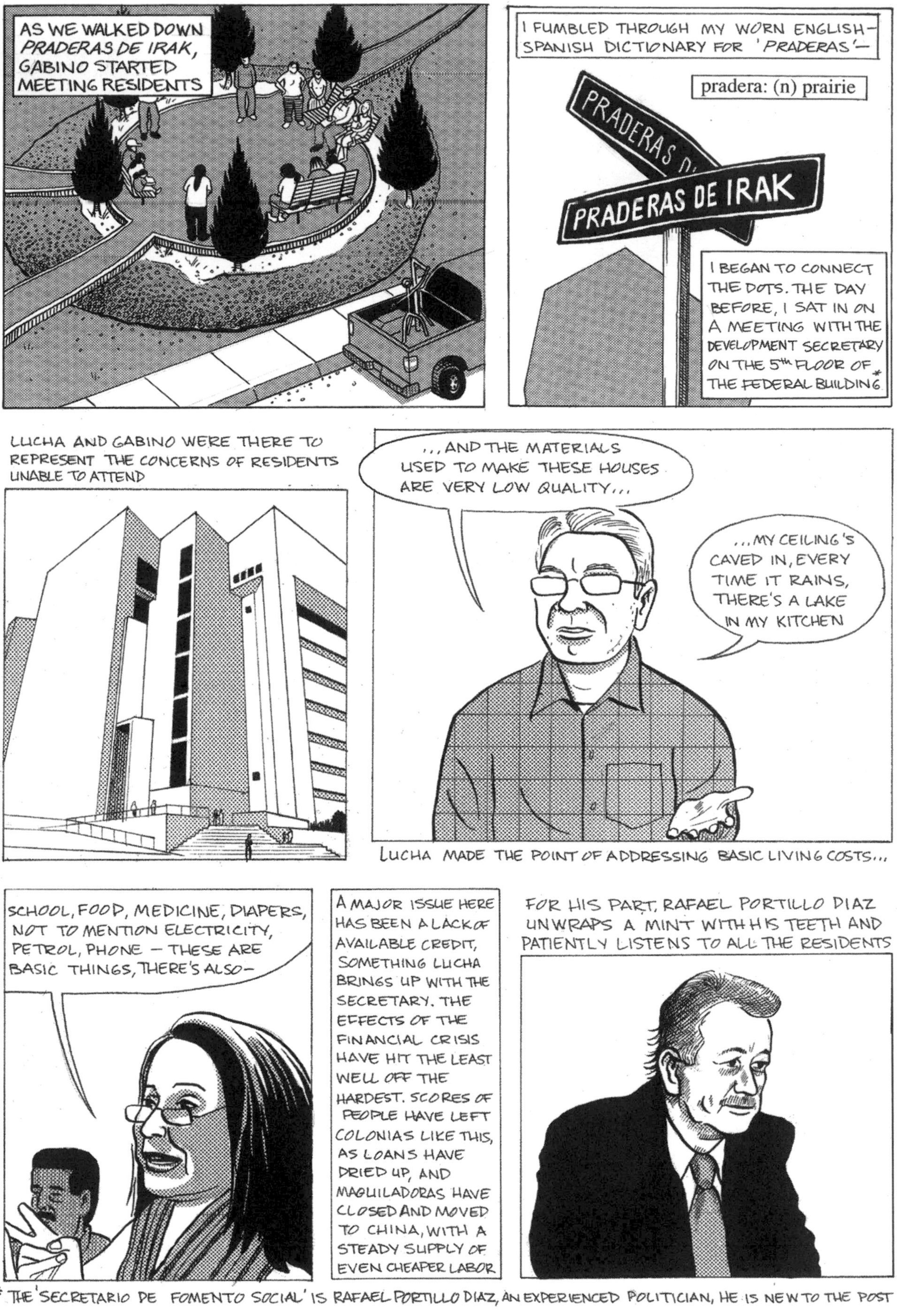
AS WE WALKED DOWN PRADERAS DE IRAK, GABINO STARTED MEETING RESIDENTS
I FUMBLED THROUGH MY WORN ENGLISH-SPANISH DICTIONARY FOR 'PRADERAS'—
pradera: (n) prairie
PRADERAS DE IRAK
I BEGAN TO CONNECT THE DOTS. THE DAY BEFORE, I SAT IN ON A MEETING WITH THE DEVELOPMENT SECRETARY ON THE 5th FLOOR OF THE FEDERAL BUILDING*
LUCHA AND GABINO WERE THERE TO REPRESENT THE CONCERNS OF RESIDENTS UNABLE TO ATTEND
...AND THE MATERIALS USED TO MAKE THESE HOUSES ARE VERY LOW QUALITY...
...MY CEILING'S CAVED IN, EVERY TIME IT RAINS, THERE'S A LAKE IN MY KITCHEN
LUCHA MADE THE POINT OF ADDRESSING BASIC LIVING COSTS...
SCHOOL, FOOD, MEDICINE, DIAPERS, NOT TO MENTION ELECTRICITY, PETROL, PHONE — THESE ARE BASIC THINGS, THERE'S ALSO—
A MAJOR ISSUE HERE HAS BEEN A LACK OF AVAILABLE CREDIT, SOMETHING LUCHA BRINGS UP WITH THE SECRETARY. THE EFFECTS OF THE FINANCIAL CRISIS HAVE HIT THE LEAST WELL OFF THE HARDEST. SCORES OF PEOPLE HAVE LEFT COLONIAS LIKE THIS, AS LOANS HAVE DRIED UP, AND MAQUILADORAS HAVE CLOSED AND MOVED TO CHINA, WITH A STEADY SUPPLY OF EVEN CHEAPER LABOR
FOR HIS PART, RAFAEL PORTILLO DIAZ UNWRAPS A MINT WITH HIS TEETH AND PATIENTLY LISTENS TO ALL THE RESIDENTS

* THE 'SECRETARIO DE FOMENTO SOCIAL' IS RAFAEL PORTILLO DIAZ, AN EXPERIENCED POLITICIAN, HE IS NEW TO THE POST

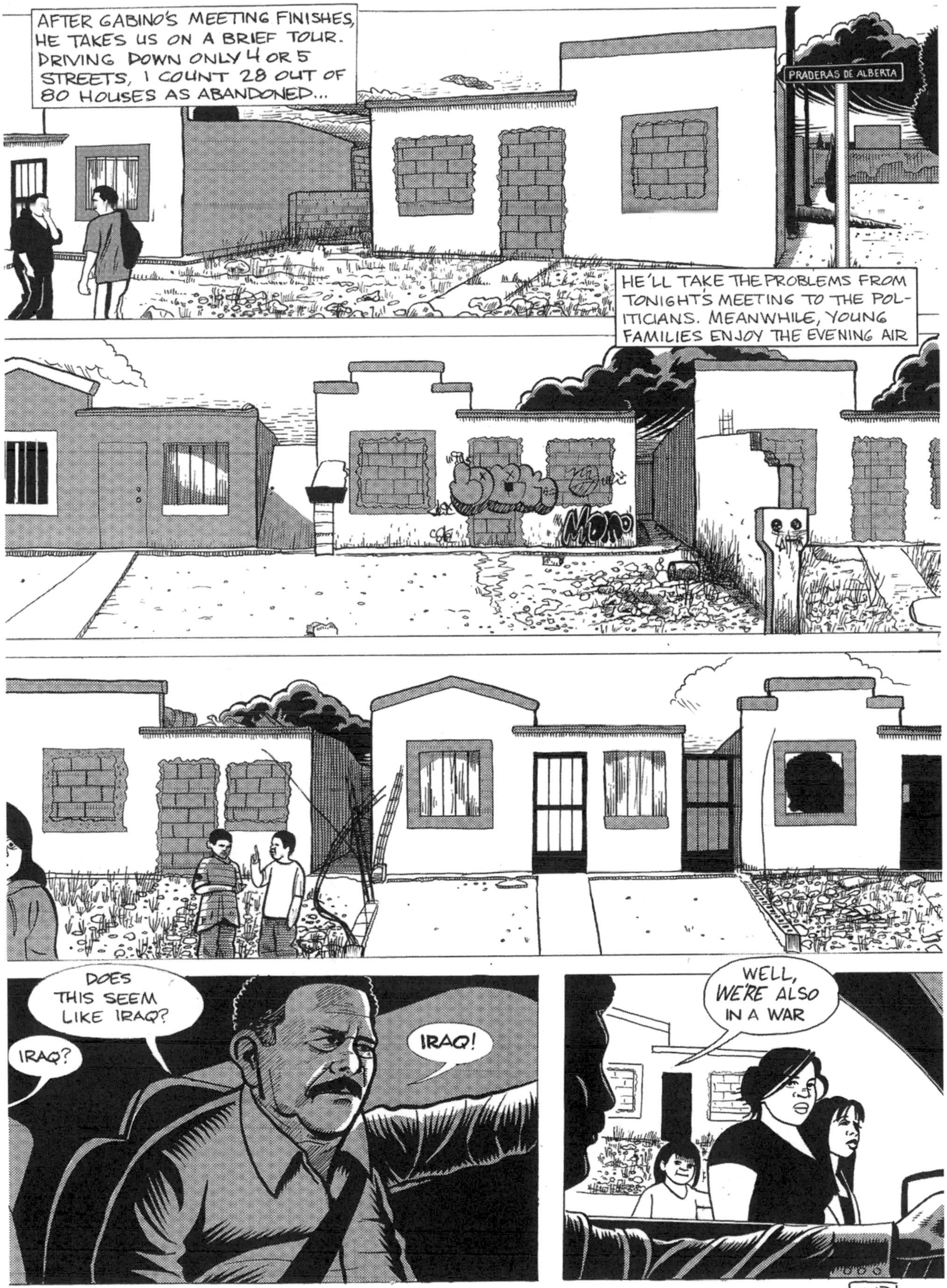
AFTER GABINO'S MEETING FINISHES, HE TAKES US ON A BRIEF TOUR. DRIVING DOWN ONLY 4 OR 5 STREETS, I COUNT 28 OUT OF 80 HOUSES AS ABANDONED...
PRADERAS DE ALBERTA
HE'LL TAKE THE PROBLEMS FROM TONIGHT'S MEETING TO THE POLITICIANS. MEANWHILE, YOUNG FAMILIES ENJOY THE EVENING AIR
MONO
DOES THIS SEEM LIKE IRAQ?
IRAQ?
IRAQ!
WELL, WE'RE ALSO IN A WAR
END

ALMA

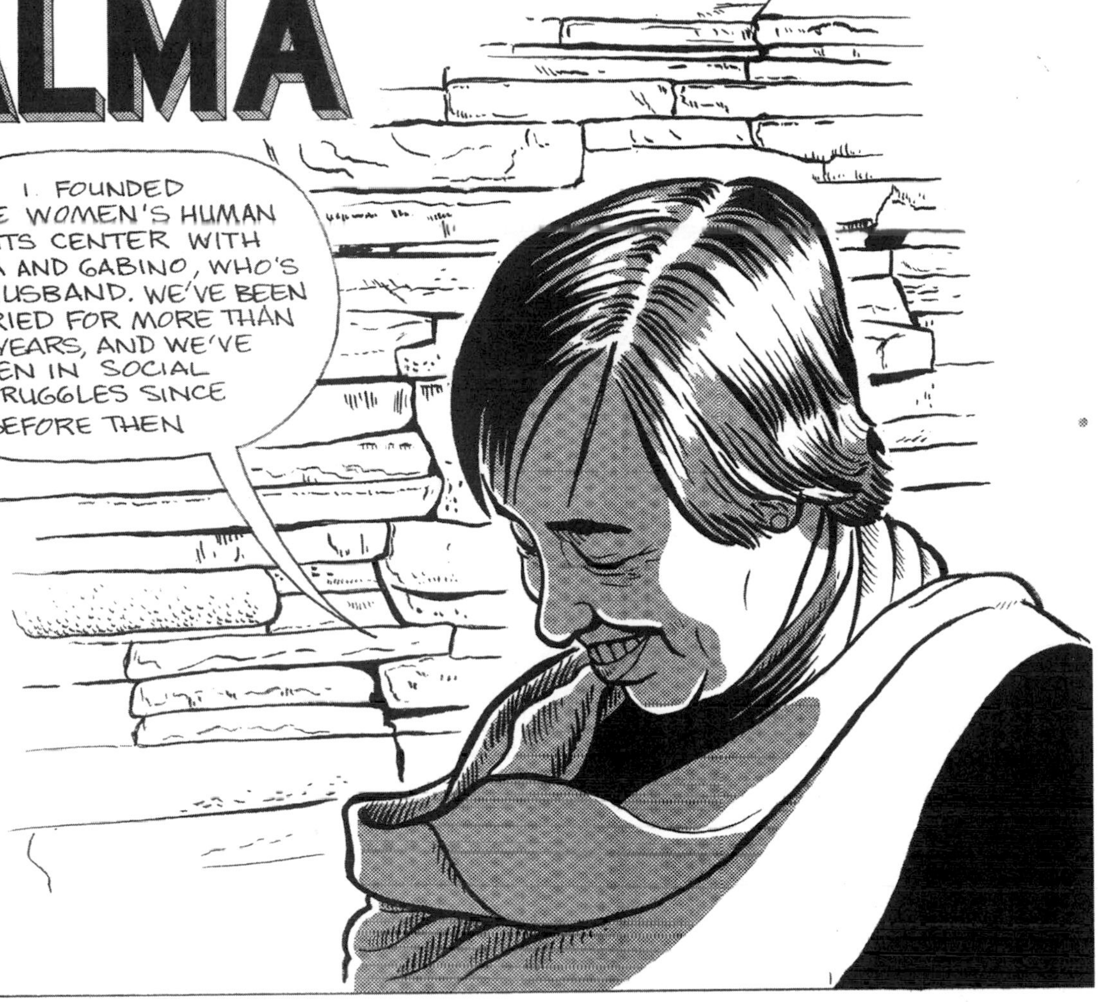
I. FOUNDED THE WOMEN'S HUMAN RIGHTS CENTER WITH LUCHA AND GABINO, WHO'S MY HUSBAND. WE'VE BEEN MARRIED FOR MORE THAN 30 YEARS, AND WE'VE BEEN IN SOCIAL STRUGGLES SINCE BEFORE THEN

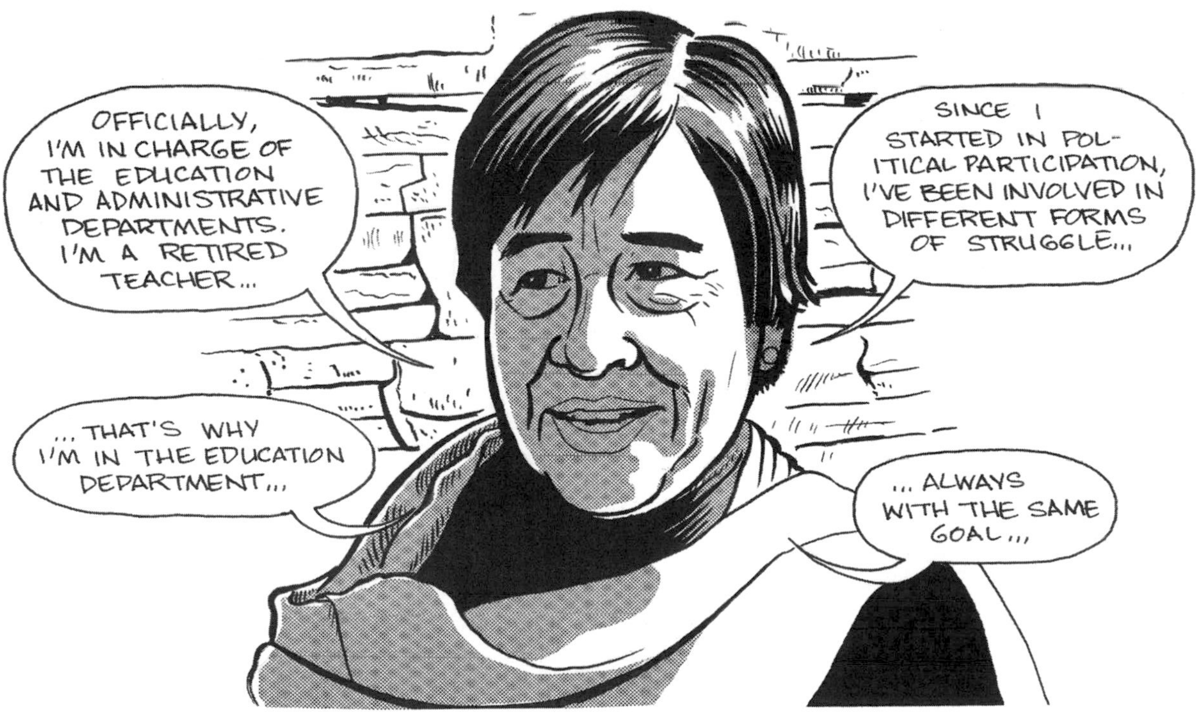
OFFICIALLY, I'M IN CHARGE OF THE EDUCATION AND ADMINISTRATIVE DEPARTMENTS. I'M A RETIRED TEACHER...
...THAT'S WHY I'M IN THE EDUCATION DEPARTMENT...
SINCE I STARTED IN POL-ITICAL PARTICIPATION, I'VE BEEN INVOLVED IN DIFFERENT FORMS OF STRUGGLE...
...ALWAYS WITH THE SAME GOAL...

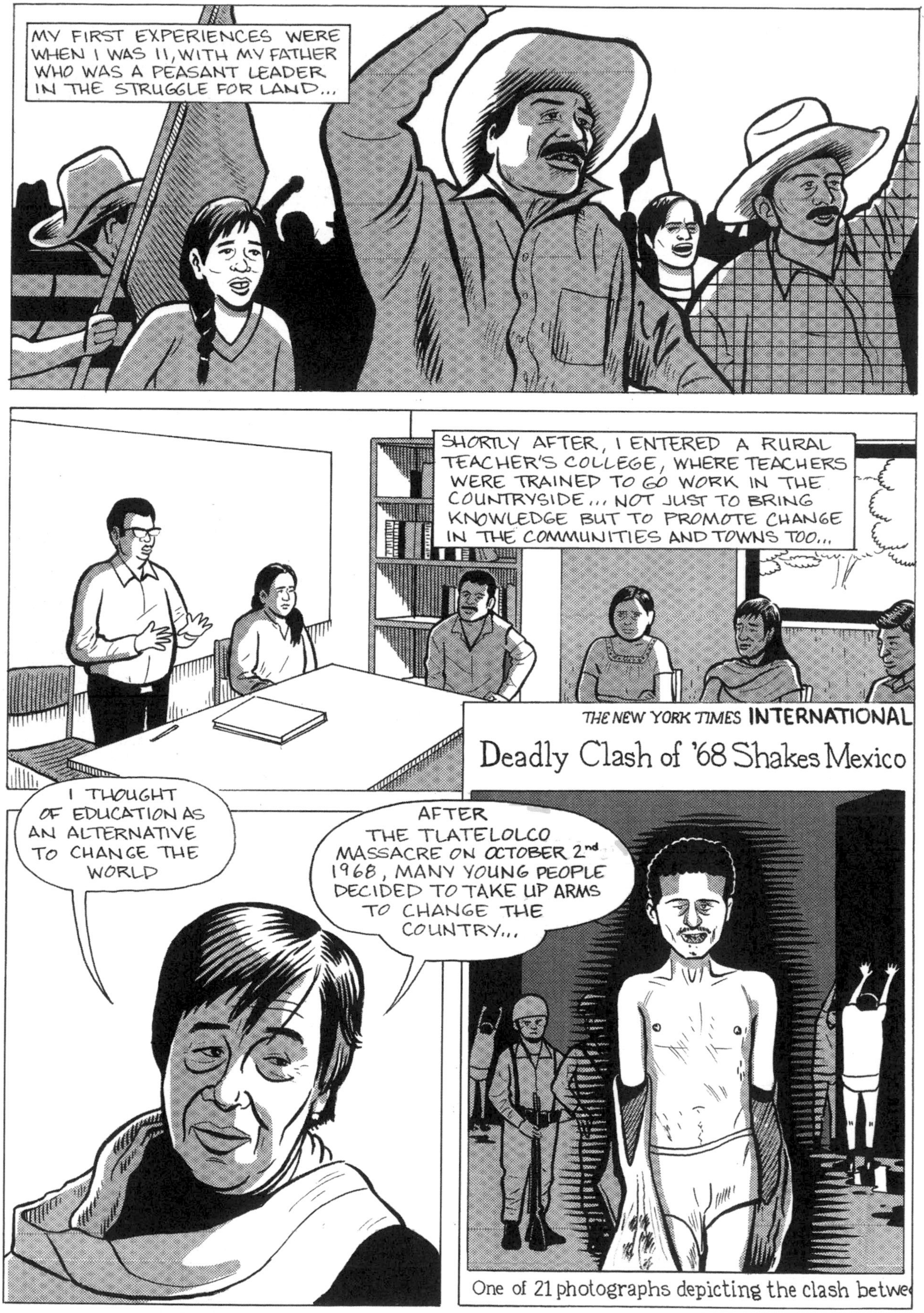
MY FIRST EXPERIENCES WERE WHEN I WAS 11, WITH MY FATHER WHO WAS A PEASANT LEADER IN THE STRUGGLE FOR LAND...
SHORTLY AFTER, I ENTERED A RURAL TEACHER'S COLLEGE, WHERE TEACHERS WERE TRAINED TO GO WORK IN THE COUNTRYSIDE... NOT JUST TO BRING KNOWLEDGE BUT TO PROMOTE CHANGE IN THE COMMUNITIES AND TOWNS TOO...
I THOUGHT OF EDUCATION AS AN ALTERNATIVE TO CHANGE THE WORLD
AFTER THE TLATELOLCO MASSACRE ON OCTOBER 2nd 1968, MANY YOUNG PEOPLE DECIDED TO TAKE UP ARMS TO CHANGE THE COUNTRY...
THE NEW YORK TIMES INTERNATIONAL
Deadly Clash of '68 Shakes Mexico
One of 21 photographs depicting the clash betwe

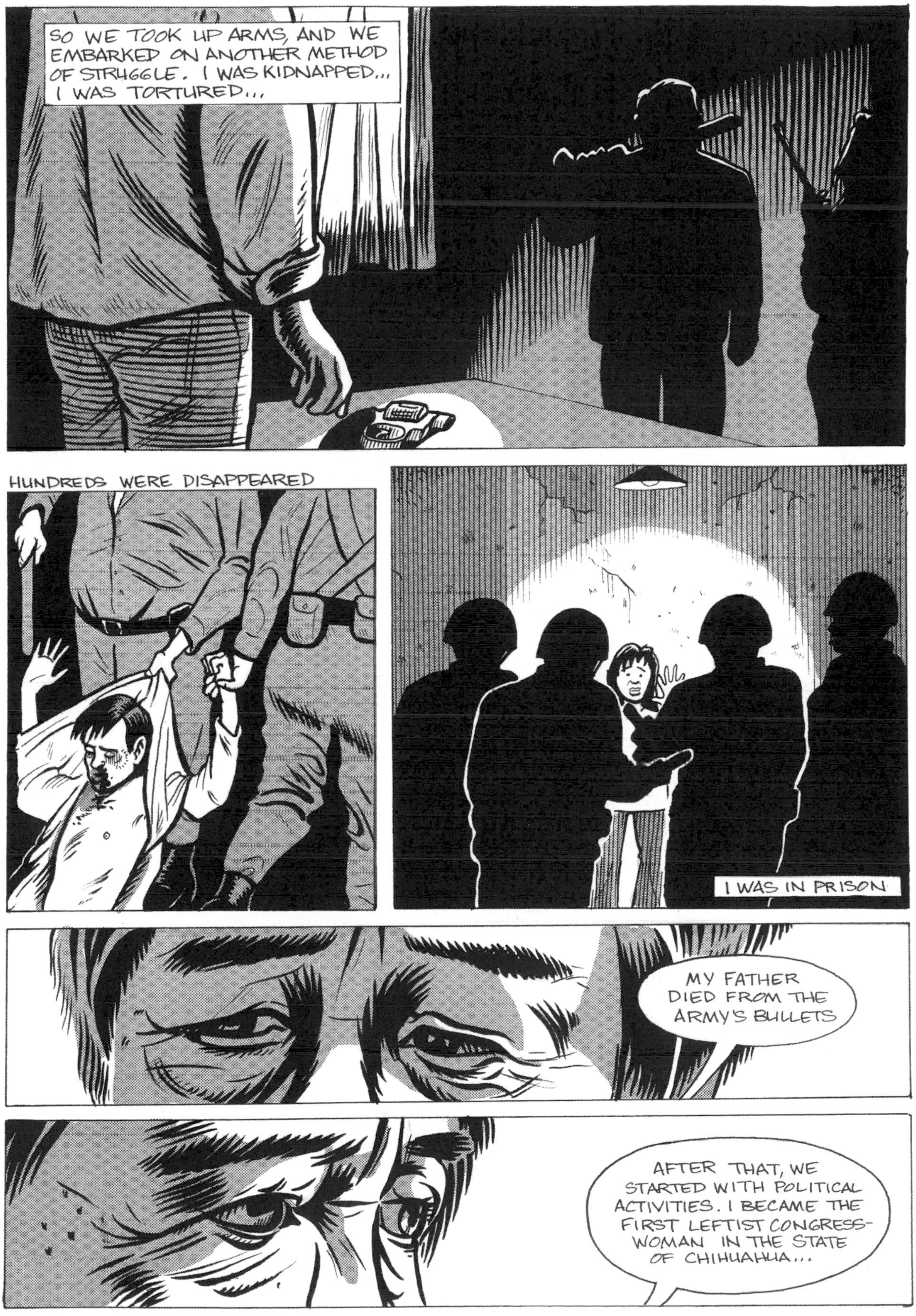

SO WE TOOK UP ARMS, AND WE EMBARKED ON ANOTHER METHOD OF STRUGGLE. I WAS KIDNAPPED... I WAS TORTURED...
HUNDREDS WERE DISAPPEARED
I WAS IN PRISON
MY FATHER DIED FROM THE ARMY'S BULLETS
AFTER THAT, WE STARTED WITH POLITICAL ACTIVITIES. I BECAME THE FIRST LEFTIST CONGRESS-WOMAN IN THE STATE OF CHIHUAHUA...

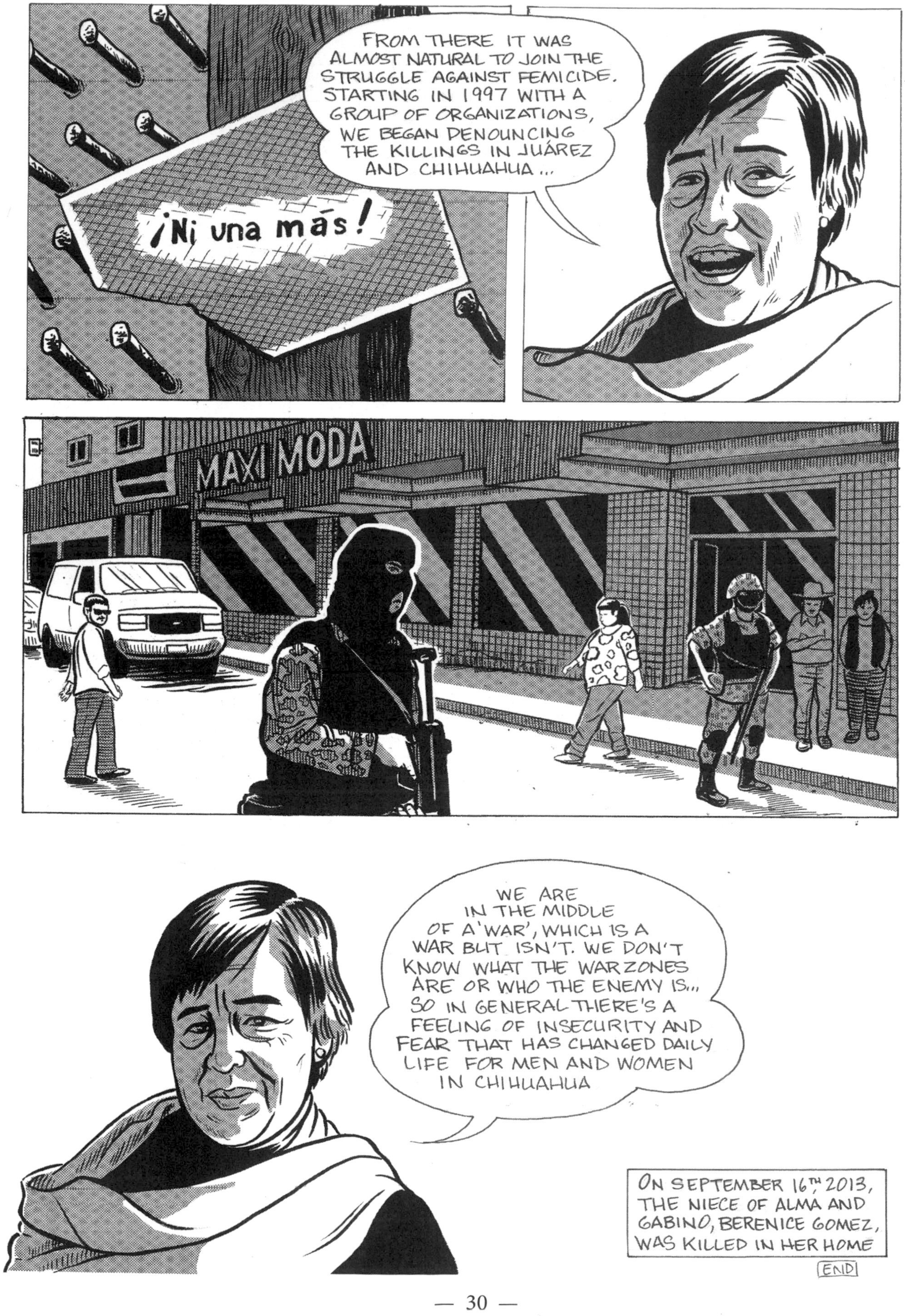
FROM THERE IT WAS ALMOST NATURAL TO JOIN THE STRUGGLE AGAINST FEMICIDE. STARTING IN 1997 WITH A GROUP OF ORGANIZATIONS, WE BEGAN DENOUNCING THE KILLINGS IN JUÁREZ AND CHIHUAHUA...
¡Ni una más!
MAXI MODA
WE ARE IN THE MIDDLE OF A 'WAR', WHICH IS A WAR BUT ISN'T. WE DON'T KNOW WHAT THE WAR ZONES ARE OR WHO THE ENEMY IS... SO IN GENERAL THERE'S A FEELING OF INSECURITY AND FEAR THAT HAS CHANGED DAILY LIFE FOR MEN AND WOMEN IN CHIHUAHUA
ON SEPTEMBER 16TH 2013, THE NIECE OF ALMA AND GABINO, BERENICE GOMEZ, WAS KILLED IN HER HOME
END

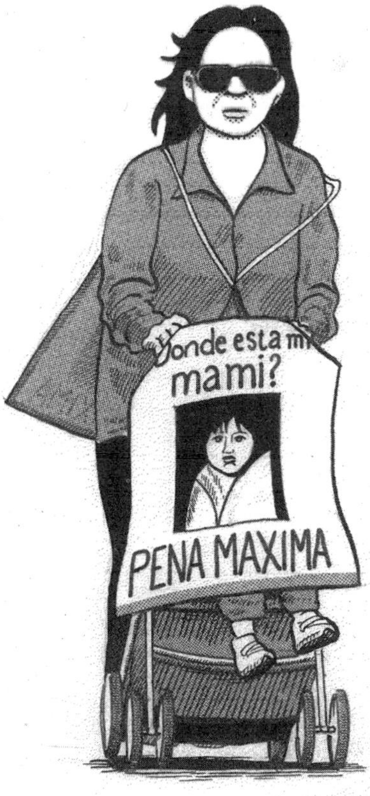
Donde esta mi
mami?
PENA MAXIMA

MARISELA

CNN México

El hijo de Marisela Escobedo señala al hombre que mató a su madre en 2010

Juan Frayre Escobedo, hijo de la act... señaló que el al asesino de su m...
...io Barraza, hermano de... marked the...

The Telegraph

Mexico in shock at murder of anti-crime

Mexico was reeling on Sunday from the brutal murder of an anti-crime campaigner and the targeting of her family that marked the...

USA TODAY

Mexico outraged by killing of anti-crime crus...

CIUDAD JUAREZ, Me...
Anger over Mexico...
over a mother wh...
daughter's killer...
herself shot to de...

proceso

A dos años de la muerte de Marisela Escobedo persiste exigencia de

EL MUNDO

Asesinada una mujer en Chihuahua por pedir justicia por la muerte de su hija

70/46° El Paso Times

Woman activist slain in Chihuahu... Quest to find daughter's killer self made investigator

A mother on a quest to find her daughter's killer was fatally shot Thursday night in front of the state capitol in Chihuahua

I WAS MARISELA ESCOBEDO'S LAWYER. BEFORE WE MET, I READ ABOUT HER PROTEST WALK FROM JUÁREZ TO MEXICO CITY, DEMANDING JUSTICE FOR THE KILLING OF HER DAUGHTER. AND I REMEMBER THINKING: HOW IS IT POSSIBLE FOR HER TO BE DOING THIS BY HERSELF?

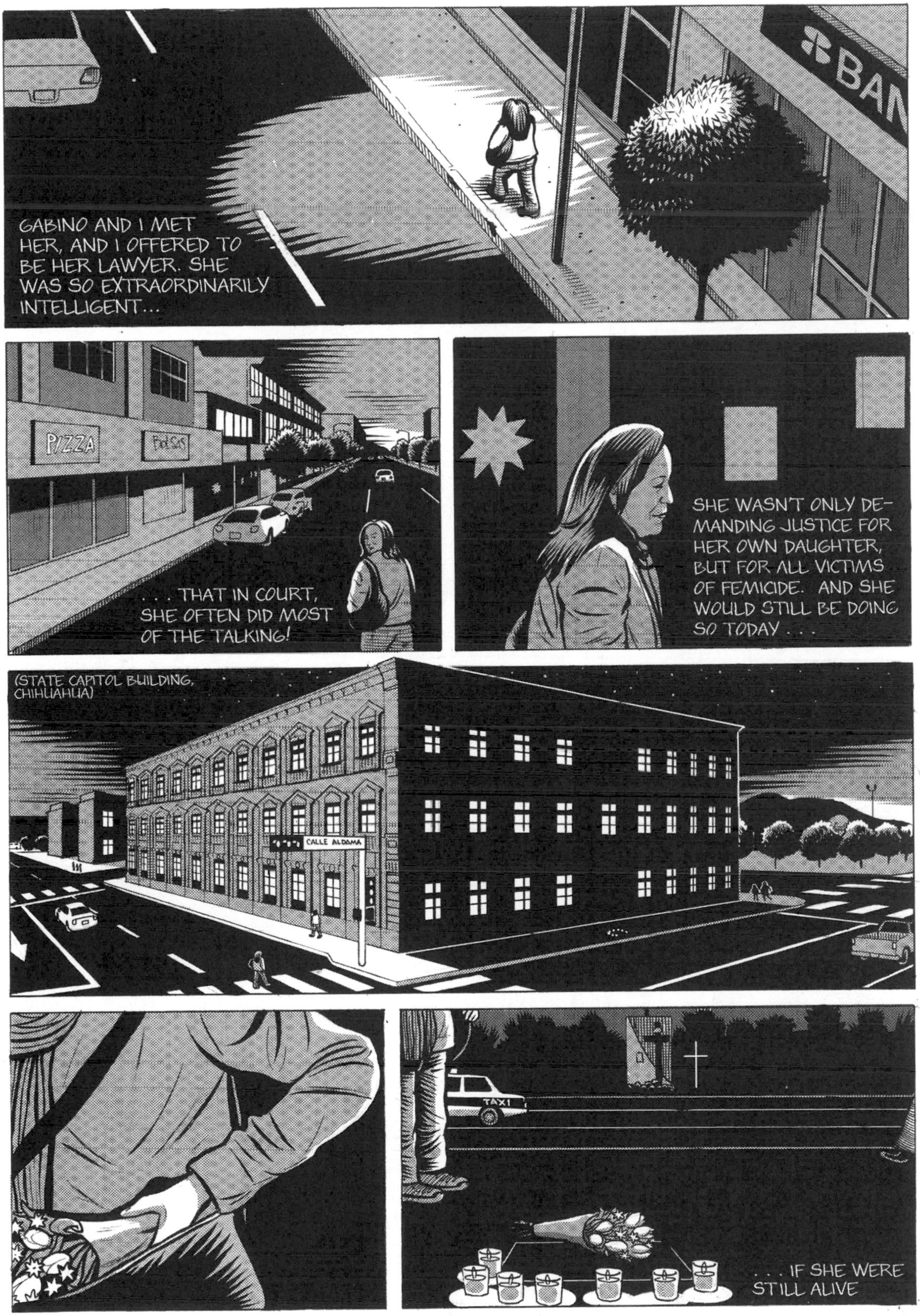
BAN
GABINO AND I MET HER, AND I OFFERED TO BE HER LAWYER. SHE WAS SO EXTRAORDINARILY INTELLIGENT...
PIZZA
. . . THAT IN COURT, SHE OFTEN DID MOST OF THE TALKING!
SHE WASN'T ONLY DE-MANDING JUSTICE FOR HER OWN DAUGHTER, BUT FOR ALL VICTIMS OF FEMICIDE. AND SHE WOULD STILL BE DOING SO TODAY . . .
(STATE CAPITOL BUILDING, CHIHUAHUA)
CALLE ALDAMA
TAXI
. . . IF SHE WERE STILL ALIVE

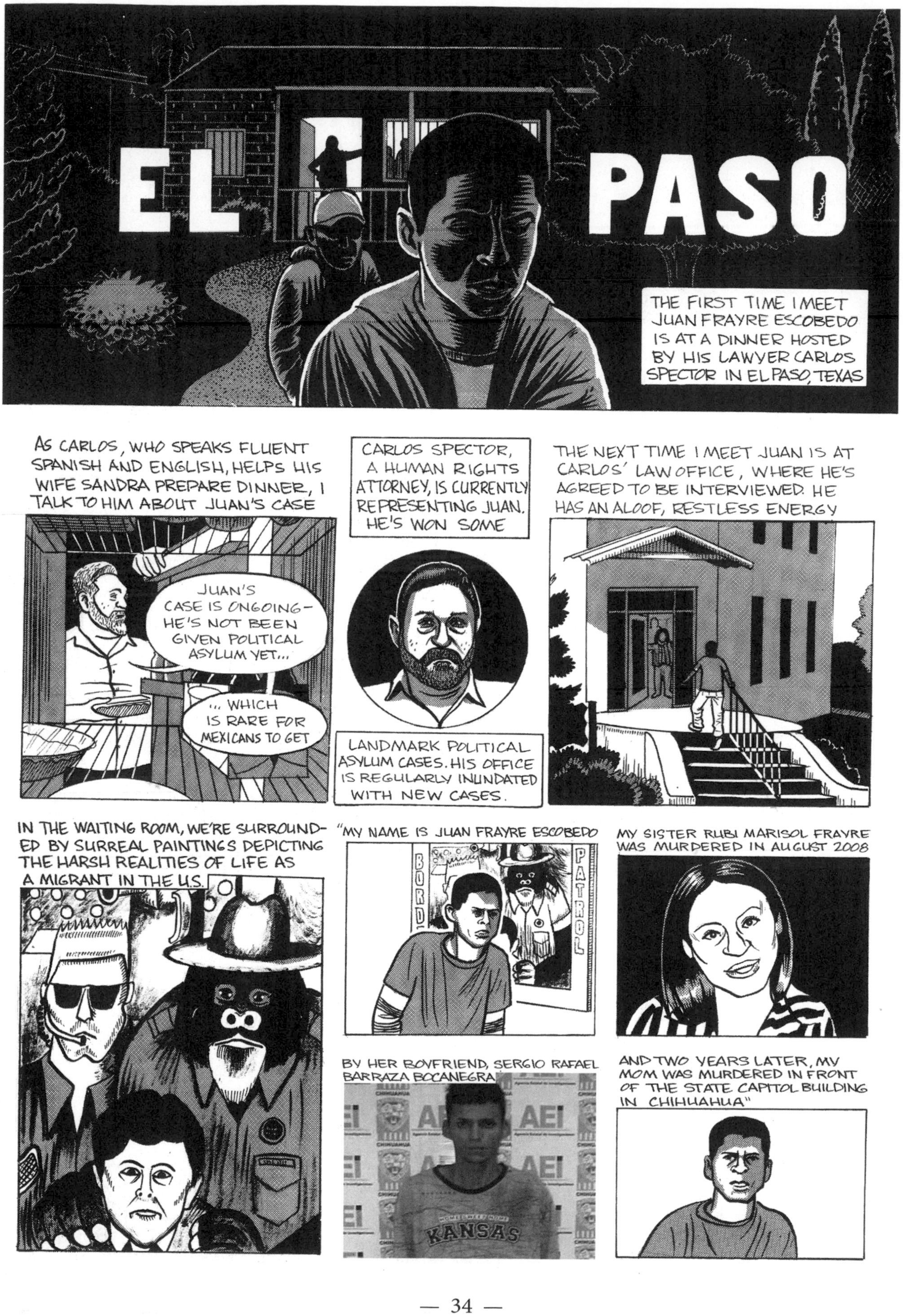
EL PASO
THE FIRST TIME I MEET JUAN FRAYRE ESCOBEDO IS AT A DINNER HOSTED BY HIS LAWYER CARLOS SPECTOR IN EL PASO, TEXAS
AS CARLOS, WHO SPEAKS FLUENT SPANISH AND ENGLISH, HELPS HIS WIFE SANDRA PREPARE DINNER, I TALK TO HIM ABOUT JUAN'S CASE
JUAN'S CASE IS ONGOING- HE'S NOT BEEN GIVEN POLITICAL ASYLUM YET...
... WHICH IS RARE FOR MEXICANS TO GET
CARLOS SPECTOR, A HUMAN RIGHTS ATTORNEY, IS CURRENTLY REPRESENTING JUAN. HE'S WON SOME
LANDMARK POLITICAL ASYLUM CASES. HIS OFFICE IS REGULARLY INUNDATED WITH NEW CASES.
THE NEXT TIME I MEET JUAN IS AT CARLOS' LAW OFFICE, WHERE HE'S AGREED TO BE INTERVIEWED. HE HAS AN ALOOF, RESTLESS ENERGY
IN THE WAITING ROOM, WE'RE SURROUND-ED BY SURREAL PAINTINGS DEPICTING THE HARSH REALITIES OF LIFE AS A MIGRANT IN THE U.S.
"MY NAME IS JUAN FRAYRE ESCOBEDO
PATROL
MY SISTER RUBI MARISOL FRAYRE WAS MURDERED IN AUGUST 2008
BY HER BOYFRIEND, SERGIO RAFAEL BARRAZA BOCANEGRA
AEI
KANSAS
AND TWO YEARS LATER, MY MOM WAS MURDERED IN FRONT OF THE STATE CAPITOL BUILDING IN CHIHUAHUA"

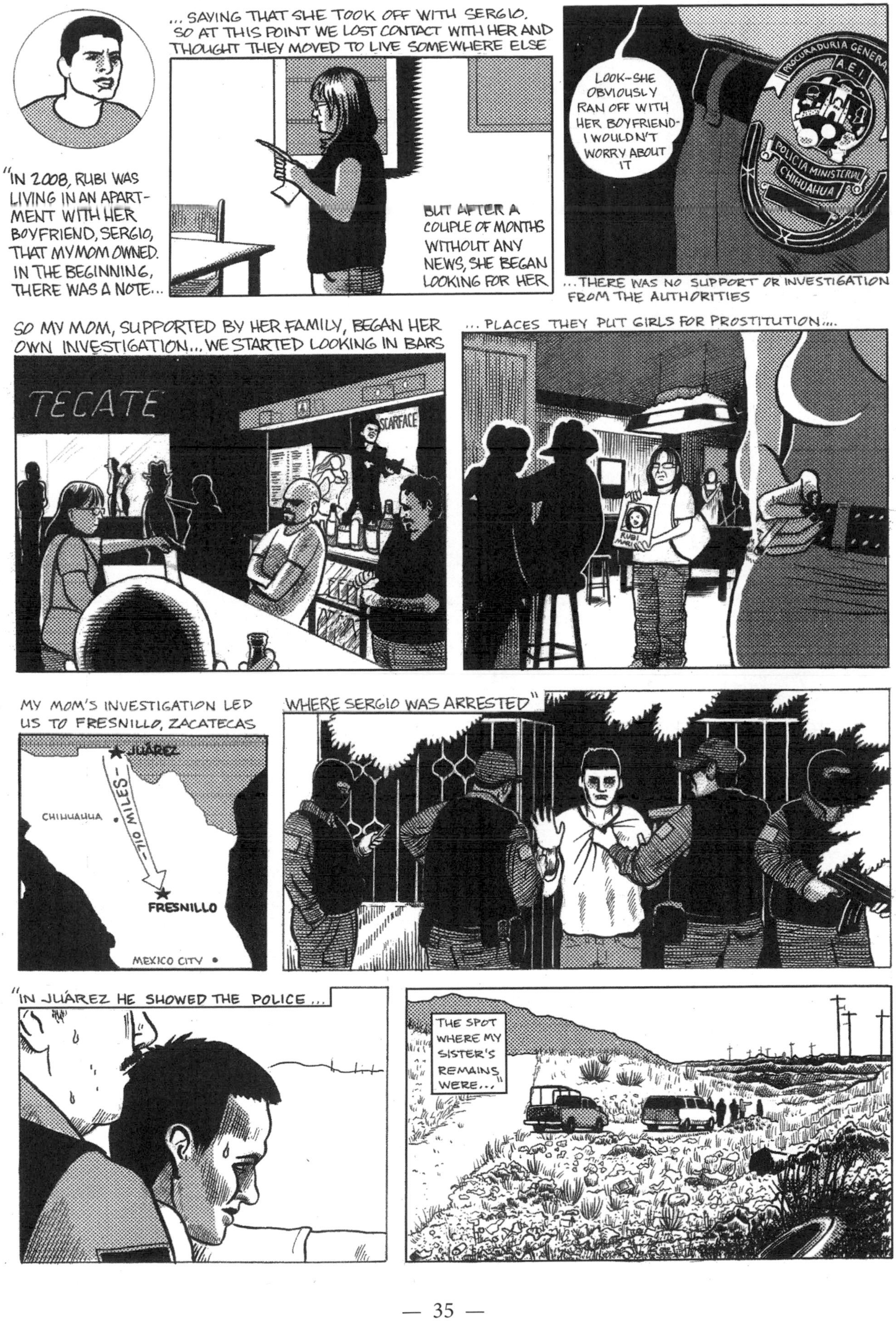

"IN 2008, RUBI WAS LIVING IN AN APARTMENT WITH HER BOYFRIEND, SERGIO, THAT MY MOM OWNED. IN THE BEGINNING, THERE WAS A NOTE...
... SAYING THAT SHE TOOK OFF WITH SERGIO, SO AT THIS POINT WE LOST CONTACT WITH HER AND THOUGHT THEY MOVED TO LIVE SOMEWHERE ELSE
BUT AFTER A COUPLE OF MONTHS WITHOUT ANY NEWS, SHE BEGAN LOOKING FOR HER
LOOK–SHE OBVIOUSLY RAN OFF WITH HER BOYFRIEND–I WOULDN'T WORRY ABOUT IT
PROCURADURIA GENERAL
A.E.I.
POLICIA MINISTERIAL
CHIHUAHUA
... THERE WAS NO SUPPORT OR INVESTIGATION FROM THE AUTHORITIES
SO MY MOM, SUPPORTED BY HER FAMILY, BEGAN HER OWN INVESTIGATION... WE STARTED LOOKING IN BARS
TECATE
SCARFACE
... PLACES THEY PUT GIRLS FOR PROSTITUTION...
MY MOM'S INVESTIGATION LED US TO FRESNILLO, ZACATECAS
JUÁREZ
CHIHUAHUA
–710 MILES–
FRESNILLO
MEXICO CITY
WHERE SERGIO WAS ARRESTED"
"IN JUÁREZ HE SHOWED THE POLICE...
THE SPOT WHERE MY SISTER'S REMAINS WERE..."

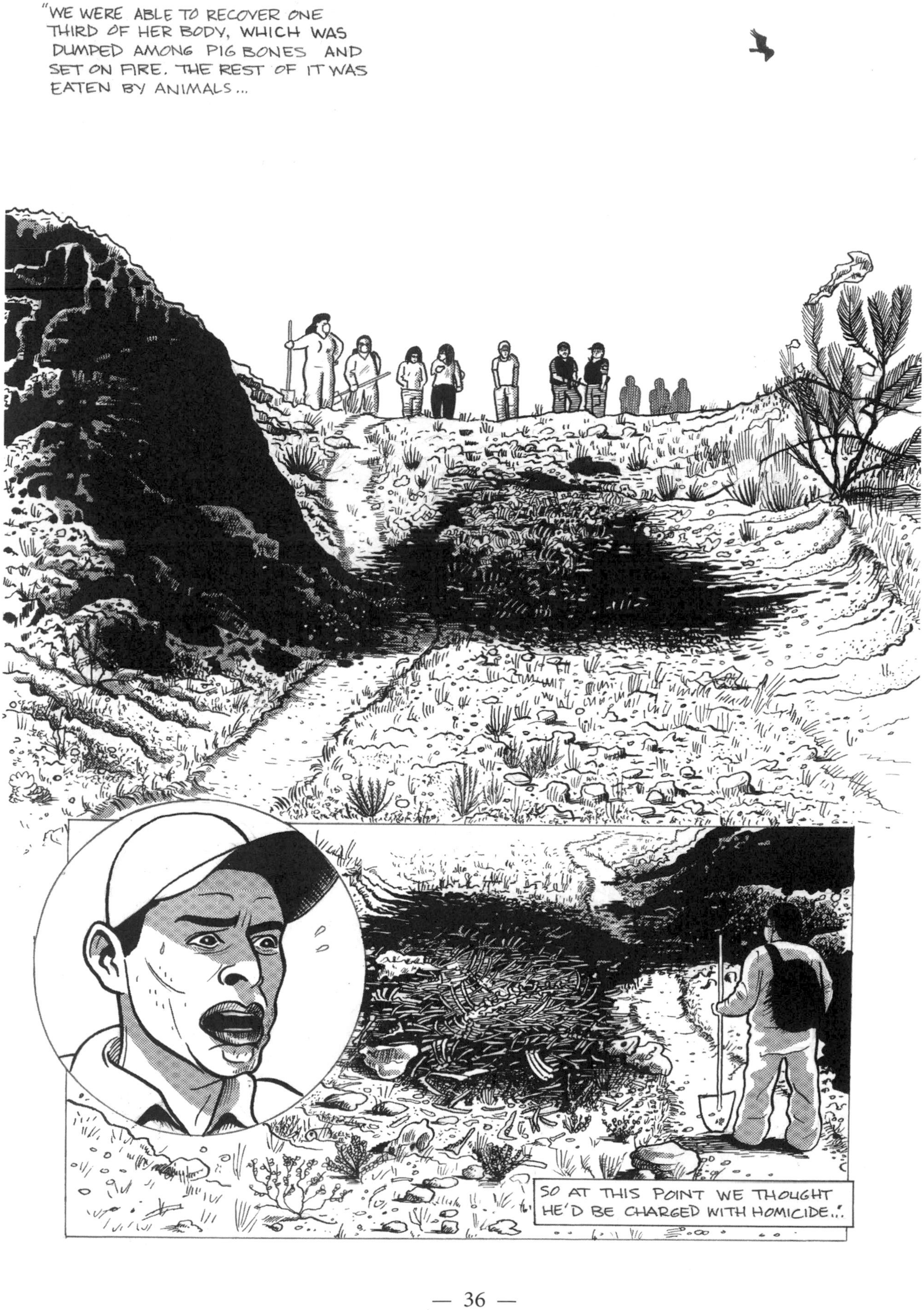
"WE WERE ABLE TO RECOVER ONE THIRD OF HER BODY, WHICH WAS DUMPED AMONG PIG BONES AND SET ON FIRE. THE REST OF IT WAS EATEN BY ANIMALS...
SO AT THIS POINT WE THOUGHT HE'D BE CHARGED WITH HOMICIDE..."

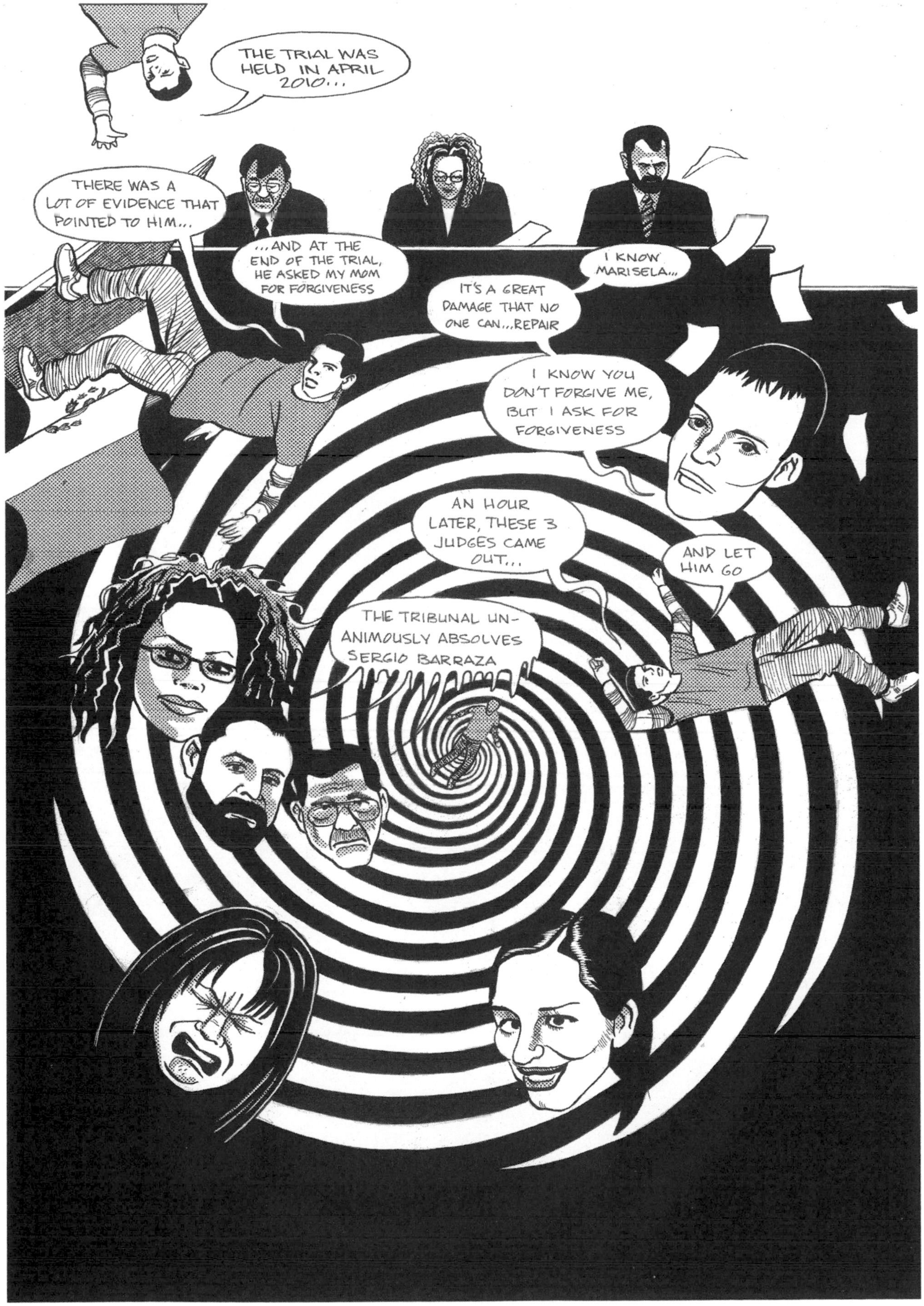
THE TRIAL WAS HELD IN APRIL 2010...
THERE WAS A LOT OF EVIDENCE THAT POINTED TO HIM...
...AND AT THE END OF THE TRIAL, HE ASKED MY MOM FOR FORGIVENESS
I KNOW MARISELA...
IT'S A GREAT DAMAGE THAT NO ONE CAN...REPAIR
I KNOW YOU DON'T FORGIVE ME, BUT I ASK FOR FORGIVENESS
AN HOUR LATER, THESE 3 JUDGES CAME OUT...
AND LET HIM GO
THE TRIBUNAL UN-ANIMOUSLY ABSOLVES SERGIO BARRAZA

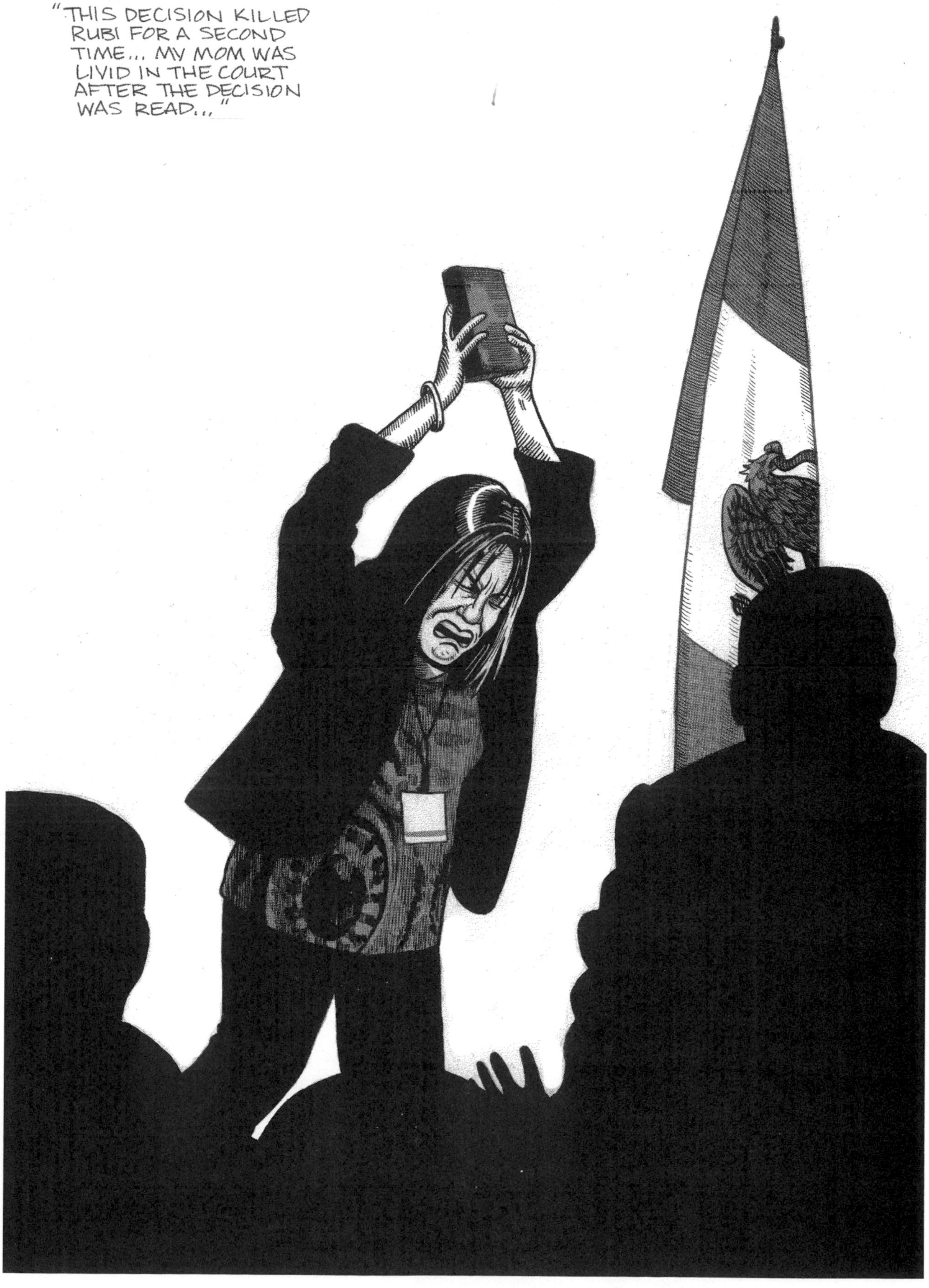
"THIS DECISION KILLED RUBI FOR A SECOND TIME... MY MOM WAS LIVID IN THE COURT AFTER THE DECISION WAS READ..."

"THEY SAID THERE WAS NOT ENOUGH EVIDENCE TO PUT HIM IN JAIL... SO ONCE AGAIN, HE WAS FREE

"AS MY MOM SCREAMED AT THE DECISION, SERGIO GOT UP AND SOUGHT REFUGE NEXT TO THE JUDGES

A MEDIA STORM SOON FOLLOWED AFTER SERGIO'S ACQUITAL, AND THE 3 JUDGES WERE SUSPENDED. ON MAY 20, 2010, SERGIO WAS FOUND GUILTY IN ABSENTIA AND SENTENCED TO 50 YEARS IN PRISON... BUT IT WAS TOO LATE - HE HAD ALREADY DISAPPEARED"

VICTIMAS SIN GARANTI

...AND ONCE AGAIN, MY MOM WAS AFTER HIM"

"WE STARTED A MARCH FROM JUÁREZ TO MEXICO CITY. ON THE WAY, WE PASSED THROUGH FRESNILLO, AND WE FOUND HIM AGAIN, LIVING WITH A NEW GIRLFRIEND

Rubi Maris años Q.E.P

PENA MAXIM

AT TIMES MY MOM WORE ONLY A PHOTO OF RUBI ON MARCHES

SO, WE CALLED THE POLICE...

←ZACATECAS
SALTILLO→

BUT THEY REFUSED TO COME ...AND HE WAS ABLE TO ESCAPE"

"WE LOOKED FOR HIM IN FRESNILLO AND THE TOWNS IN THAT AREA, WITH NO RESULT..."

SO WE CONTINUED TO MEXICO CITY...

...TO DEMAND AN AUDIENCE WITH PRESIDENT CALDERON

RECOMPENSA $250,000

Rubi Maris años Q.E.

SINO

"WHEN WE GOT THERE

HE REFUSED TO MEET MY MOM...

SO WE CAME BACK TO JUÁREZ AND WAITED 30 DAYS TO SEE WHAT WAS GOING TO HAPPEN WITH THE AUTHORITIES... AND SAW THEY WEREN'T GOING TO DO ANYTHING"

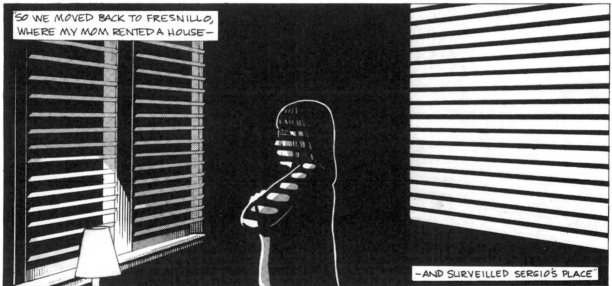

"SO WE MOVED BACK TO FRESNILLO, WHERE MY MOM RENTED A HOUSE—

—AND SURVEILLED SERGIO'S PLACE"

"HE WASN'T THERE

BUT WE KNEW HE'D COME BACK

AS HIS GIRLFRIEND WAS THERE"

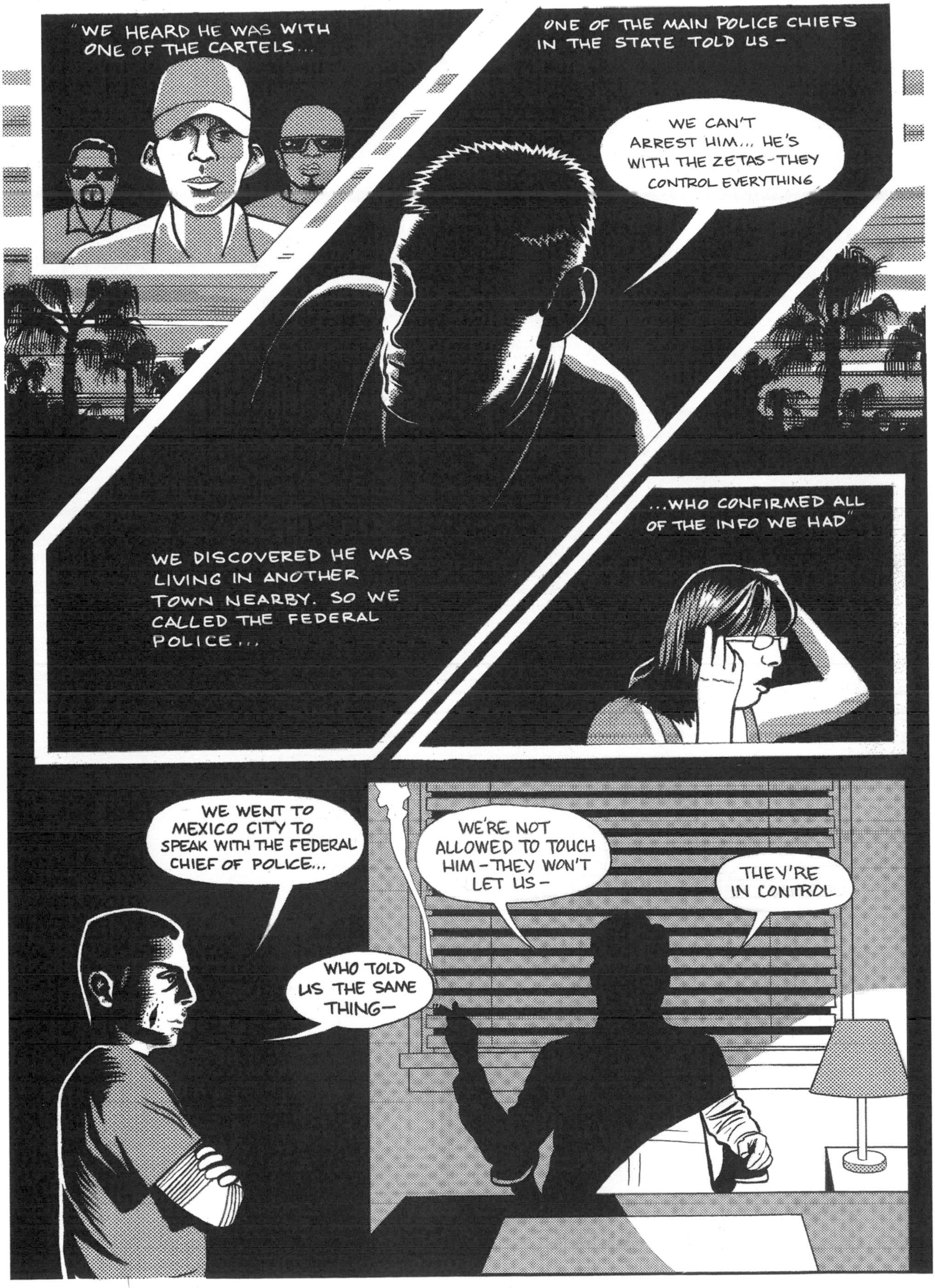
"WE HEARD HE WAS WITH ONE OF THE CARTELS...
ONE OF THE MAIN POLICE CHIEFS IN THE STATE TOLD US –
WE CAN'T ARREST HIM... HE'S WITH THE ZETAS – THEY CONTROL EVERYTHING
WE DISCOVERED HE WAS LIVING IN ANOTHER TOWN NEARBY. SO WE CALLED THE FEDERAL POLICE...
...WHO CONFIRMED ALL OF THE INFO WE HAD"
WE WENT TO MEXICO CITY TO SPEAK WITH THE FEDERAL CHIEF OF POLICE...
WHO TOLD US THE SAME THING–
WE'RE NOT ALLOWED TO TOUCH HIM – THEY WON'T LET US –
THEY'RE IN CONTROL

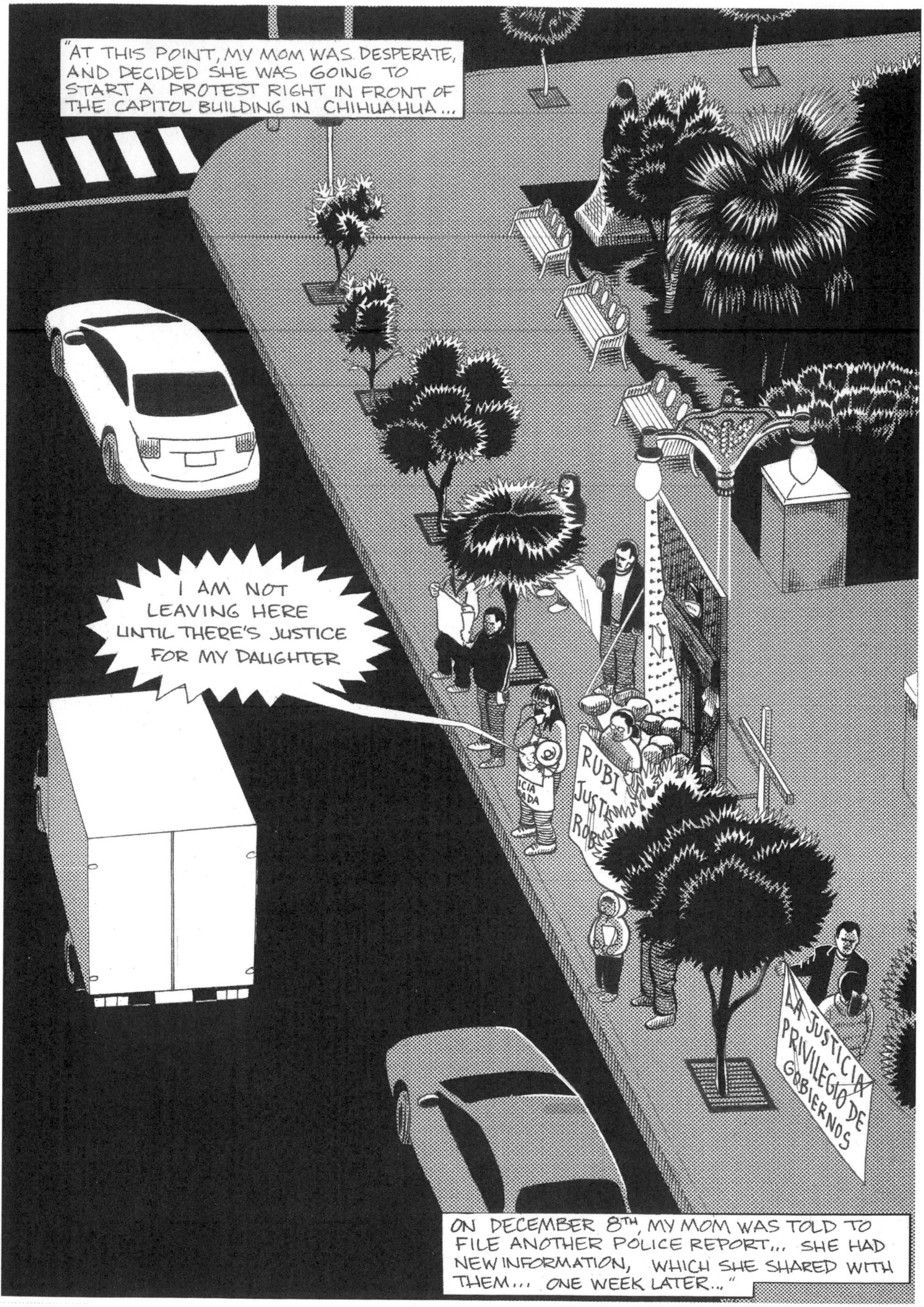
"AT THIS POINT, MY MOM WAS DESPERATE, AND DECIDED SHE WAS GOING TO START A PROTEST RIGHT IN FRONT OF THE CAPITOL BUILDING IN CHIHUAHUA...
I AM NOT LEAVING HERE UNTIL THERE'S JUSTICE FOR MY DAUGHTER
RUBI
LA JUSTICIA PRIVILEGIO DE GOBIERNOS
ON DECEMBER 8TH, MY MOM WAS TOLD TO FILE ANOTHER POLICE REPORT... SHE HAD NEW INFORMATION, WHICH SHE SHARED WITH THEM... ONE WEEK LATER..."

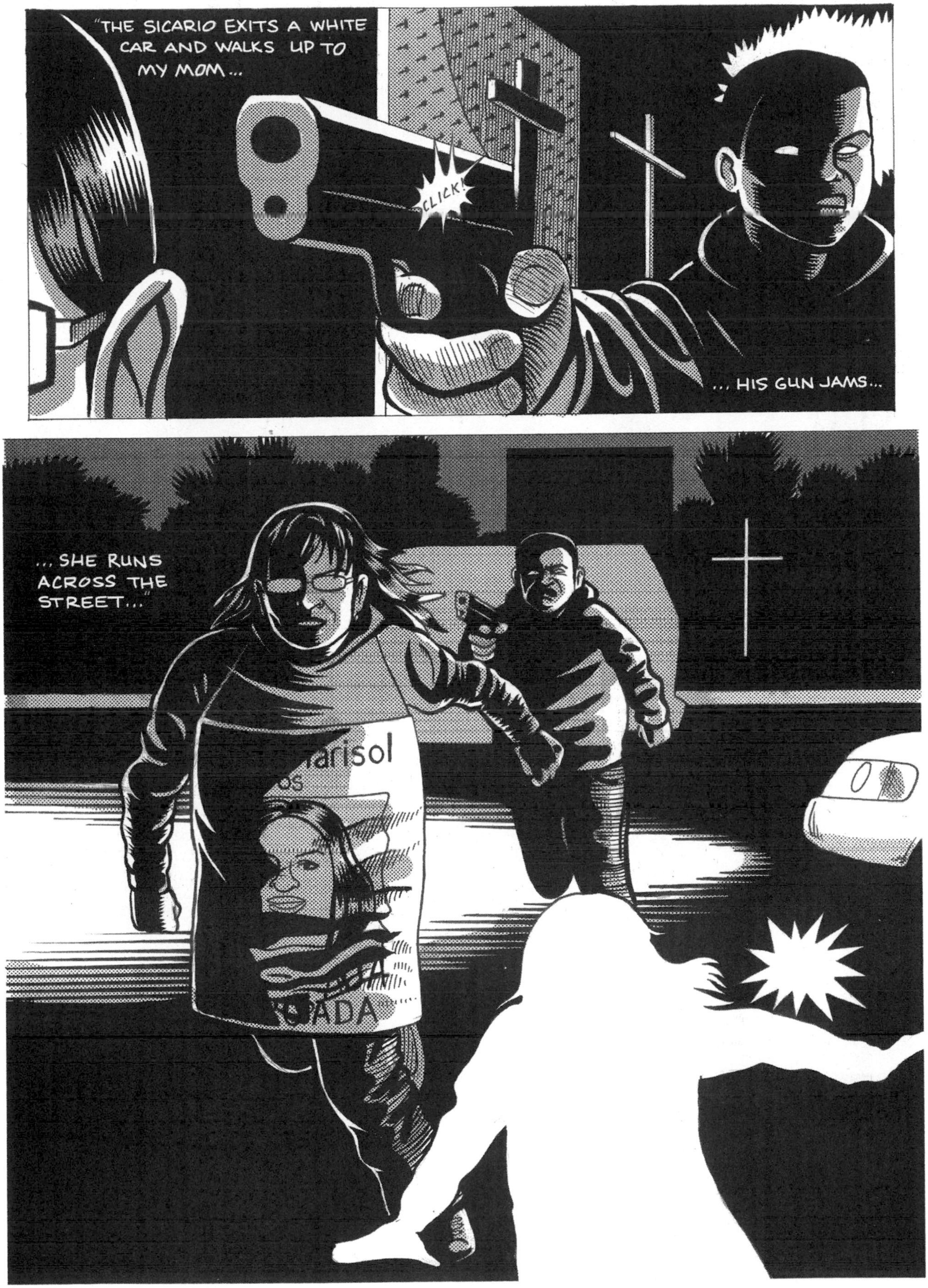
"THE SICARIO EXITS A WHITE CAR AND WALKS UP TO MY MOM...
CLICK!
... HIS GUN JAMS...
... SHE RUNS ACROSS THE STREET..."

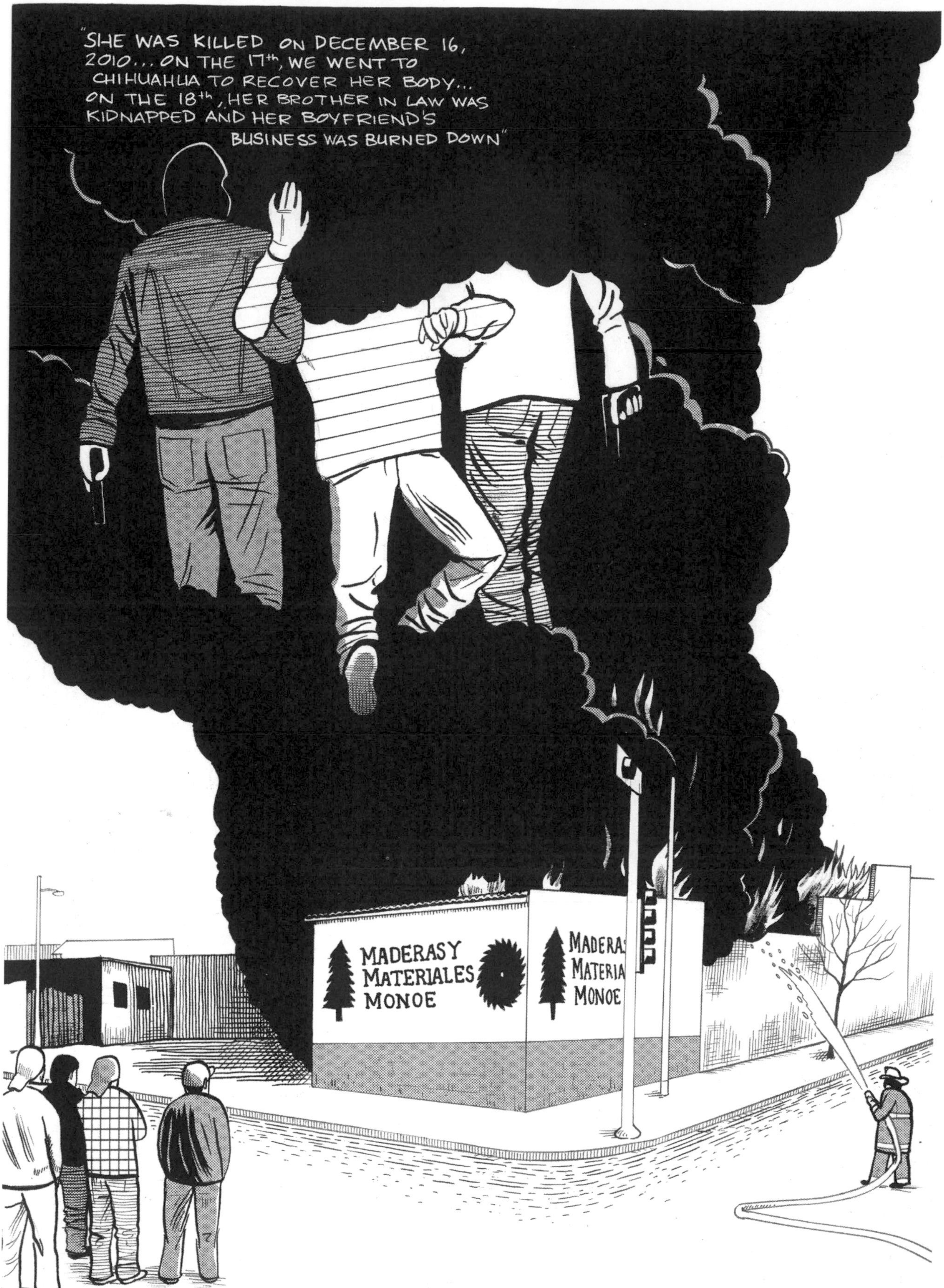
"SHE WAS KILLED ON DECEMBER 16, 2010... ON THE 17th, WE WENT TO CHIHUAHUA TO RECOVER HER BODY... ON THE 18th, HER BROTHER IN LAW WAS KIDNAPPED AND HER BOYFRIEND'S BUSINESS WAS BURNED DOWN"
MADERAS Y MATERIALES MONOE
MADERAS MATERIA MONOE

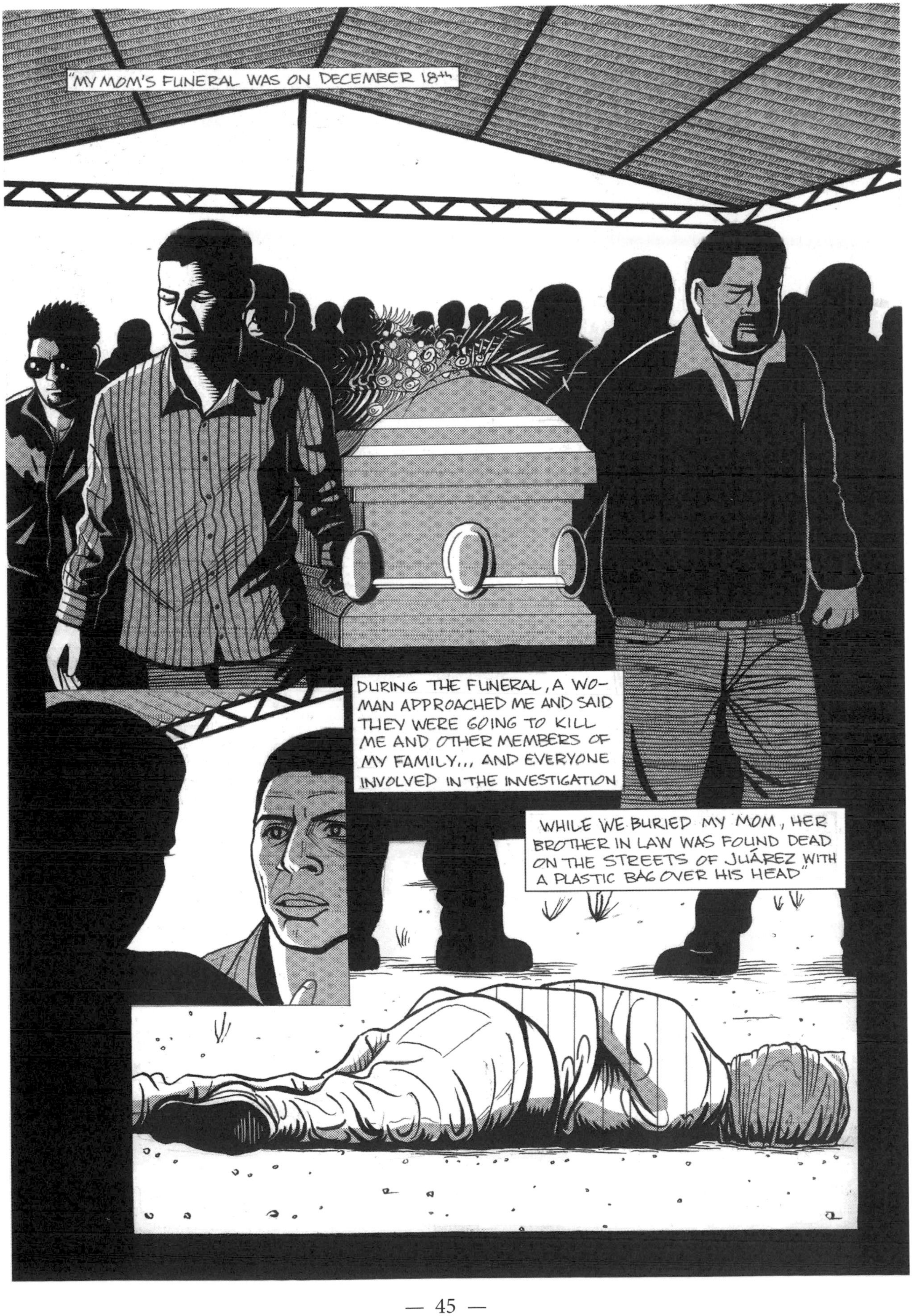
"MY MOM'S FUNERAL WAS ON DECEMBER 18th
DURING THE FUNERAL, A WOMAN APPROACHED ME AND SAID THEY WERE GOING TO KILL ME AND OTHER MEMBERS OF MY FAMILY..., AND EVERYONE INVOLVED IN THE INVESTIGATION
WHILE WE BURIED MY MOM, HER BROTHER IN LAW WAS FOUND DEAD ON THE STREETS OF JUÁREZ WITH A PLASTIC BAG OVER HIS HEAD"

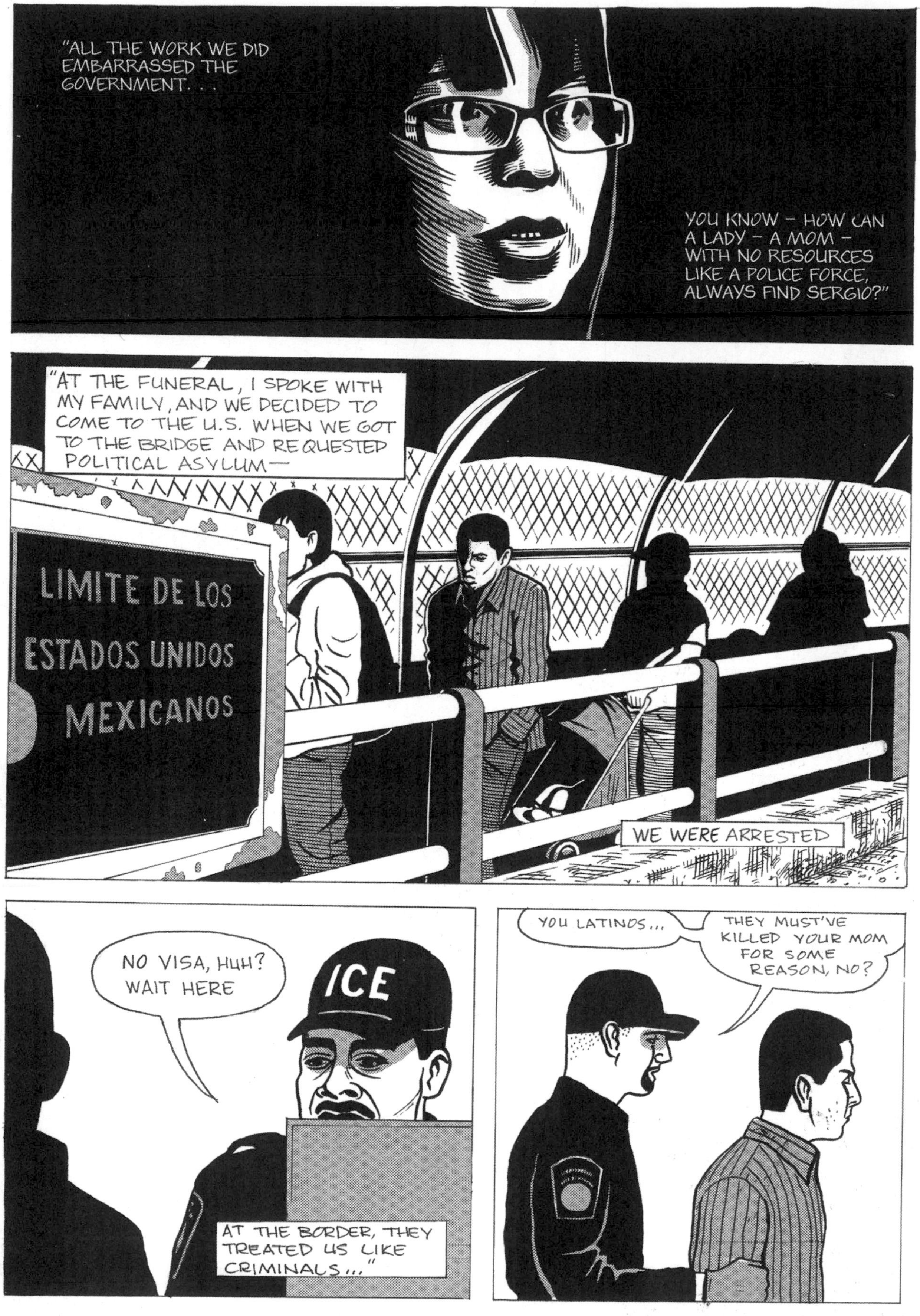
"ALL THE WORK WE DID EMBARRASSED THE GOVERNMENT. . .
YOU KNOW – HOW CAN A LADY – A MOM – WITH NO RESOURCES LIKE A POLICE FORCE, ALWAYS FIND SERGIO?"
"AT THE FUNERAL, I SPOKE WITH MY FAMILY, AND WE DECIDED TO COME TO THE U.S. WHEN WE GOT TO THE BRIDGE AND REQUESTED POLITICAL ASYLUM—
LIMITE DE LOS ESTADOS UNIDOS MEXICANOS
WE WERE ARRESTED
NO VISA, HUH? WAIT HERE
ICE
AT THE BORDER, THEY TREATED US LIKE CRIMINALS..."
YOU LATINOS...
THEY MUST'VE KILLED YOUR MOM FOR SOME REASON, NO?

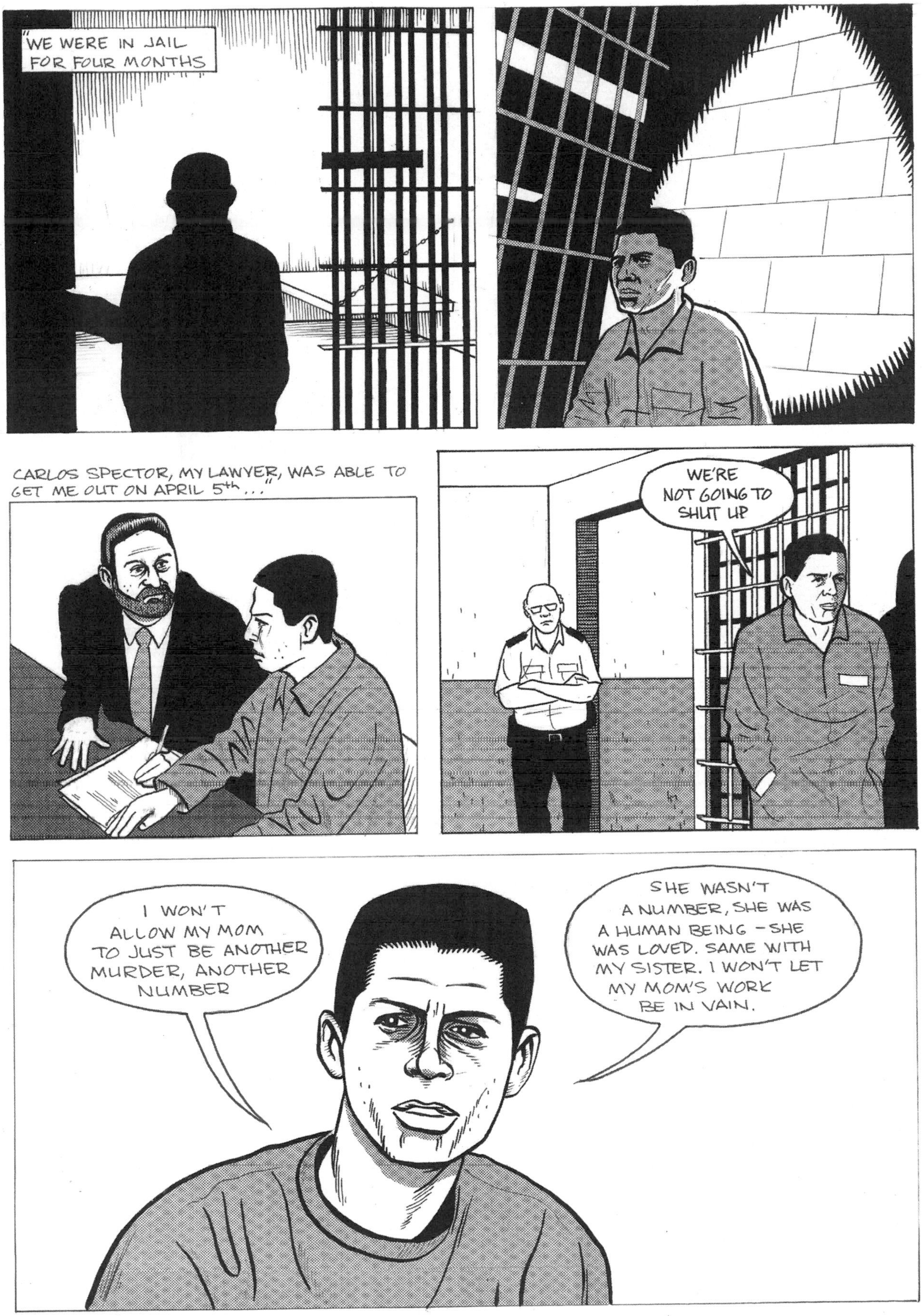
"WE WERE IN JAIL FOR FOUR MONTHS
CARLOS SPECTOR, MY LAWYER, WAS ABLE TO GET ME OUT ON APRIL 5th..."
WE'RE NOT GOING TO SHUT UP
I WON'T ALLOW MY MOM TO JUST BE ANOTHER MURDER, ANOTHER NUMBER
SHE WASN'T A NUMBER, SHE WAS A HUMAN BEING - SHE WAS LOVED. SAME WITH MY SISTER. I WON'T LET MY MOM'S WORK BE IN VAIN.

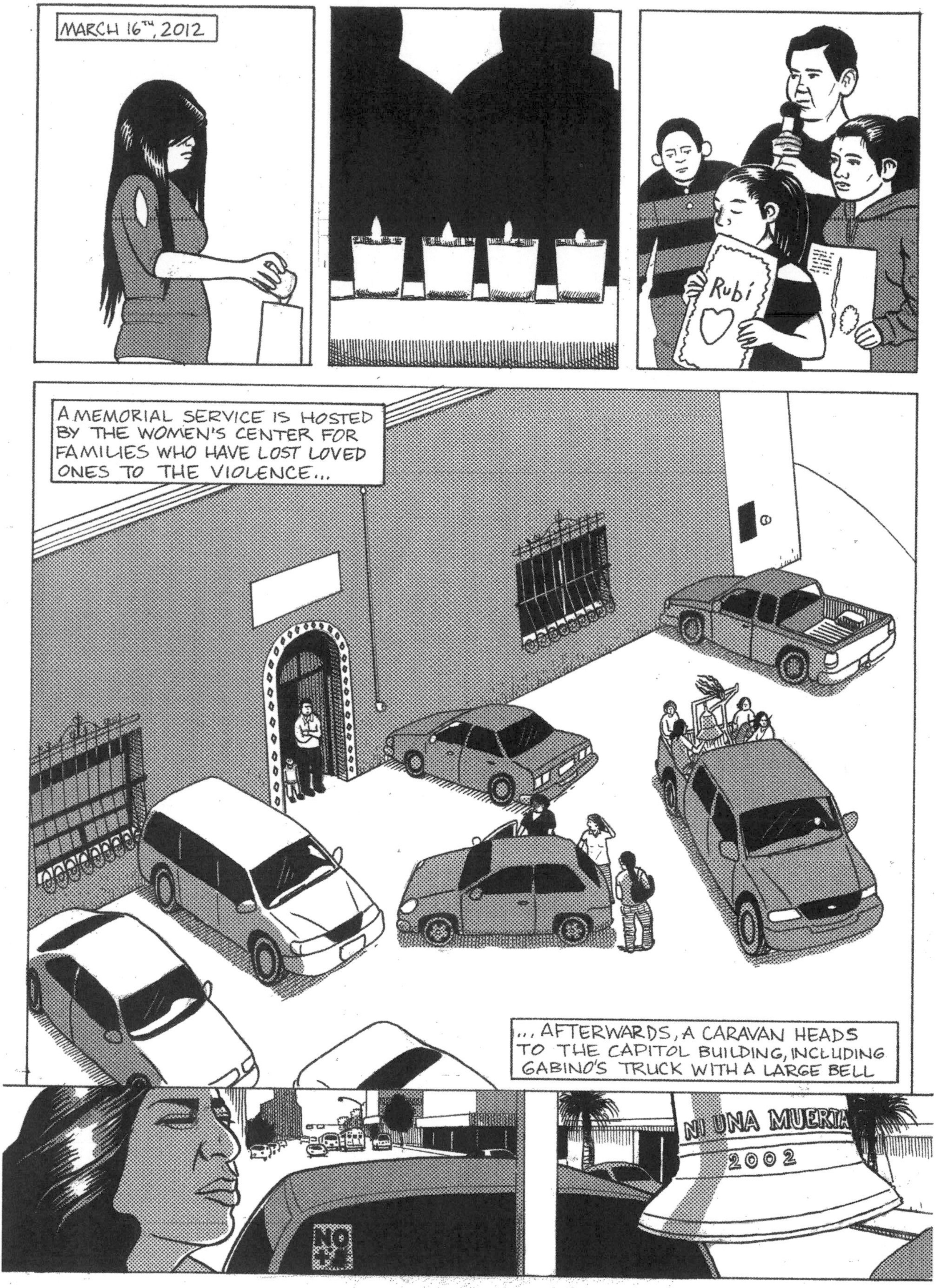
MARCH 16TH, 2012
Rubí
A MEMORIAL SERVICE IS HOSTED BY THE WOMEN'S CENTER FOR FAMILIES WHO HAVE LOST LOVED ONES TO THE VIOLENCE...
...AFTERWARDS, A CARAVAN HEADS TO THE CAPITOL BUILDING, INCLUDING GABINO'S TRUCK WITH A LARGE BELL
NI UNA MUERTA
2002

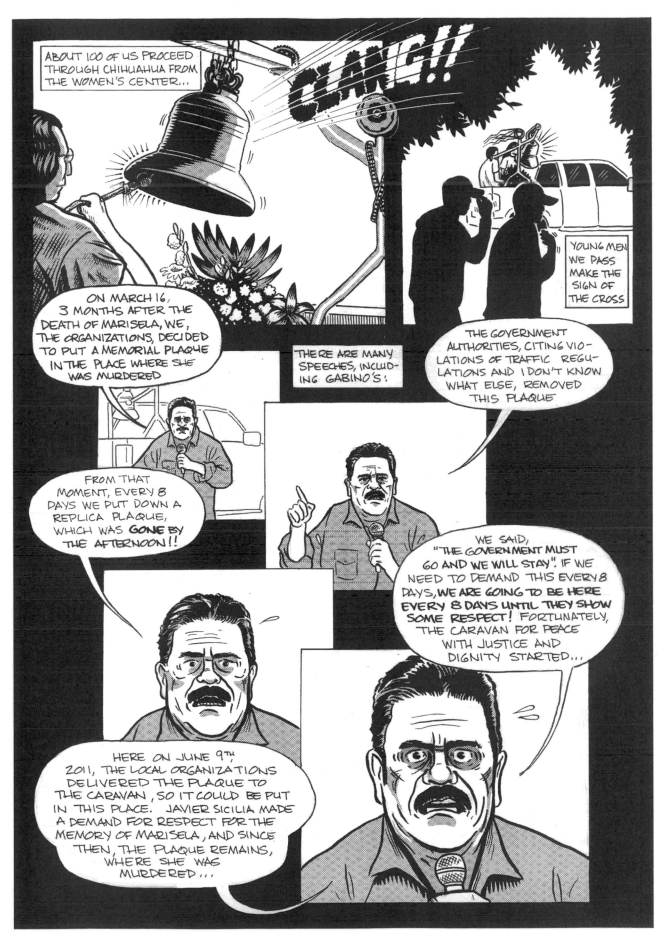

ABOUT 100 OF US PROCEED THROUGH CHIHUAHUA FROM THE WOMEN'S CENTER...

CLANG!!

YOUNG MEN WE PASS MAKE THE SIGN OF THE CROSS

ON MARCH 16, 3 MONTHS AFTER THE DEATH OF MARISELA, WE, THE ORGANIZATIONS, DECIDED TO PUT A MEMORIAL PLAQUE IN THE PLACE WHERE SHE WAS MURDERED

THERE ARE MANY SPEECHES, INCLUDING GABINO'S:

THE GOVERNMENT AUTHORITIES, CITING VIOLATIONS OF TRAFFIC REGULATIONS AND I DON'T KNOW WHAT ELSE, REMOVED THIS PLAQUE

FROM THAT MOMENT, EVERY 8 DAYS WE PUT DOWN A REPLICA PLAQUE, WHICH WAS GONE BY THE AFTERNOON!!

WE SAID, "THE GOVERNMENT MUST GO AND WE WILL STAY". IF WE NEED TO DEMAND THIS EVERY 8 DAYS, WE ARE GOING TO BE HERE EVERY 8 DAYS UNTIL THEY SHOW SOME RESPECT! FORTUNATELY, THE CARAVAN FOR PEACE WITH JUSTICE AND DIGNITY STARTED...

HERE ON JUNE 9TH, 2011, THE LOCAL ORGANIZATIONS DELIVERED THE PLAQUE TO THE CARAVAN, SO IT COULD BE PUT IN THIS PLACE. JAVIER SICILIA MADE A DEMAND FOR RESPECT FOR THE MEMORY OF MARISELA, AND SINCE THEN, THE PLAQUE REMAINS, WHERE SHE WAS MURDERED...

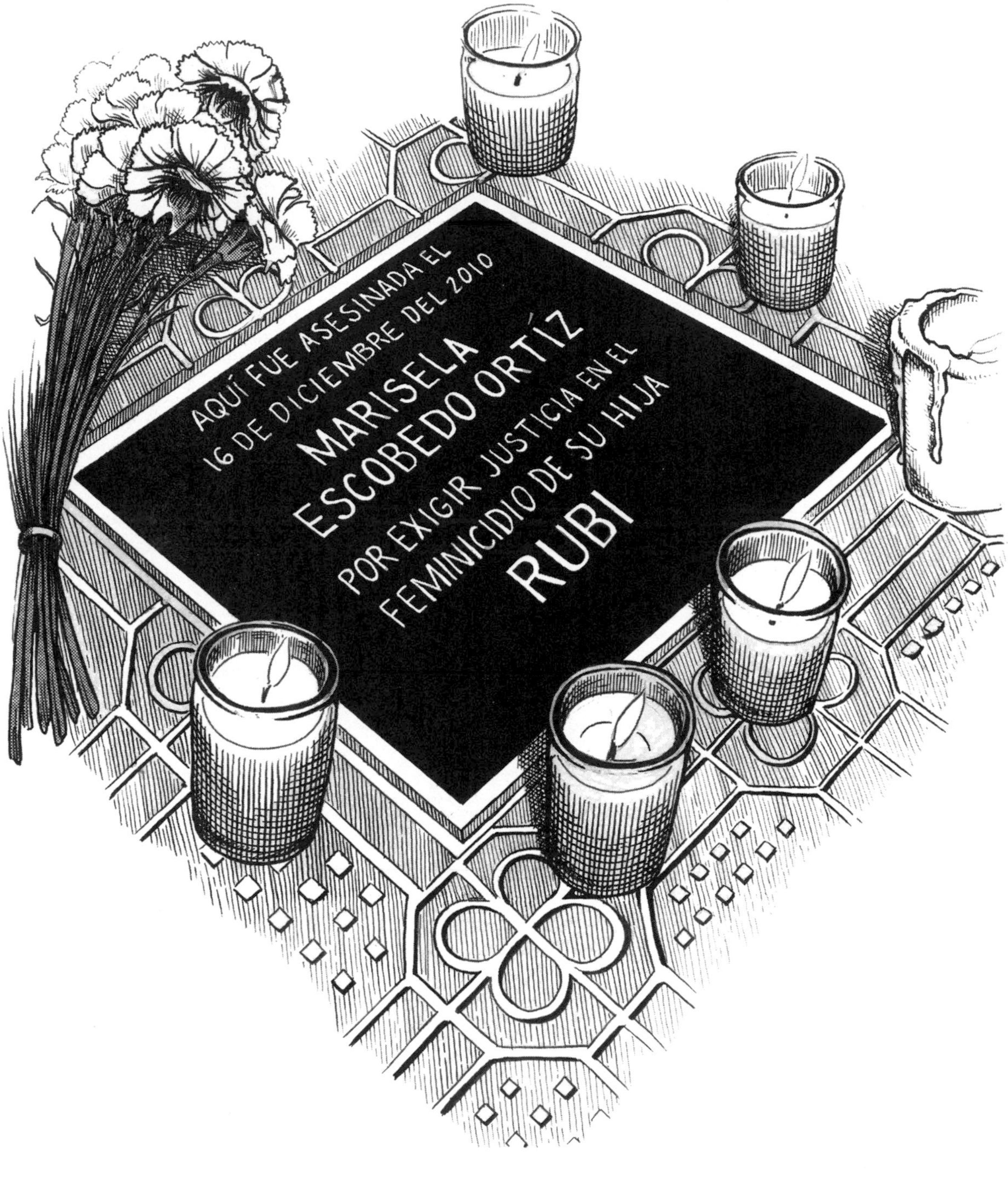
AQUÍ FUE ASESINADA EL
16 DE DICIEMBRE DEL 2010
MARISELA
ESCOBEDO ORTÍZ
POR EXIGIR JUSTICIA EN EL
FEMINICIDIO DE SU HIJA
RUBI

END

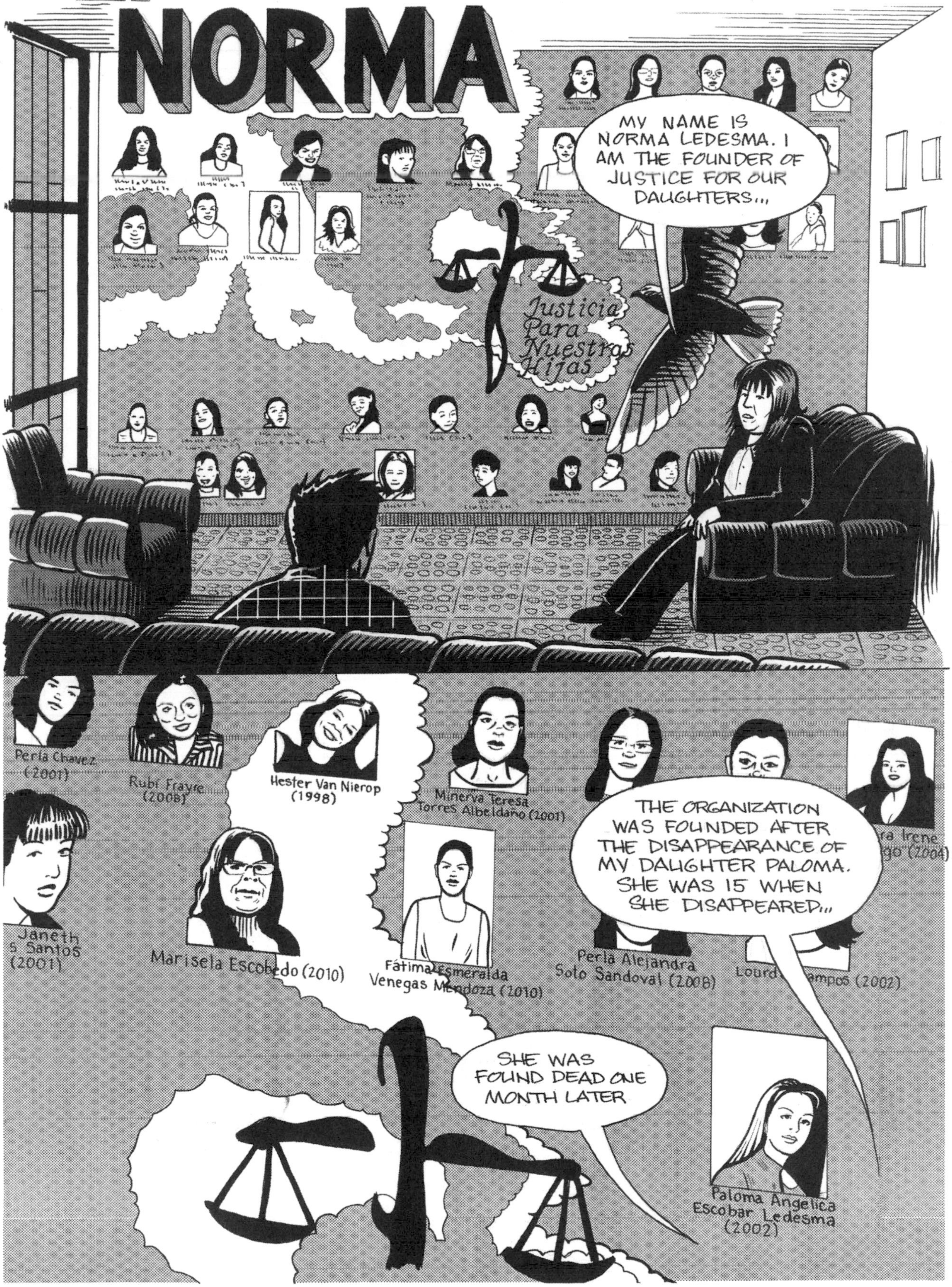

NORMA
MY NAME IS NORMA LEDESMA. I AM THE FOUNDER OF JUSTICE FOR OUR DAUGHTERS...
Justicia Para Nuestras Hijas
Perla Chavez (2001)
Rubi Frayre (2008)
Hester Van Nierop (1998)
Minerva Teresa Torres Albeldaño (2001)
THE ORGANIZATION WAS FOUNDED AFTER THE DISAPPEARANCE OF MY DAUGHTER PALOMA. SHE WAS 15 WHEN SHE DISAPPEARED...
Janeth s Santos (2001)
Marisela Escobedo (2010)
Fátima Esmeralda Venegas Mendoza (2010)
Perla Alejandra Soto Sandoval (2008)
SHE WAS FOUND DEAD ONE MONTH LATER
Paloma Angelica Escobar Ledesma (2002)

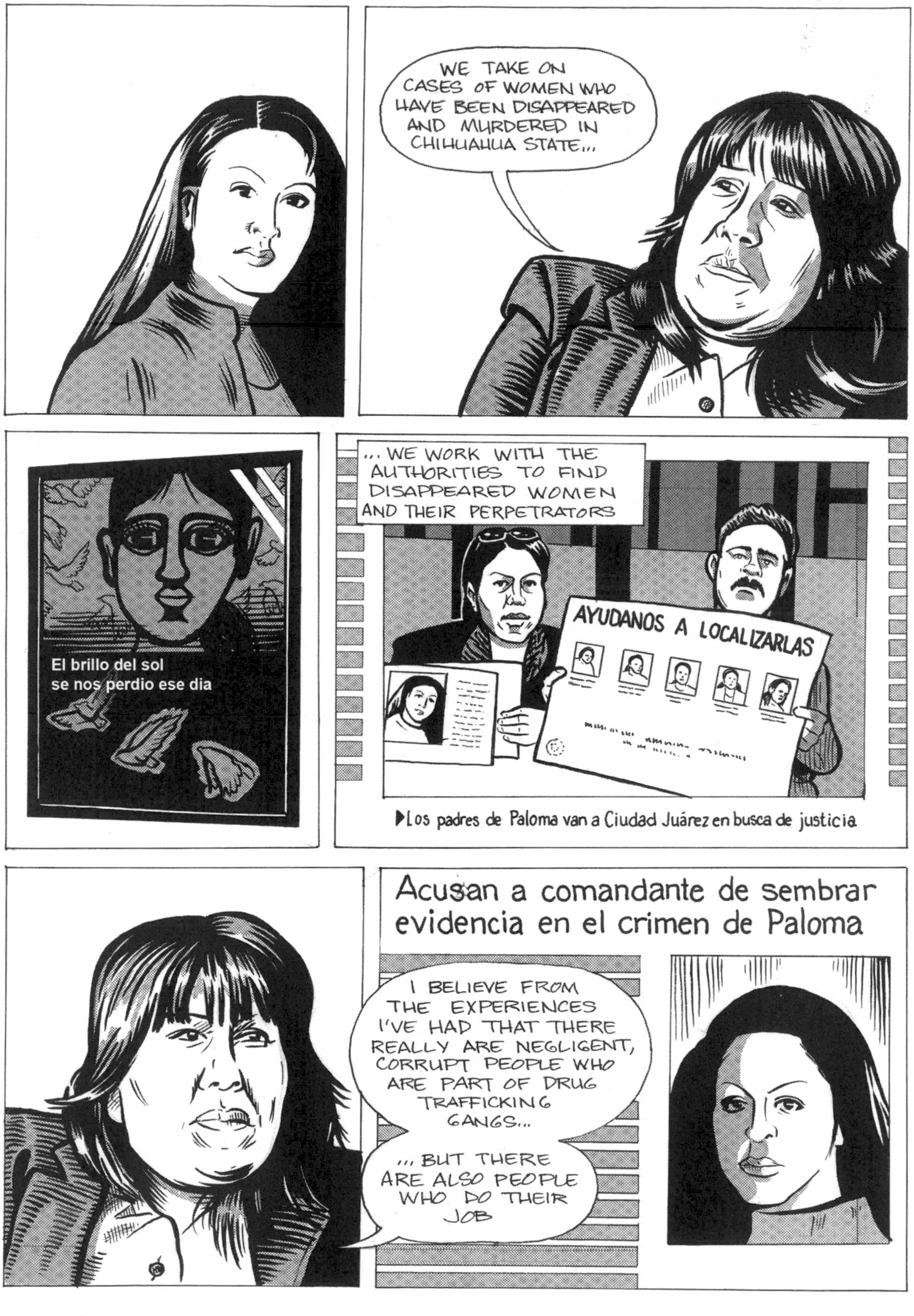
WE TAKE ON CASES OF WOMEN WHO HAVE BEEN DISAPPEARED AND MURDERED IN CHIHUAHUA STATE...
El brillo del sol se nos perdio ese dia
...WE WORK WITH THE AUTHORITIES TO FIND DISAPPEARED WOMEN AND THEIR PERPETRATORS
AYUDANOS A LOCALIZARLAS
Los padres de Paloma van a Ciudad Juárez en busca de justicia
Acusan a comandante de sembrar evidencia en el crimen de Paloma
I BELIEVE FROM THE EXPERIENCES I'VE HAD THAT THERE REALLY ARE NEGLIGENT, CORRUPT PEOPLE WHO ARE PART OF DRUG TRAFFICKING GANGS...
...BUT THERE ARE ALSO PEOPLE WHO DO THEIR JOB

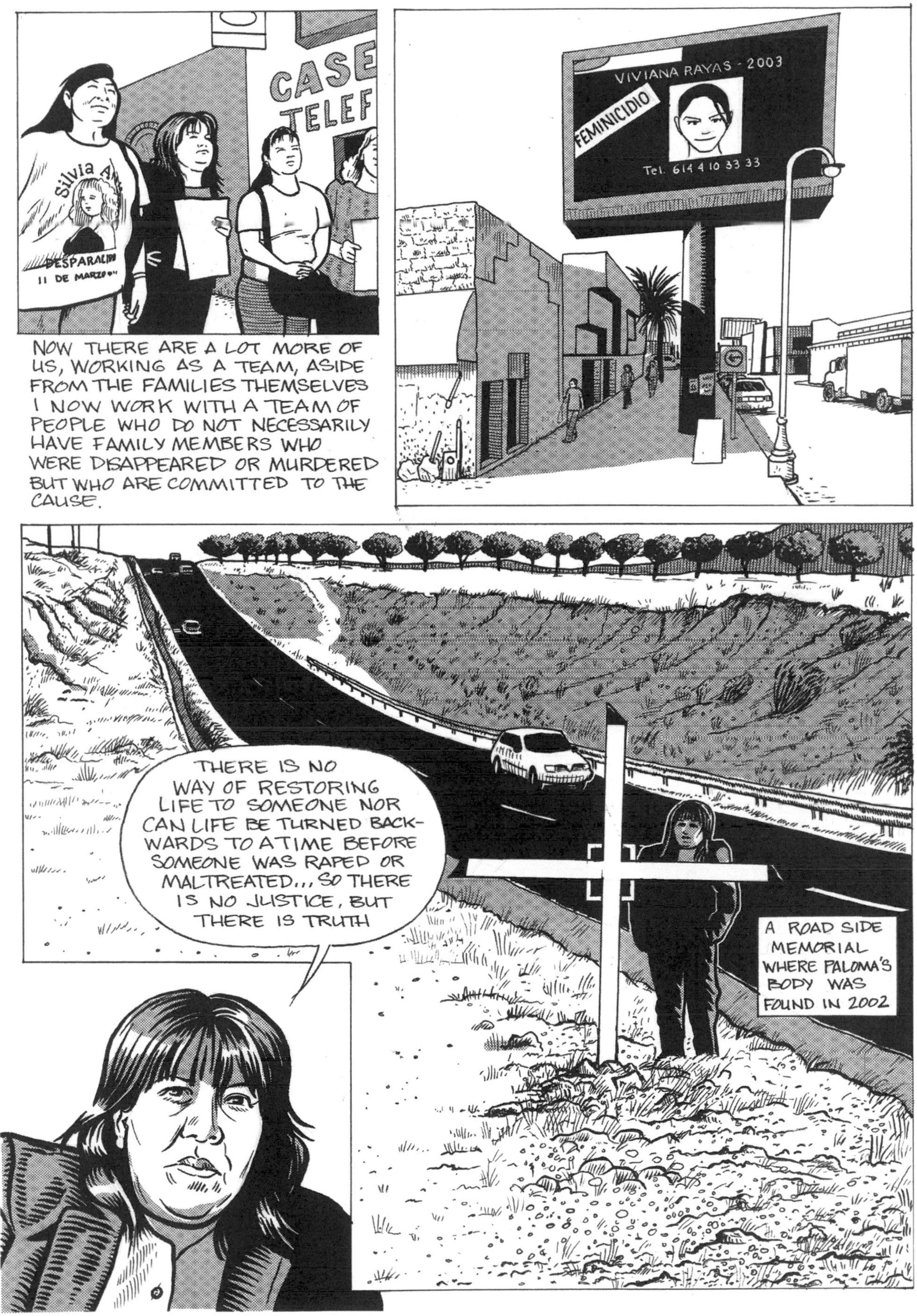
NOW THERE ARE A LOT MORE OF US, WORKING AS A TEAM, ASIDE FROM THE FAMILIES THEMSELVES I NOW WORK WITH A TEAM OF PEOPLE WHO DO NOT NECESSARILY HAVE FAMILY MEMBERS WHO WERE DISAPPEARED OR MURDERED BUT WHO ARE COMMITTED TO THE CAUSE.
VIVIANA RAYAS - 2003
FEMINICIDIO
Tel. 614 4 10 33 33
THERE IS NO WAY OF RESTORING LIFE TO SOMEONE NOR CAN LIFE BE TURNED BACK-WARDS TO A TIME BEFORE SOMEONE WAS RAPED OR MALTREATED... SO THERE IS NO JUSTICE, BUT THERE IS TRUTH
A ROAD SIDE MEMORIAL WHERE PALOMA'S BODY WAS FOUND IN 2002

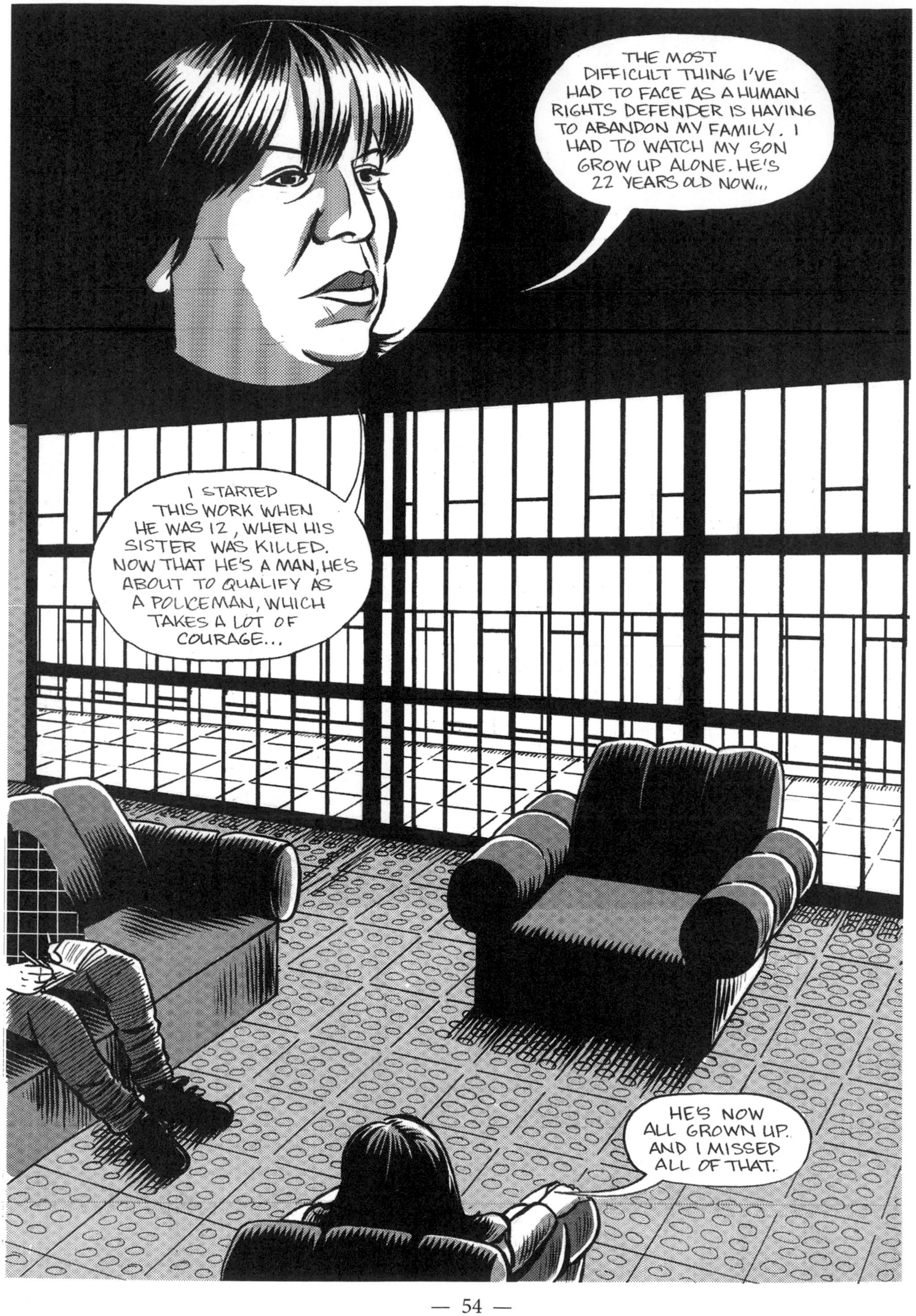
THE MOST DIFFICULT THING I'VE HAD TO FACE AS A HUMAN RIGHTS DEFENDER IS HAVING TO ABANDON MY FAMILY. I HAD TO WATCH MY SON GROW UP ALONE. HE'S 22 YEARS OLD NOW...
I STARTED THIS WORK WHEN HE WAS 12, WHEN HIS SISTER WAS KILLED. NOW THAT HE'S A MAN, HE'S ABOUT TO QUALIFY AS A POLICEMAN, WHICH TAKES A LOT OF COURAGE...
HE'S NOW ALL GROWN UP. AND I MISSED ALL OF THAT.

EMILIA

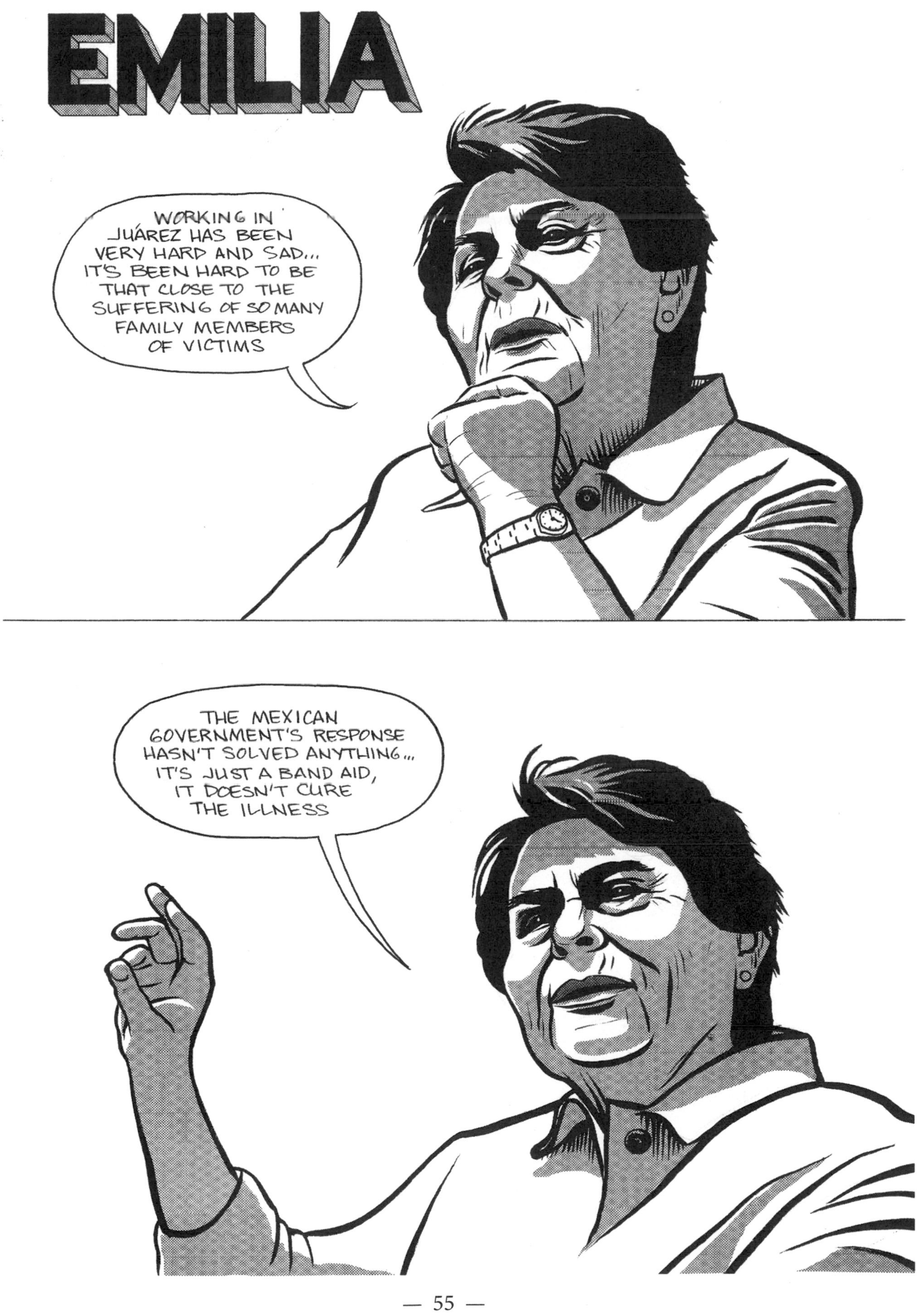

WORKING IN JUÁREZ HAS BEEN VERY HARD AND SAD... IT'S BEEN HARD TO BE THAT CLOSE TO THE SUFFERING OF SO MANY FAMILY MEMBERS OF VICTIMS
THE MEXICAN GOVERNMENT'S RESPONSE HASN'T SOLVED ANYTHING... IT'S JUST A BAND AID, IT DOESN'T CURE THE ILLNESS

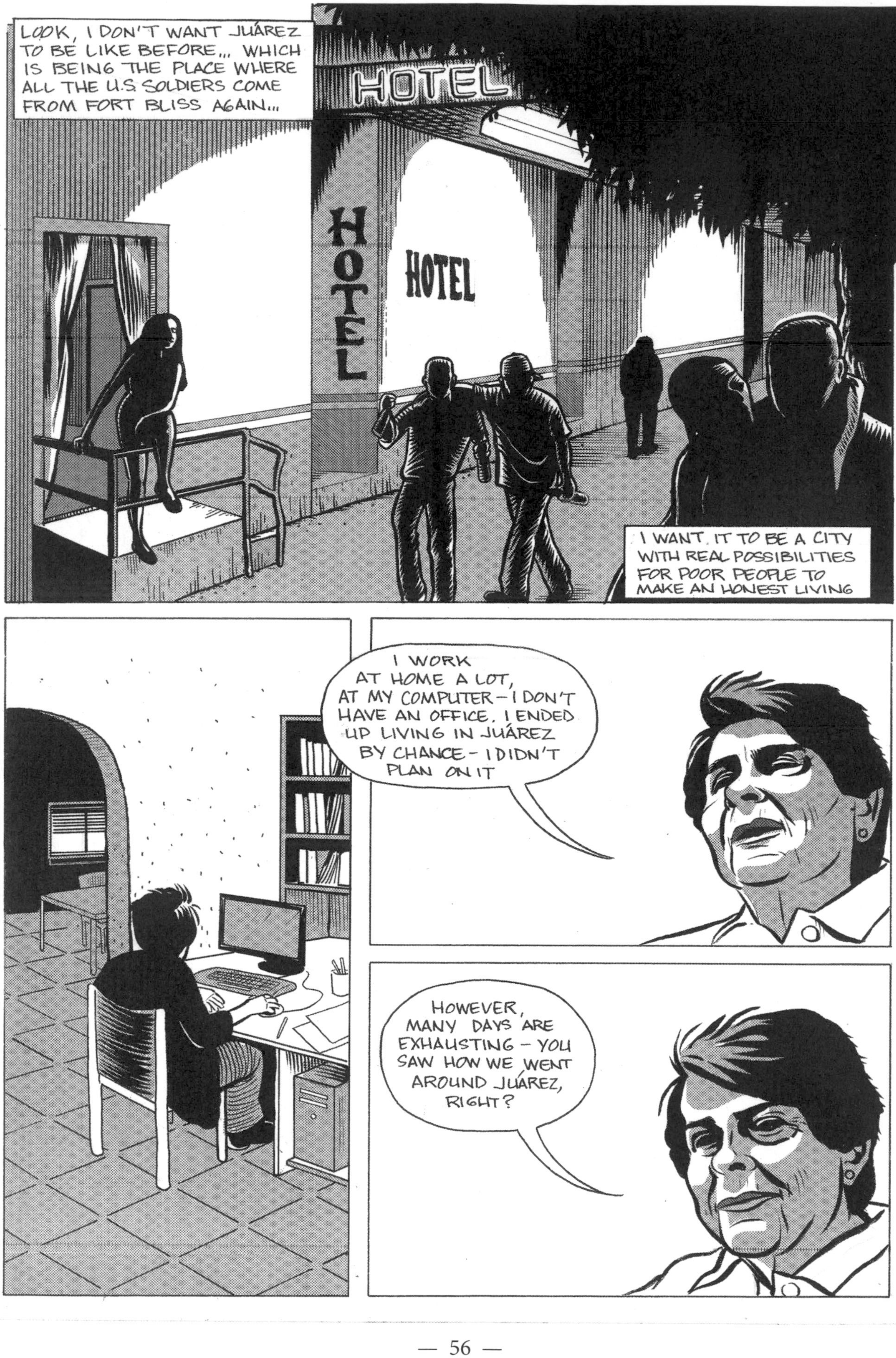
LOOK, I DON'T WANT JUÁREZ TO BE LIKE BEFORE... WHICH IS BEING THE PLACE WHERE ALL THE U.S SOLDIERS COME FROM FORT BLISS AGAIN...
HOTEL
HOTEL
HOTEL
I WANT IT TO BE A CITY WITH REAL POSSIBILITIES FOR POOR PEOPLE TO MAKE AN HONEST LIVING
I WORK AT HOME A LOT, AT MY COMPUTER – I DON'T HAVE AN OFFICE. I ENDED UP LIVING IN JUÁREZ BY CHANCE – I DIDN'T PLAN ON IT
HOWEVER, MANY DAYS ARE EXHAUSTING – YOU SAW HOW WE WENT AROUND JUÁREZ, RIGHT?

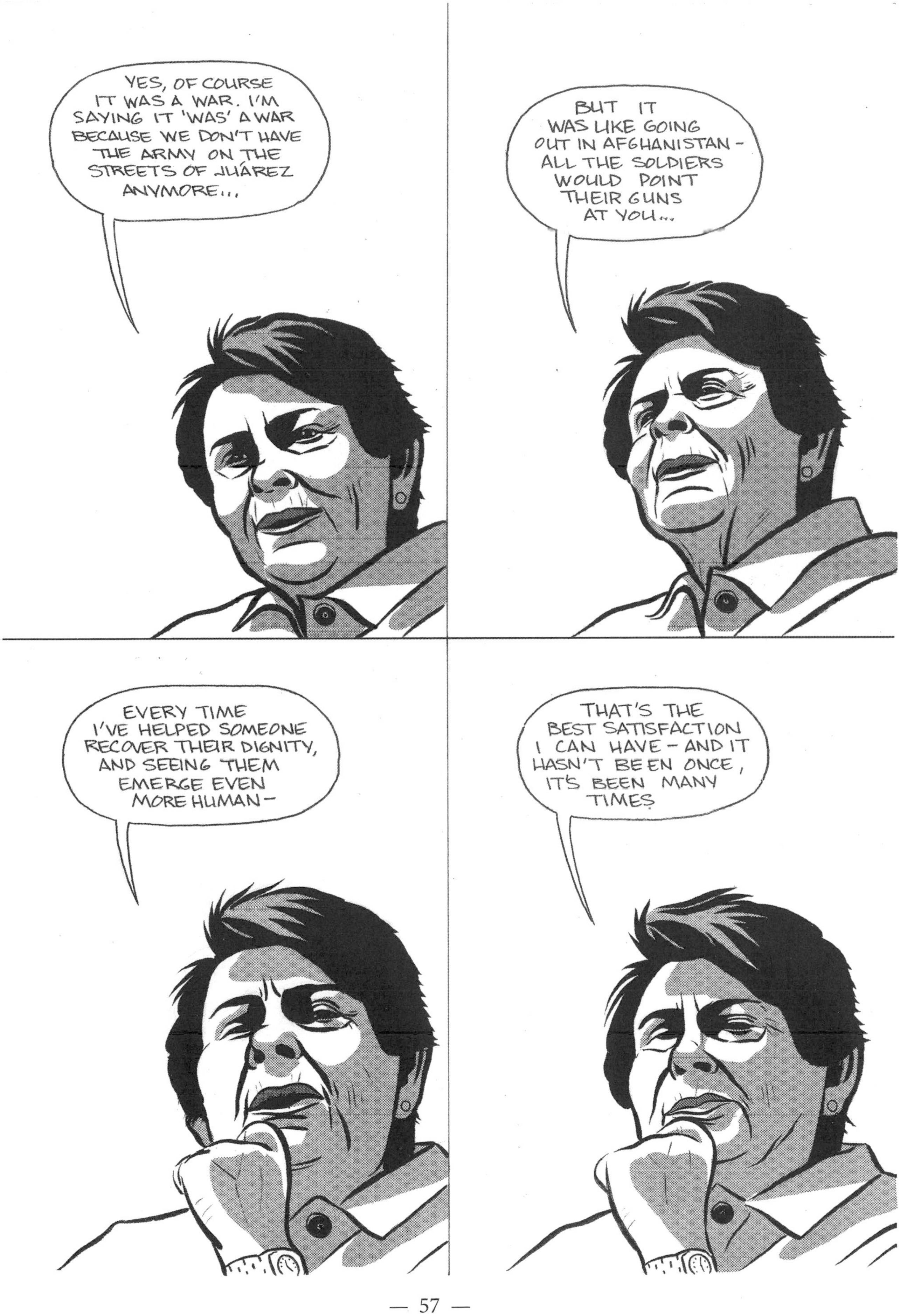
YES, OF COURSE IT WAS A WAR. I'M SAYING IT 'WAS' A WAR BECAUSE WE DON'T HAVE THE ARMY ON THE STREETS OF JUÁREZ ANYMORE...
BUT IT WAS LIKE GOING OUT IN AFGHANISTAN - ALL THE SOLDIERS WOULD POINT THEIR GUNS AT YOU...
EVERY TIME I'VE HELPED SOMEONE RECOVER THEIR DIGNITY, AND SEEING THEM EMERGE EVEN MORE HUMAN -
THAT'S THE BEST SATISFACTION I CAN HAVE - AND IT HASN'T BEEN ONCE, IT'S BEEN MANY TIMES

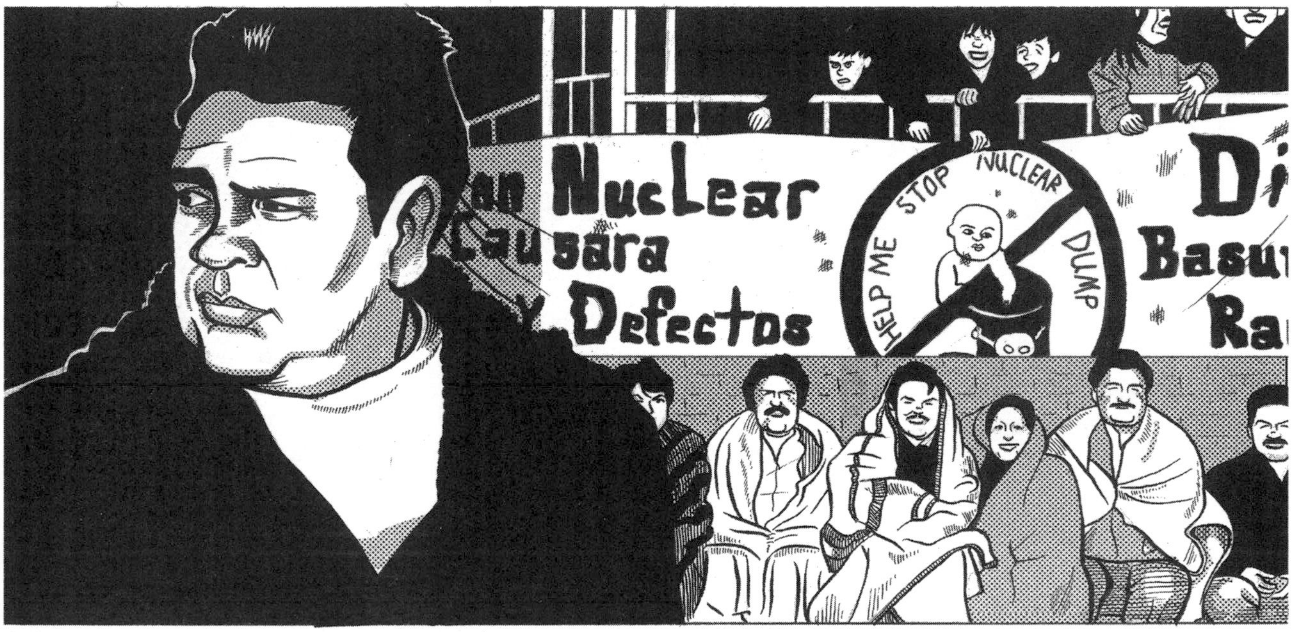
Nuclear
Defectos
HELP ME STOP NUCLEAR DUMP

JOSEFINA

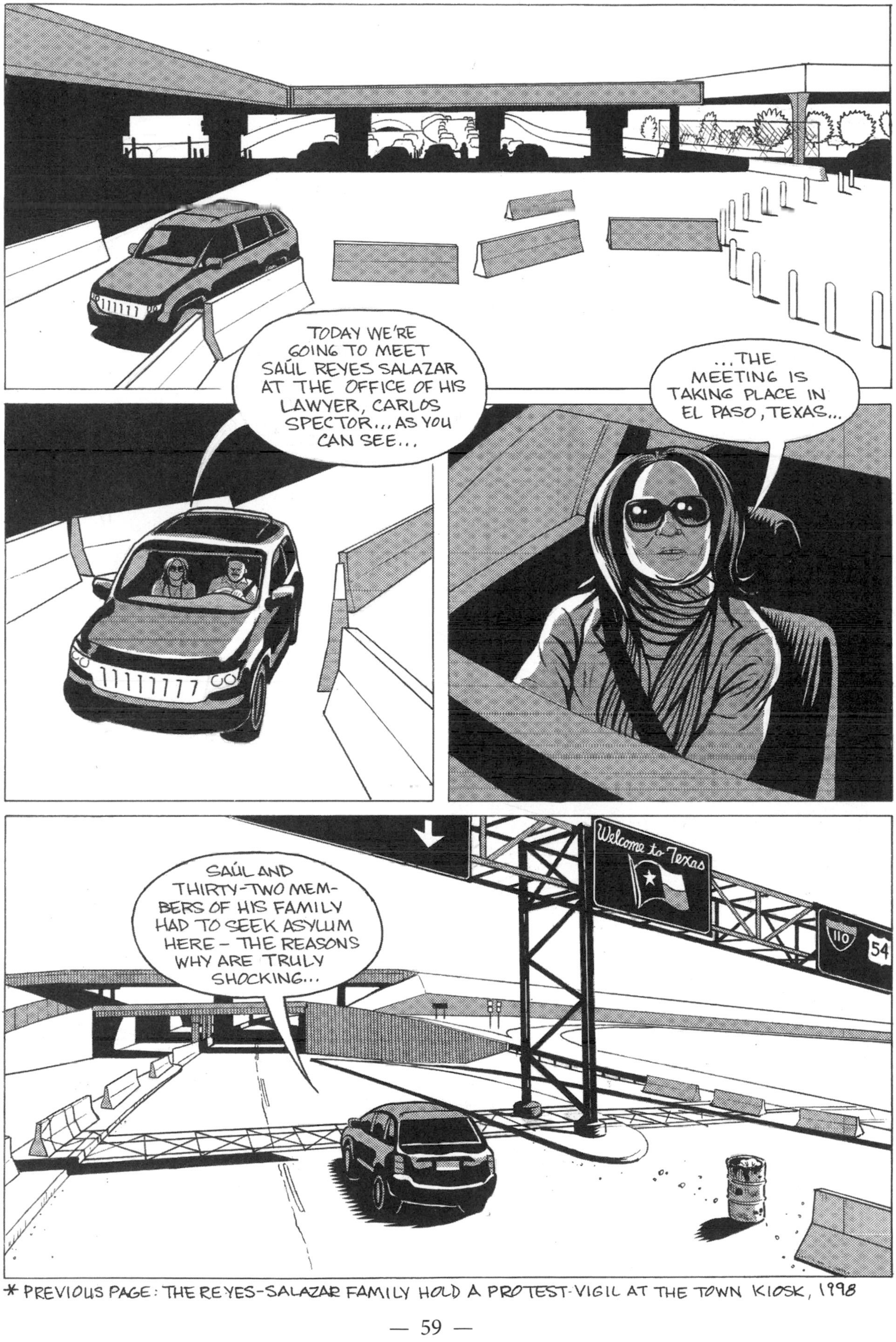
TODAY WE'RE GOING TO MEET SAÚL REYES SALAZAR AT THE OFFICE OF HIS LAWYER, CARLOS SPECTOR... AS YOU CAN SEE...
...THE MEETING IS TAKING PLACE IN EL PASO, TEXAS...
Welcome to Texas
110
54
SAÚL AND THIRTY-TWO MEMBERS OF HIS FAMILY HAD TO SEEK ASYLUM HERE – THE REASONS WHY ARE TRULY SHOCKING...

* PREVIOUS PAGE: THE REYES-SALAZAR FAMILY HOLD A PROTEST-VIGIL AT THE TOWN KIOSK, 1998

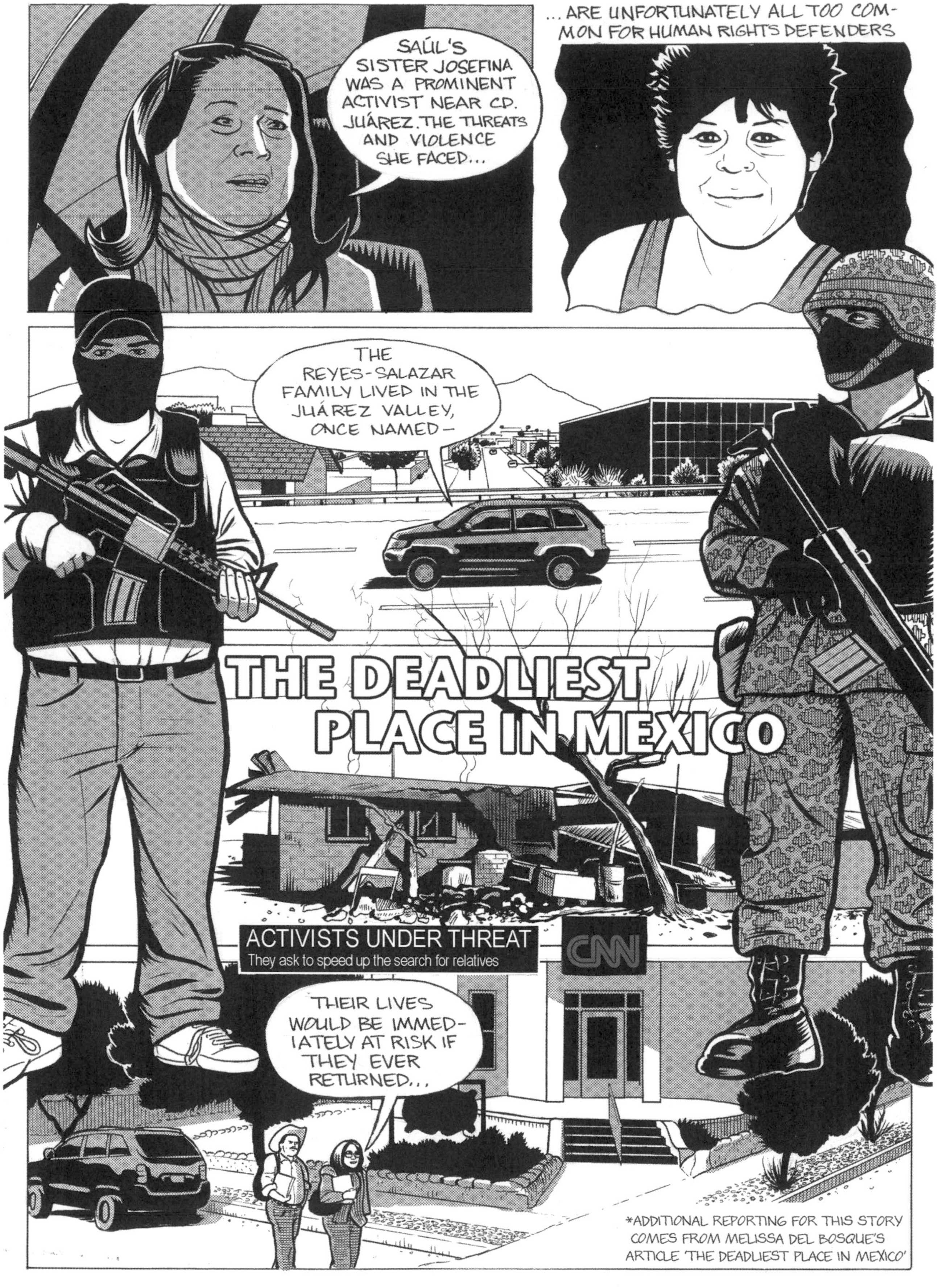
SAÚL'S SISTER JOSEFINA WAS A PROMINENT ACTIVIST NEAR CD. JUÁREZ. THE THREATS AND VIOLENCE SHE FACED...
...ARE UNFORTUNATELY ALL TOO COMMON FOR HUMAN RIGHTS DEFENDERS
THE REYES-SALAZAR FAMILY LIVED IN THE JUÁREZ VALLEY, ONCE NAMED –
THE DEADLIEST PLACE IN MEXICO
ACTIVISTS UNDER THREAT
They ask to speed up the search for relatives
CNN
THEIR LIVES WOULD BE IMMEDIATELY AT RISK IF THEY EVER RETURNED...
*ADDITIONAL REPORTING FOR THIS STORY COMES FROM MELISSA DEL BOSQUE'S ARTICLE 'THE DEADLIEST PLACE IN MEXICO'

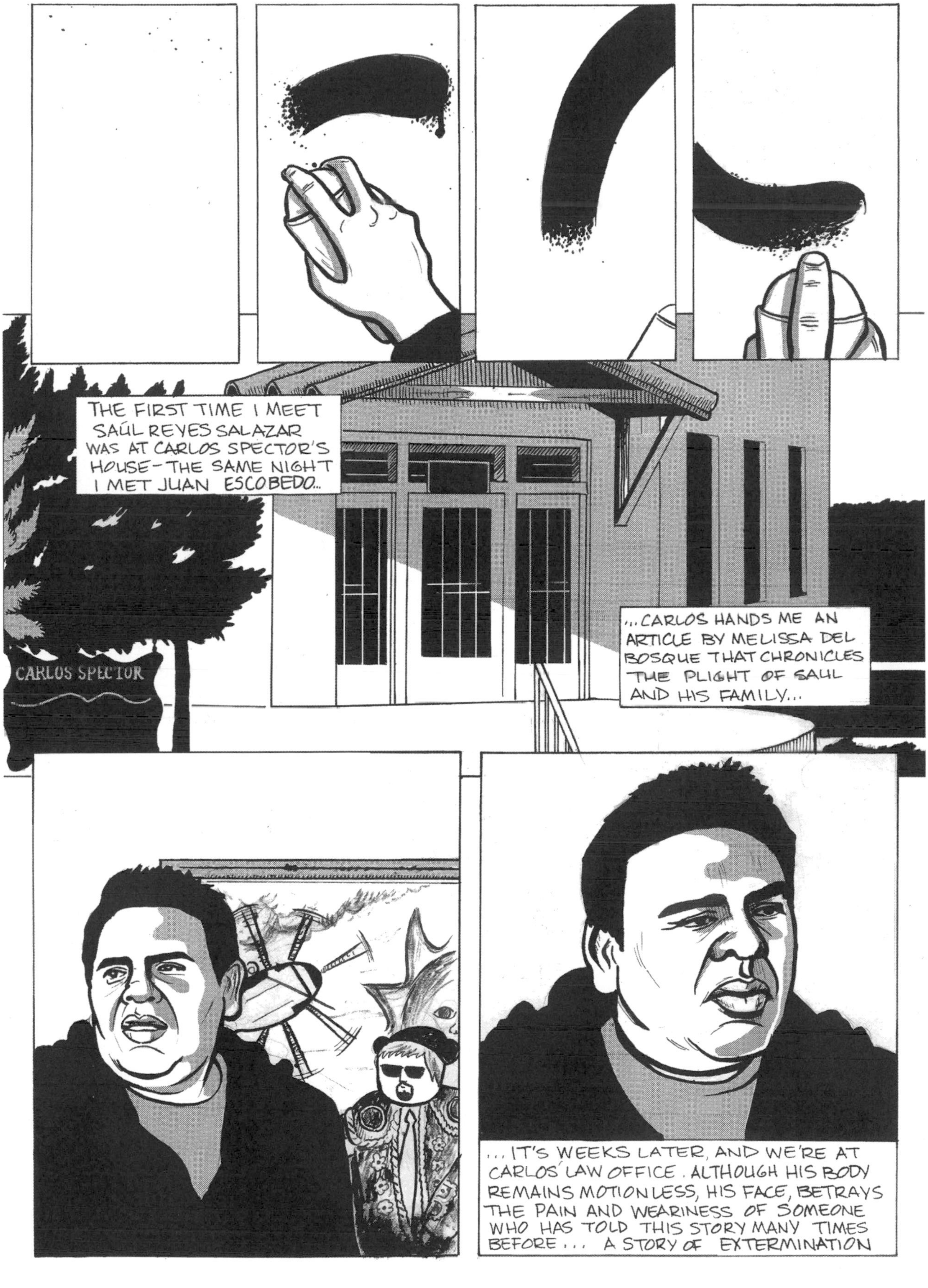
THE FIRST TIME I MEET SAÚL REYES SALAZAR WAS AT CARLOS SPECTOR'S HOUSE– THE SAME NIGHT I MET JUAN ESCOBEDO...
CARLOS SPECTOR
...CARLOS HANDS ME AN ARTICLE BY MELISSA DEL BOSQUE THAT CHRONICLES THE PLIGHT OF SAÚL AND HIS FAMILY...
...IT'S WEEKS LATER, AND WE'RE AT CARLOS' LAW OFFICE. ALTHOUGH HIS BODY REMAINS MOTIONLESS, HIS FACE, BETRAYS THE PAIN AND WEARINESS OF SOMEONE WHO HAS TOLD THIS STORY MANY TIMES BEFORE... A STORY OF EXTERMINATION

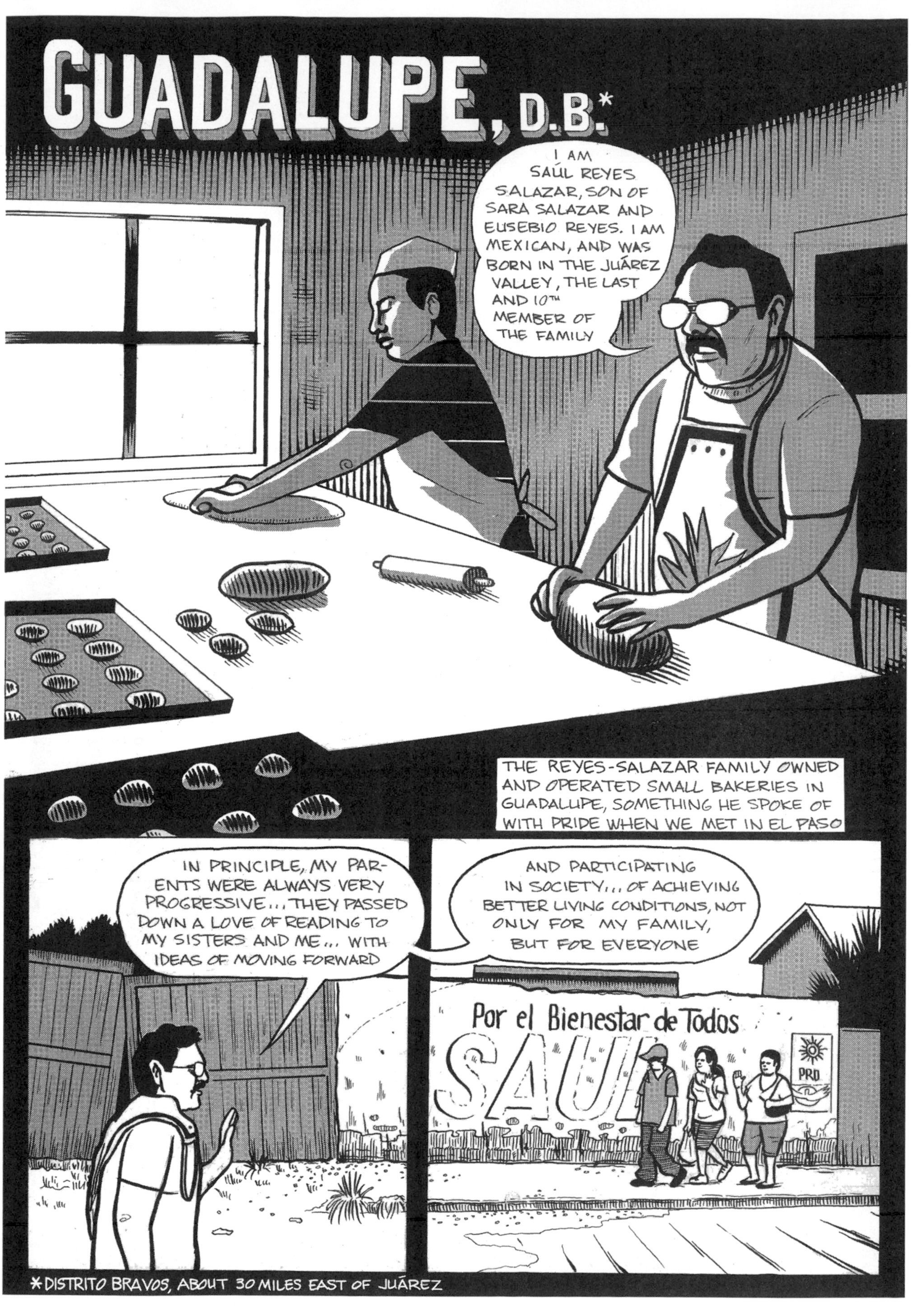
GUADALUPE, D.B.*
I AM SAÚL REYES SALAZAR, SON OF SARA SALAZAR AND EUSEBIO REYES. I AM MEXICAN, AND WAS BORN IN THE JUÁREZ VALLEY, THE LAST AND 10TH MEMBER OF THE FAMILY
THE REYES-SALAZAR FAMILY OWNED AND OPERATED SMALL BAKERIES IN GUADALUPE, SOMETHING HE SPOKE OF WITH PRIDE WHEN WE MET IN EL PASO
IN PRINCIPLE, MY PARENTS WERE ALWAYS VERY PROGRESSIVE... THEY PASSED DOWN A LOVE OF READING TO MY SISTERS AND ME... WITH IDEAS OF MOVING FORWARD
AND PARTICIPATING IN SOCIETY... OF ACHIEVING BETTER LIVING CONDITIONS, NOT ONLY FOR MY FAMILY, BUT FOR EVERYONE
Por el Bienestar de Todos
SAÚL
PRD
*DISTRITO BRAVOS, ABOUT 30 MILES EAST OF JUÁREZ

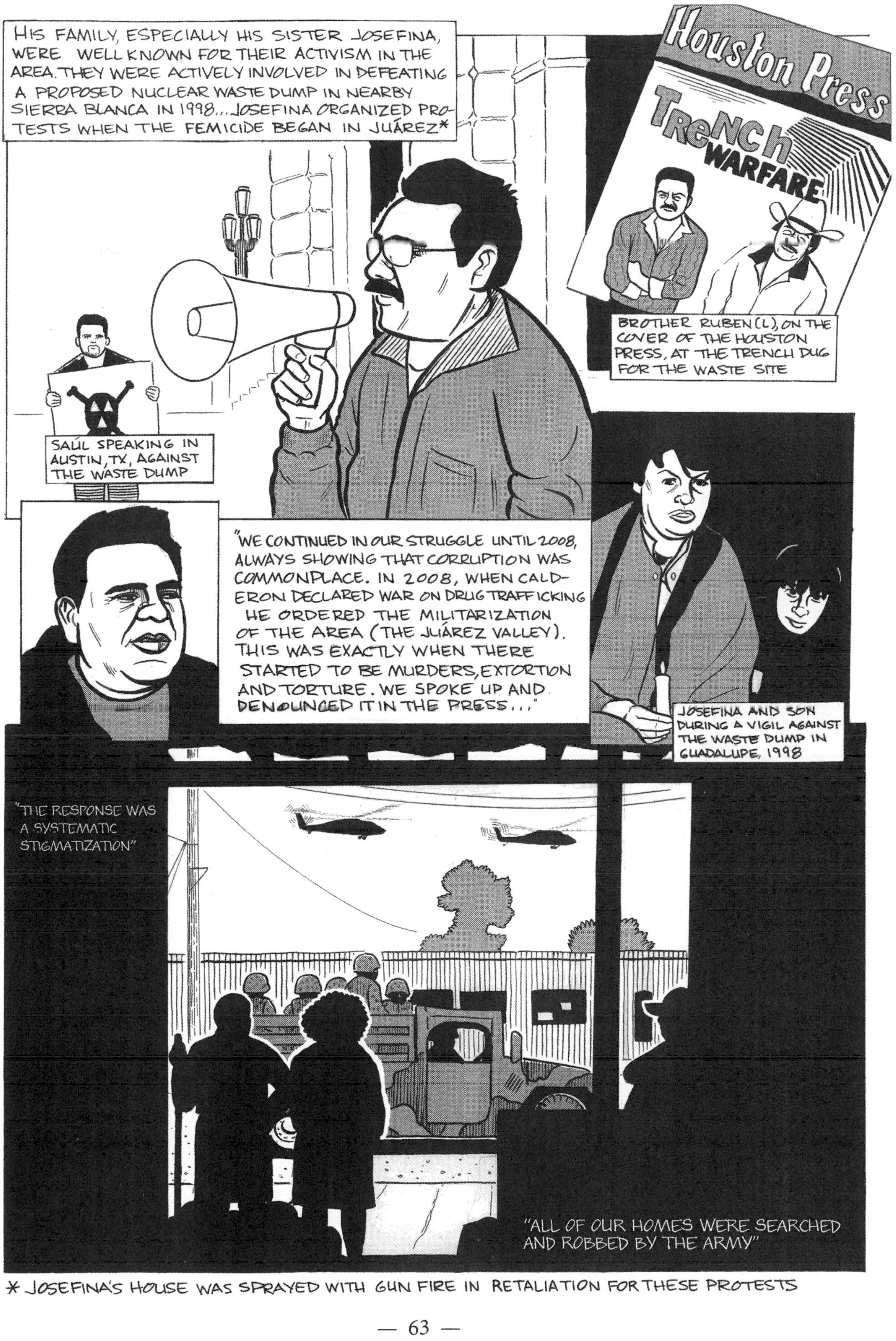

HIS FAMILY, ESPECIALLY HIS SISTER JOSEFINA, WERE WELL KNOWN FOR THEIR ACTIVISM IN THE AREA. THEY WERE ACTIVELY INVOLVED IN DEFEATING A PROPOSED NUCLEAR WASTE DUMP IN NEARBY SIERRA BLANCA IN 1998... JOSEFINA ORGANIZED PROTESTS WHEN THE FEMICIDE BEGAN IN JUÁREZ*
Houston Press
TRENCH WARFARE
BROTHER RUBEN (L), ON THE COVER OF THE HOUSTON PRESS, AT THE TRENCH DUG FOR THE WASTE SITE
SAÚL SPEAKING IN AUSTIN, TX, AGAINST THE WASTE DUMP
"WE CONTINUED IN OUR STRUGGLE UNTIL 2008, ALWAYS SHOWING THAT CORRUPTION WAS COMMONPLACE. IN 2008, WHEN CALDERON DECLARED WAR ON DRUG TRAFFICKING HE ORDERED THE MILITARIZATION OF THE AREA (THE JUÁREZ VALLEY). THIS WAS EXACTLY WHEN THERE STARTED TO BE MURDERS, EXTORTION AND TORTURE. WE SPOKE UP AND DENOUNCED IT IN THE PRESS..."
JOSEFINA AND SON DURING A VIGIL AGAINST THE WASTE DUMP IN GUADALUPE, 1998
"THE RESPONSE WAS A SYSTEMATIC STIGMATIZATION"
"ALL OF OUR HOMES WERE SEARCHED AND ROBBED BY THE ARMY"

* JOSEFINA'S HOUSE WAS SPRAYED WITH GUN FIRE IN RETALIATION FOR THESE PROTESTS

SHORTLY AFTER THE ARMY ARRIVED IN GUADALUPE AS PART OF 'OPERATION CHIHUAHUA', 13 OF JOSEFINA'S NEIGHBORS WERE ARRESTED AND DETAINED WITHOUT CHARGE BY THE ARMY. NEIGHBORS BEGAN KNOCKING ON JOSEFINA'S DOOR, SEEKING HELP

MY SON— HE'S GONE!

JOSEFINA JOINED A HUMAN RIGHTS DELEGATION THAT MET WITH SENATOR ROSARIO IBARRA IN MEXICO CITY, TO PRESSURE THE ARMY TO RELEASE THOSE DETAINED

IN AUGUST 2008, JOSEFINA SPOKE AT A FORUM AGAINST MILITARISATION AND REPRESSION

I'M HERE AS AN ACTIVIST UNDER ATTACK BY THE MILITARY...

RO CONTRA LA
ON Y REPRESIÓN

... AND AFTERWARDS LED A MARCH THROUGH JUÁREZ AGAINST THE ARMY'S PRESENCE IN GUADALUPE

¡BASTA YA! DE VIOLENCIA

A WEEK LATER, THE MILITARY DISAPPEARED HER SON, MIGUEL ANGEL

DISCO BAR EXTASIS
Verduras
CHULETA DISCADA POLLO
"HE WAS MISSING FOR 16 DAYS AND WE BLAMED THE MEXICAN ARMY, BECAUSE WE HAD PROOF. HE WAS RELEASED 16 DAYS LATER, AND HE HAD BEEN TORTURED AND PSYCHOLOGICALLY ABUSED AS WELL.. HE HAD 2 FRACTURED RIBS, A BROKEN NOSE, AND THE SOLES OF HIS FEET HAD BEEN BURNT FROM ELECTRICAL SHOCKS."
NOOOOOOOOOO!
AGAIN
FREE MIGUEL!
GIMNASIO MUNICIPAL
HUELGA DE HAMBRE
3 MONTHS LATER...
...GUNMEN ENTERED A WEDDING PARTY...
...AND ORDERED EVERYONE TO GET ON THE GROUND...

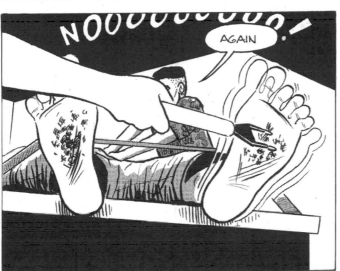

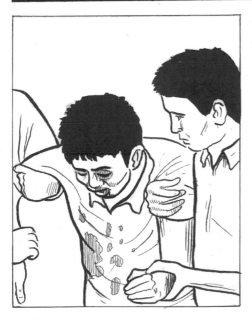

THEY SEARCHED THE CROWD...

...AND WHEN THEY FOUND JOSEFINA'S OTHER SON, JULIO CESAR—

IS THAT HIM?

YEAH

—THEY FIRED ONE SHOT...

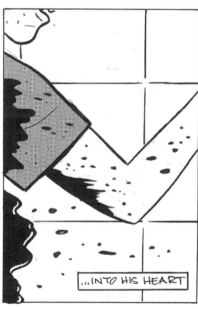

...INTO HIS HEART

"LESS THAN 500 METERS AWAY, THERE WAS A MILITARY VEHICLE WITH SOLDIERS. AND NEITHER — UPON HEARING THE SHOT

BANG!

NOR AFTER—

DID THEY DO ANYTHING...

LINEA DE POLICIA N

THE MILITARY, CLAIMS SARA SALAZAR, THE FAMILY MATRIARCH, PUT UP YELLOW POLICE TAPE AND LEFT...

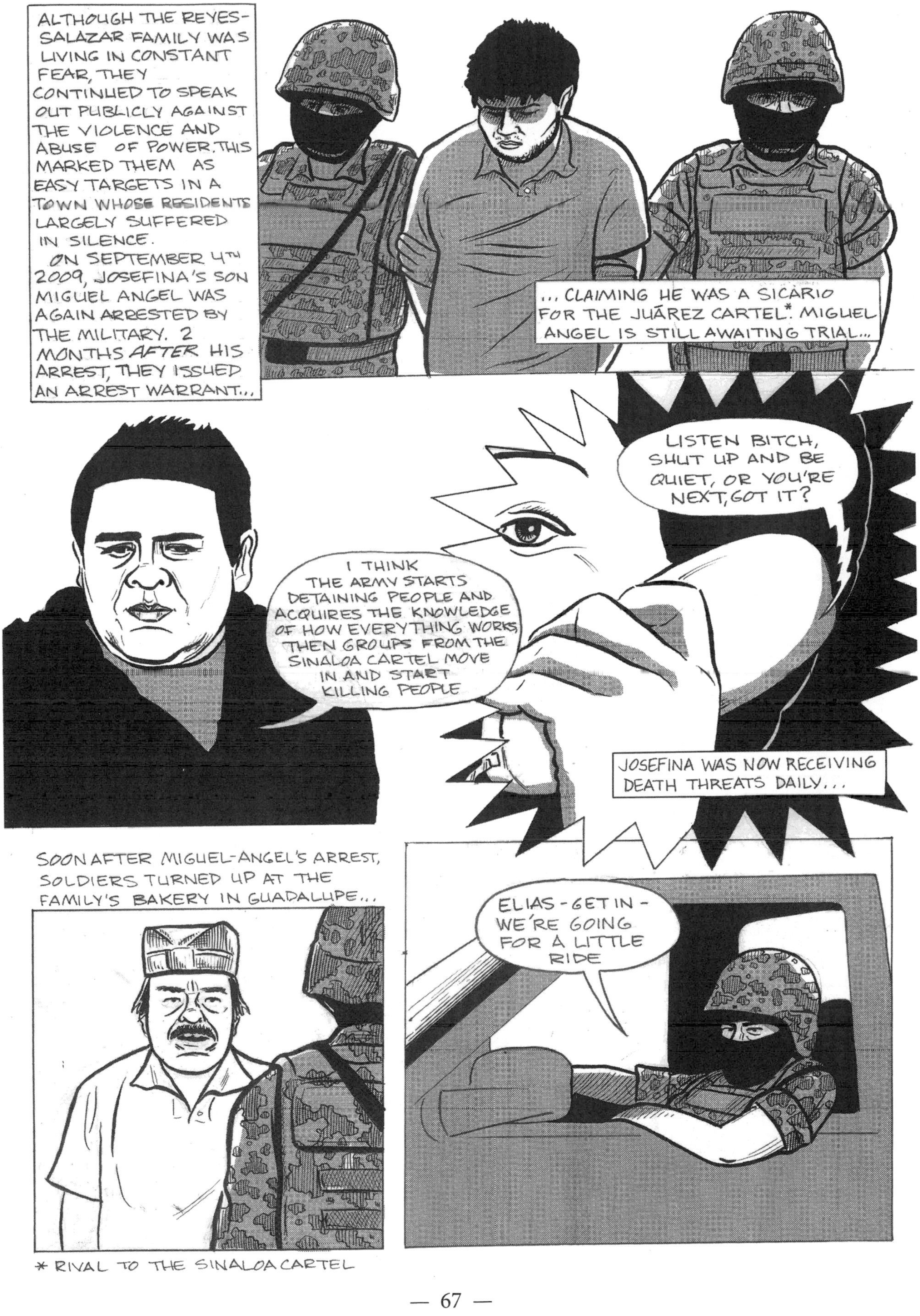
ALTHOUGH THE REYES-SALAZAR FAMILY WAS LIVING IN CONSTANT FEAR, THEY CONTINUED TO SPEAK OUT PUBLICLY AGAINST THE VIOLENCE AND ABUSE OF POWER. THIS MARKED THEM AS EASY TARGETS IN A TOWN WHOSE RESIDENTS LARGELY SUFFERED IN SILENCE.
ON SEPTEMBER 4TH 2009, JOSEFINA'S SON MIGUEL ANGEL WAS AGAIN ARRESTED BY THE MILITARY. 2 MONTHS AFTER HIS ARREST, THEY ISSUED AN ARREST WARRANT...
...CLAIMING HE WAS A SICARIO FOR THE JUÁREZ CARTEL*. MIGUEL ANGEL IS STILL AWAITING TRIAL...
I THINK THE ARMY STARTS DETAINING PEOPLE AND ACQUIRES THE KNOWLEDGE OF HOW EVERYTHING WORKS THEN GROUPS FROM THE SINALOA CARTEL MOVE IN AND START KILLING PEOPLE
LISTEN BITCH, SHUT UP AND BE QUIET, OR YOU'RE NEXT, GOT IT?
JOSEFINA WAS NOW RECEIVING DEATH THREATS DAILY...
SOON AFTER MIGUEL-ANGEL'S ARREST, SOLDIERS TURNED UP AT THE FAMILY'S BAKERY IN GUADALUPE...
ELIAS - GET IN - WE'RE GOING FOR A LITTLE RIDE
* RIVAL TO THE SINALOA CARTEL

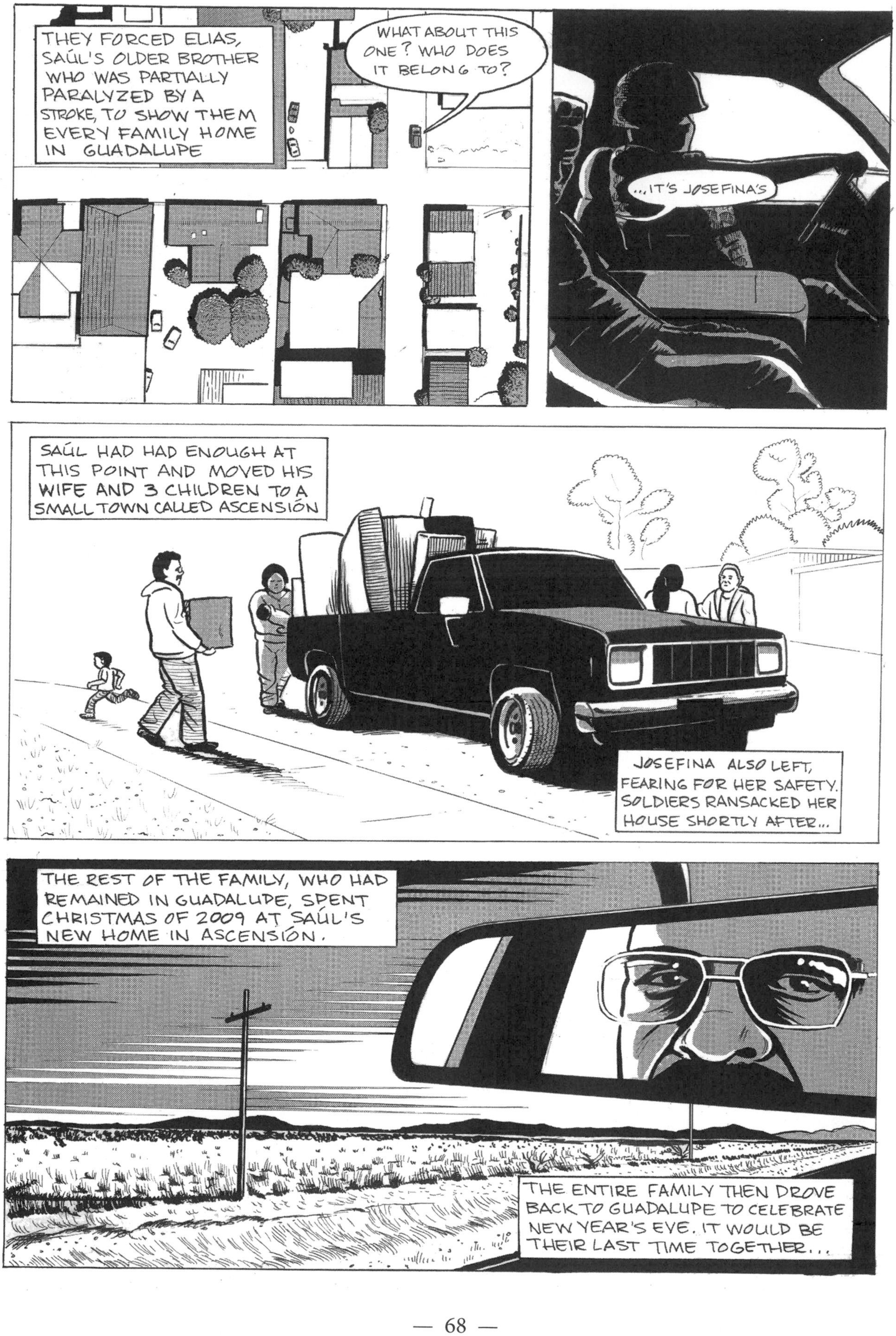
THEY FORCED ELIAS, SAÚL'S OLDER BROTHER WHO WAS PARTIALLY PARALYZED BY A STROKE, TO SHOW THEM EVERY FAMILY HOME IN GUADALUPE
WHAT ABOUT THIS ONE? WHO DOES IT BELONG TO?
...IT'S JOSEFINA'S
SAÚL HAD HAD ENOUGH AT THIS POINT AND MOVED HIS WIFE AND 3 CHILDREN TO A SMALL TOWN CALLED ASCENSIÓN
JOSEFINA ALSO LEFT, FEARING FOR HER SAFETY. SOLDIERS RANSACKED HER HOUSE SHORTLY AFTER...
THE REST OF THE FAMILY, WHO HAD REMAINED IN GUADALUPE, SPENT CHRISTMAS OF 2009 AT SAÚL'S NEW HOME IN ASCENSIÓN.
THE ENTIRE FAMILY THEN DROVE BACK TO GUADALUPE TO CELEBRATE NEW YEAR'S EVE. IT WOULD BE THEIR LAST TIME TOGETHER...

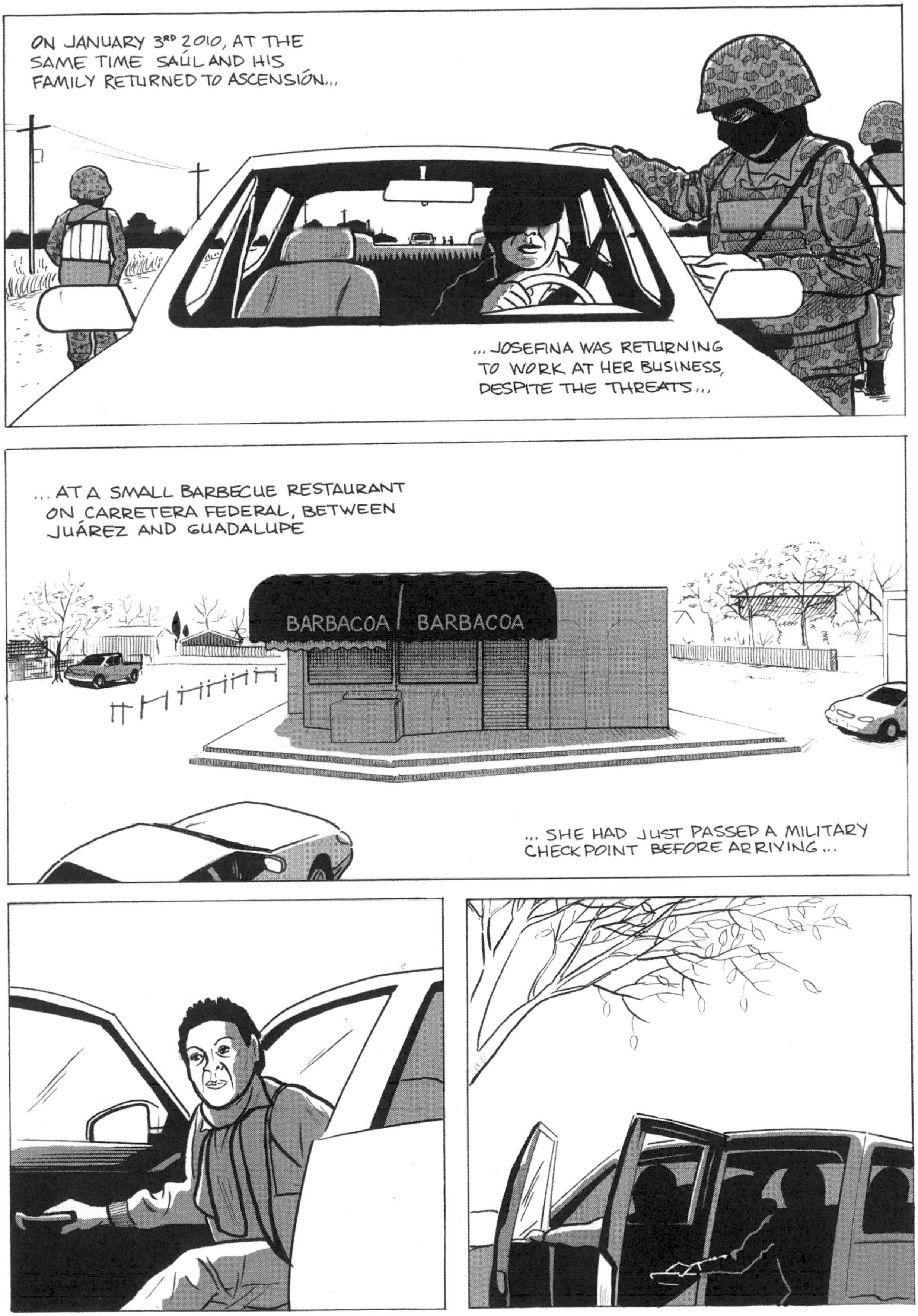
ON JANUARY 3RD 2010, AT THE SAME TIME SAÚL AND HIS FAMILY RETURNED TO ASCENSIÓN...
...JOSEFINA WAS RETURNING TO WORK AT HER BUSINESS, DESPITE THE THREATS...
...AT A SMALL BARBECUE RESTAURANT ON CARRETERA FEDERAL, BETWEEN JUÁREZ AND GUADALUPE
BARBACOA BARBACOA
...SHE HAD JUST PASSED A MILITARY CHECKPOINT BEFORE ARRIVING...

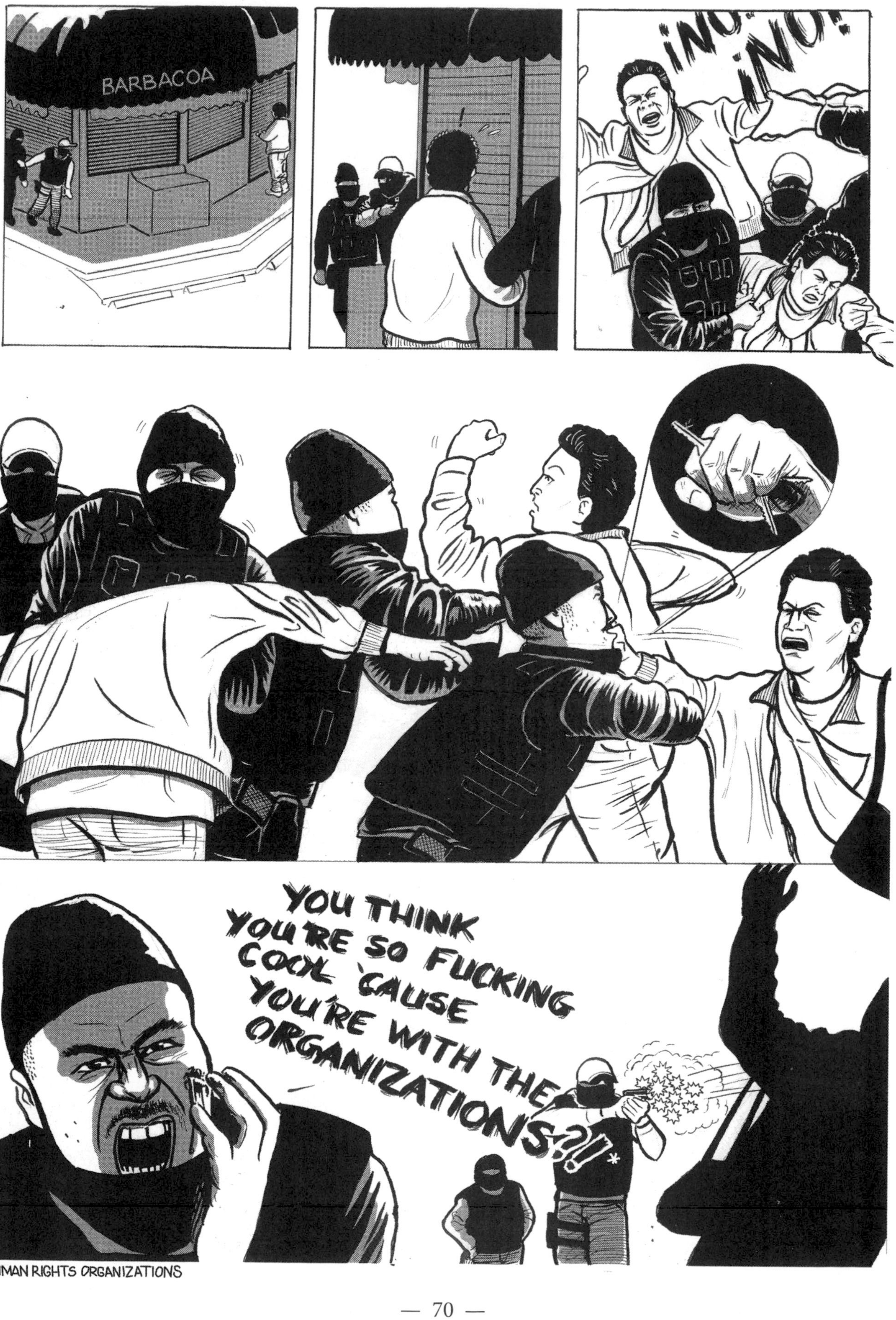
BARBACOA
¡NO! ¡NO!
YOU THINK YOU'RE SO FUCKING COOL 'CAUSE YOU'RE WITH THE ORGANIZATIONS*?!!

* HUMAN RIGHTS ORGANIZATIONS

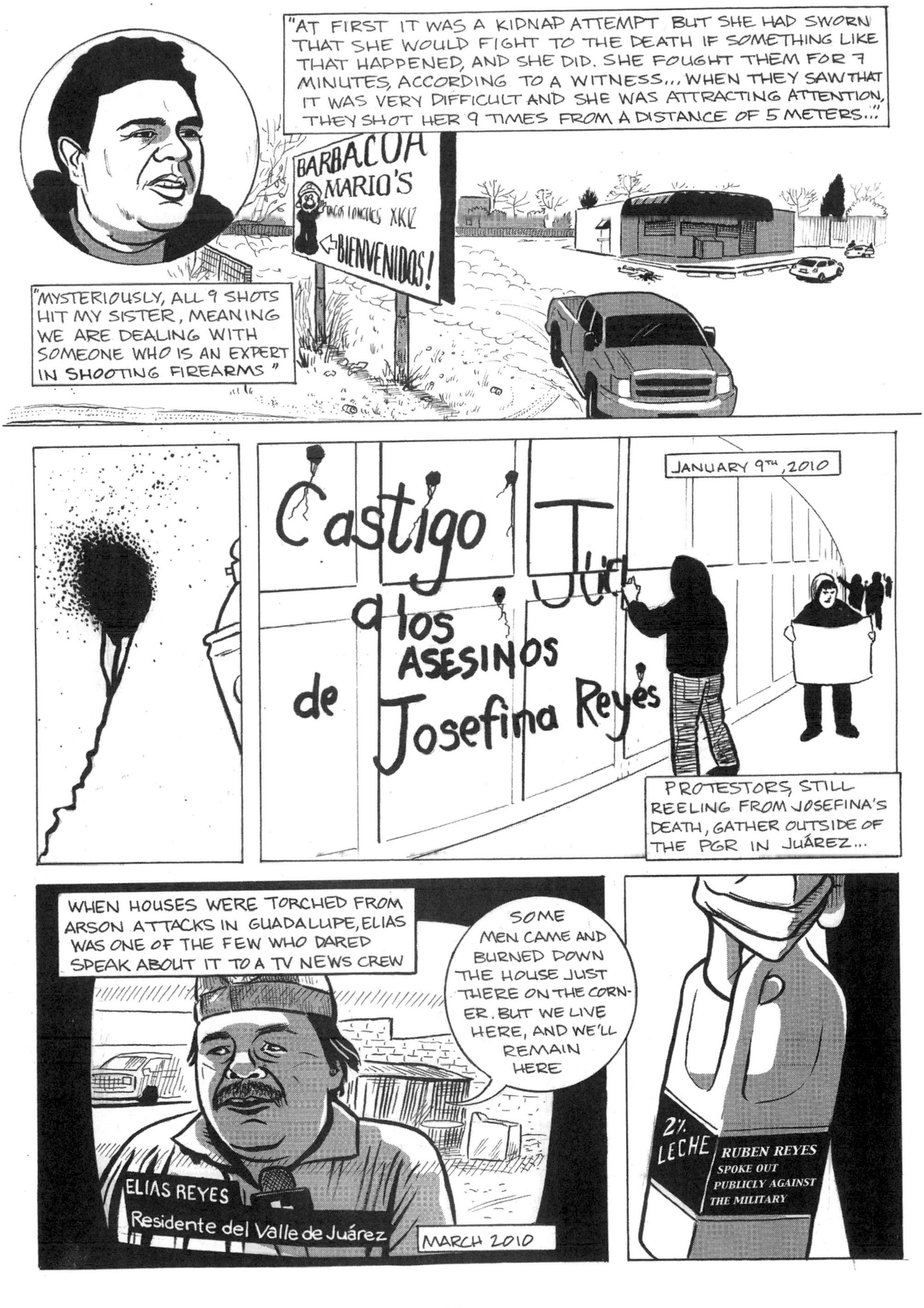
"AT FIRST IT WAS A KIDNAP ATTEMPT BUT SHE HAD SWORN THAT SHE WOULD FIGHT TO THE DEATH IF SOMETHING LIKE THAT HAPPENED, AND SHE DID. SHE FOUGHT THEM FOR 7 MINUTES, ACCORDING TO A WITNESS... WHEN THEY SAW THAT IT WAS VERY DIFFICULT AND SHE WAS ATTRACTING ATTENTION, THEY SHOT HER 9 TIMES FROM A DISTANCE OF 5 METERS..."
BARBACOA
MARIO'S
BIENVENIDOS!
"MYSTERIOUSLY, ALL 9 SHOTS HIT MY SISTER, MEANING WE ARE DEALING WITH SOMEONE WHO IS AN EXPERT IN SHOOTING FIREARMS"
JANUARY 9TH, 2010
Castigo Jui
a los
ASESINOS
de
Josefina Reyes
PROTESTORS, STILL REELING FROM JOSEFINA'S DEATH, GATHER OUTSIDE OF THE PGR IN JUÁREZ...
WHEN HOUSES WERE TORCHED FROM ARSON ATTACKS IN GUADALUPE, ELIAS WAS ONE OF THE FEW WHO DARED SPEAK ABOUT IT TO A TV NEWS CREW
SOME MEN CAME AND BURNED DOWN THE HOUSE JUST THERE ON THE CORNER. BUT WE LIVE HERE, AND WE'LL REMAIN HERE
ELIAS REYES
Residente del Valle de Juárez
MARCH 2010
2% LECHE
RUBEN REYES SPOKE OUT PUBLICLY AGAINST THE MILITARY

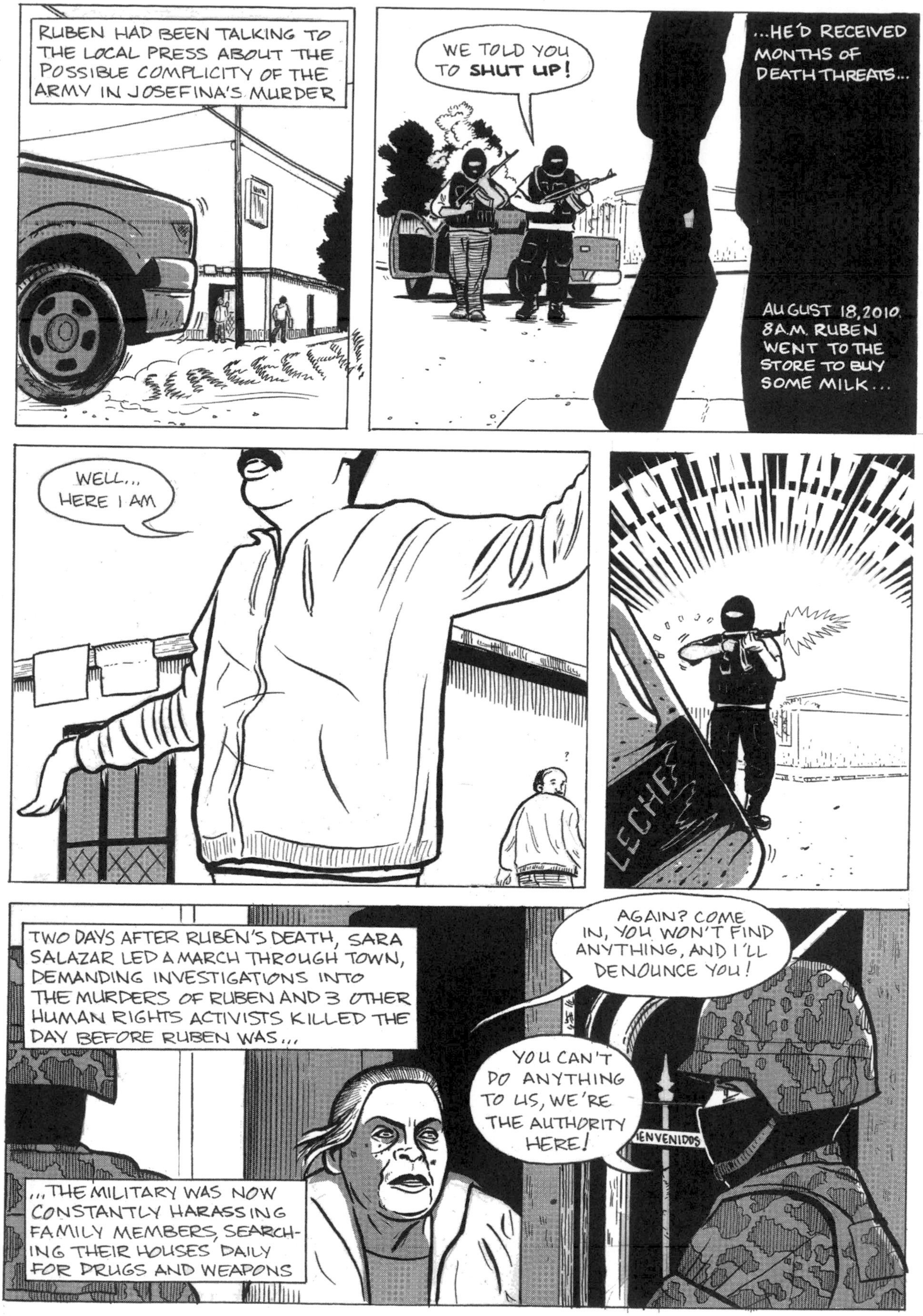
RUBEN HAD BEEN TALKING TO THE LOCAL PRESS ABOUT THE POSSIBLE COMPLICITY OF THE ARMY IN JOSEFINA'S MURDER
WE TOLD YOU TO SHUT UP!
...HE'D RECEIVED MONTHS OF DEATH THREATS...
AUGUST 18, 2010. 8 A.M. RUBEN WENT TO THE STORE TO BUY SOME MILK...
WELL... HERE I AM
?
LECHES
TWO DAYS AFTER RUBEN'S DEATH, SARA SALAZAR LED A MARCH THROUGH TOWN, DEMANDING INVESTIGATIONS INTO THE MURDERS OF RUBEN AND 3 OTHER HUMAN RIGHTS ACTIVISTS KILLED THE DAY BEFORE RUBEN WAS...
AGAIN? COME IN, YOU WON'T FIND ANYTHING, AND I'LL DENOUNCE YOU!
YOU CAN'T DO ANYTHING TO US, WE'RE THE AUTHORITY HERE!
...THE MILITARY WAS NOW CONSTANTLY HARASSING FAMILY MEMBERS, SEARCHING THEIR HOUSES DAILY FOR DRUGS AND WEAPONS

AS THE SINALOA CARTEL MOVED IN TO CONTROL THE PLAZA, A POLITICAL AND POLICING VACUUM ENSUED. JOURNALISTS, HUMAN RIGHTS DEFENDERS AND POLITICIANS WERE BEING MURDERED IN BROAD DAYLIGHT. 20 YEAR OLD MARISOL VALLES GARCIA MADE INTERNATIONAL HEADLINES AFTER ASSUMING THE ROLE OF POLICE CHIEF IN NEIGHBORING PRAXÉDIS G. GUERRERO. HER PREDECESSOR'S HEAD HAD BEEN LEFT IN FRONT OF THE POLICE STATION. SHE FLED TO THE U.S. AFTER ONLY 5 MONTHS. A MASS EXODUS WAS UNFOLDING – PEOPLE WERE WALKING OR DRIVING AWAY WITH WHATEVER THEY COULD BRING AS THE SMOKE FROM BURNING HOUSES WAFTED ACROSS THE BORDER INTO THE U.S., LESS THAN A MILE AWAY...

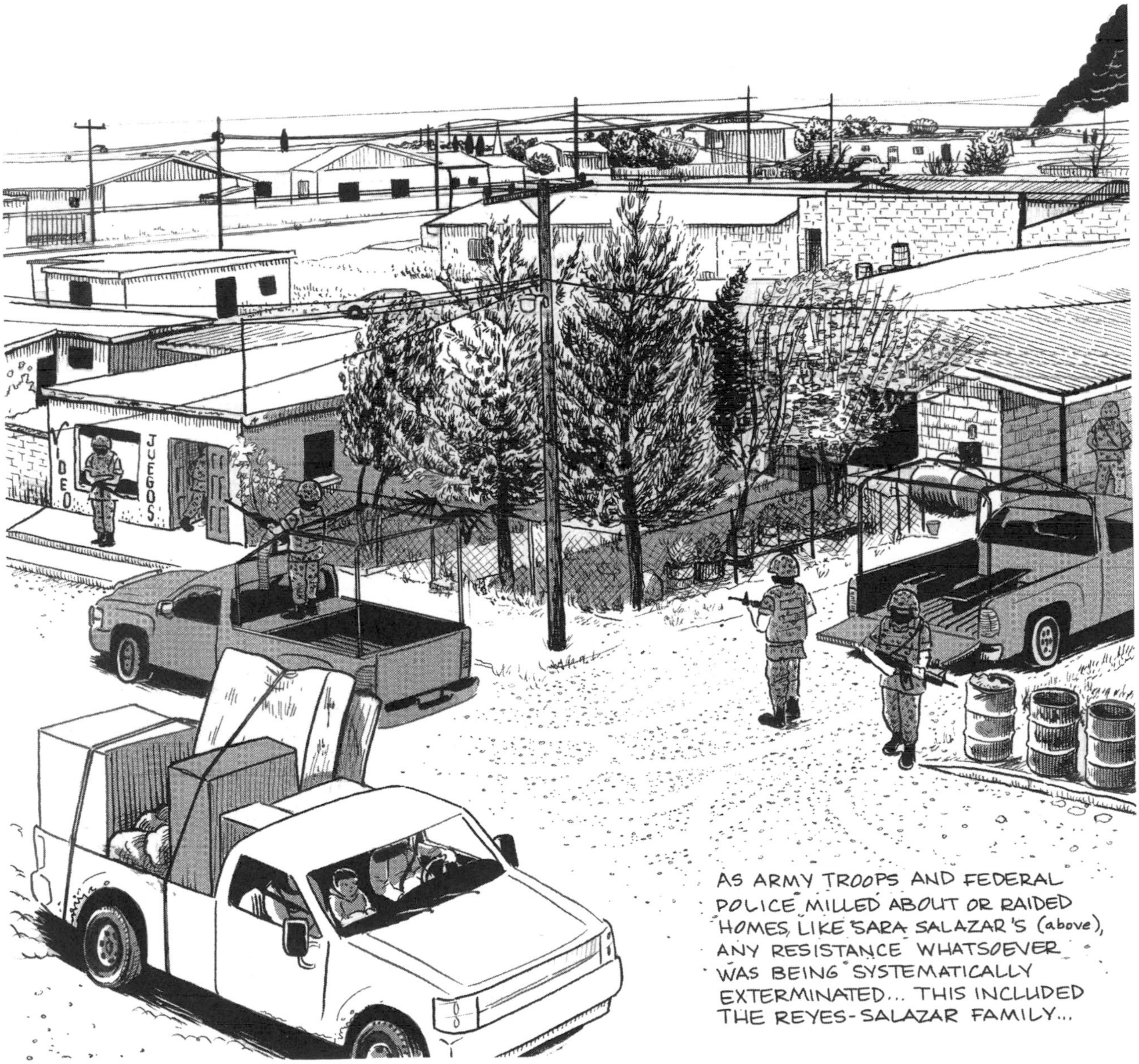
VIDEO
JUEGOS
AS ARMY TROOPS AND FEDERAL POLICE MILLED ABOUT OR RAIDED HOMES, LIKE SARA SALAZAR'S (above), ANY RESISTANCE WHATSOEVER WAS BEING SYSTEMATICALLY EXTERMINATED... THIS INCLUDED THE REYES-SALAZAR FAMILY...

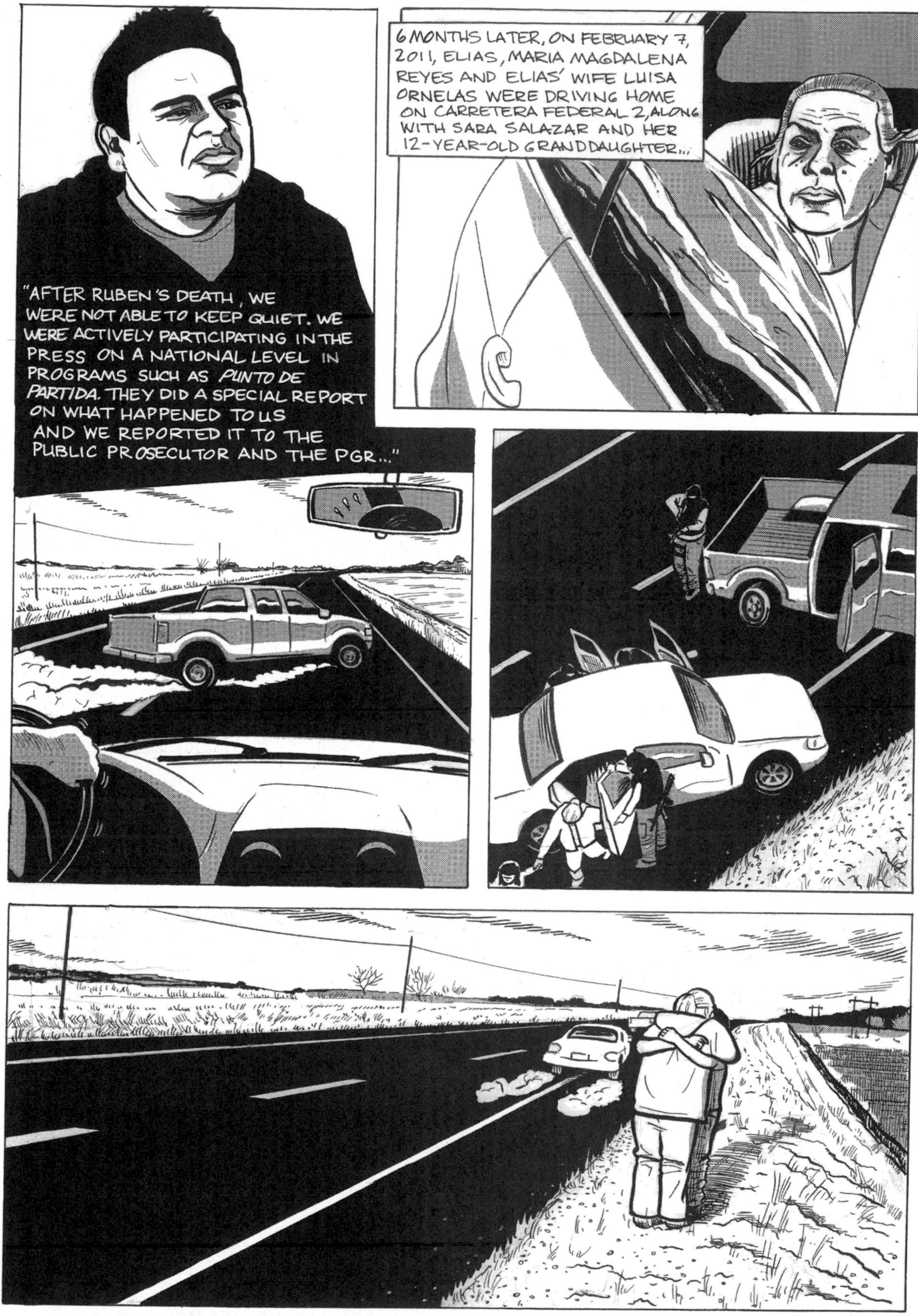
"AFTER RUBEN'S DEATH, WE WERE NOT ABLE TO KEEP QUIET. WE WERE ACTIVELY PARTICIPATING IN THE PRESS ON A NATIONAL LEVEL IN PROGRAMS SUCH AS *PUNTO DE PARTIDA*. THEY DID A SPECIAL REPORT ON WHAT HAPPENED TO US AND WE REPORTED IT TO THE PUBLIC PROSECUTOR AND THE PGR..."
6 MONTHS LATER, ON FEBRUARY 7, 2011, ELIAS, MARIA MAGDALENA REYES AND ELIAS' WIFE LUISA ORNELAS WERE DRIVING HOME ON CARRETERA FEDERAL 2, ALONG WITH SARA SALAZAR AND HER 12-YEAR-OLD GRANDDAUGHTER...

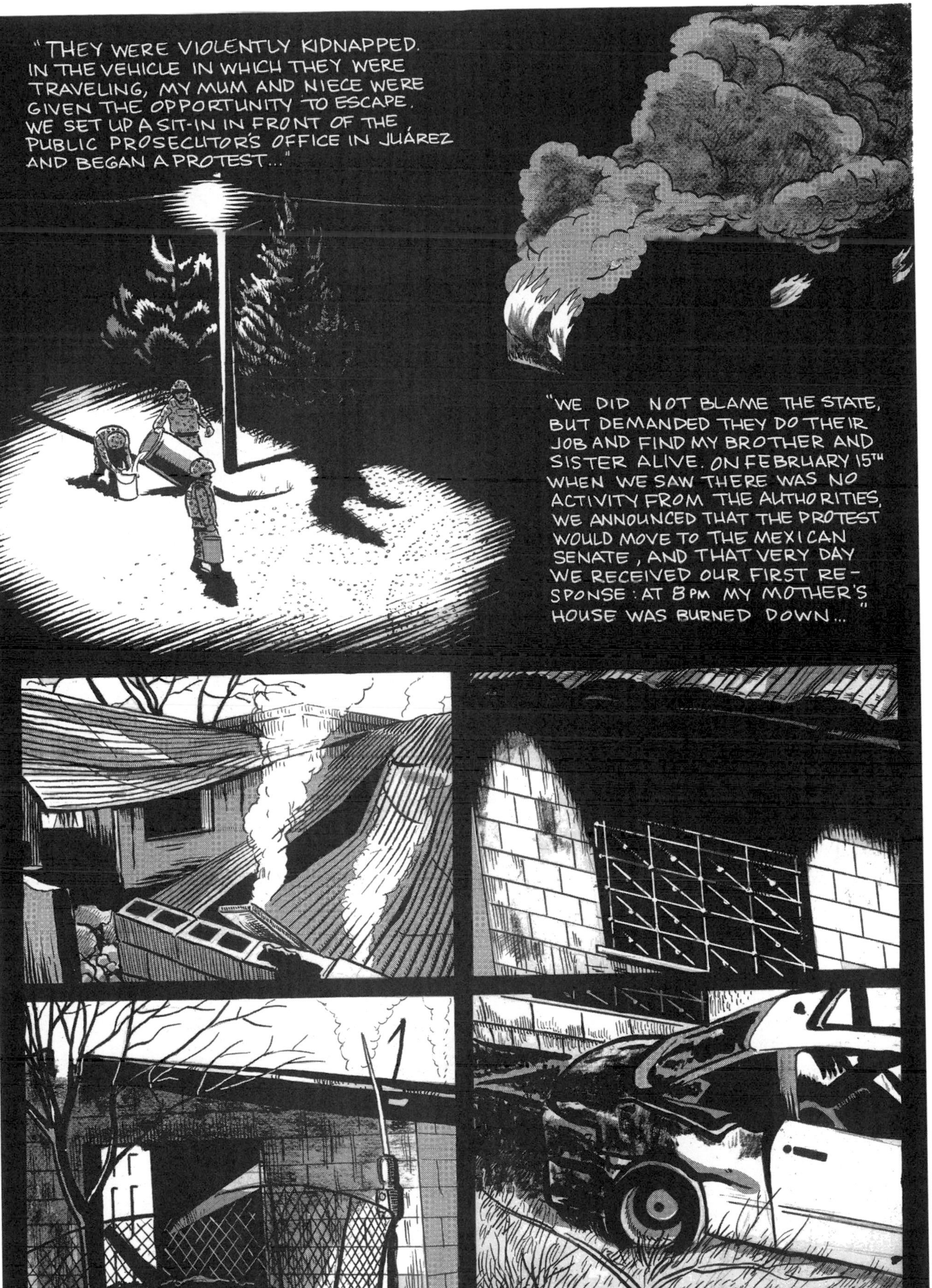
"THEY WERE VIOLENTLY KIDNAPPED. IN THE VEHICLE IN WHICH THEY WERE TRAVELING, MY MUM AND NIECE WERE GIVEN THE OPPORTUNITY TO ESCAPE. WE SET UP A SIT-IN IN FRONT OF THE PUBLIC PROSECUTOR'S OFFICE IN JUÁREZ AND BEGAN A PROTEST..."
"WE DID NOT BLAME THE STATE, BUT DEMANDED THEY DO THEIR JOB AND FIND MY BROTHER AND SISTER ALIVE. ON FEBRUARY 15TH WHEN WE SAW THERE WAS NO ACTIVITY FROM THE AUTHORITIES, WE ANNOUNCED THAT THE PROTEST WOULD MOVE TO THE MEXICAN SENATE, AND THAT VERY DAY WE RECEIVED OUR FIRST RESPONSE: AT 8 PM MY MOTHER'S HOUSE WAS BURNED DOWN..."

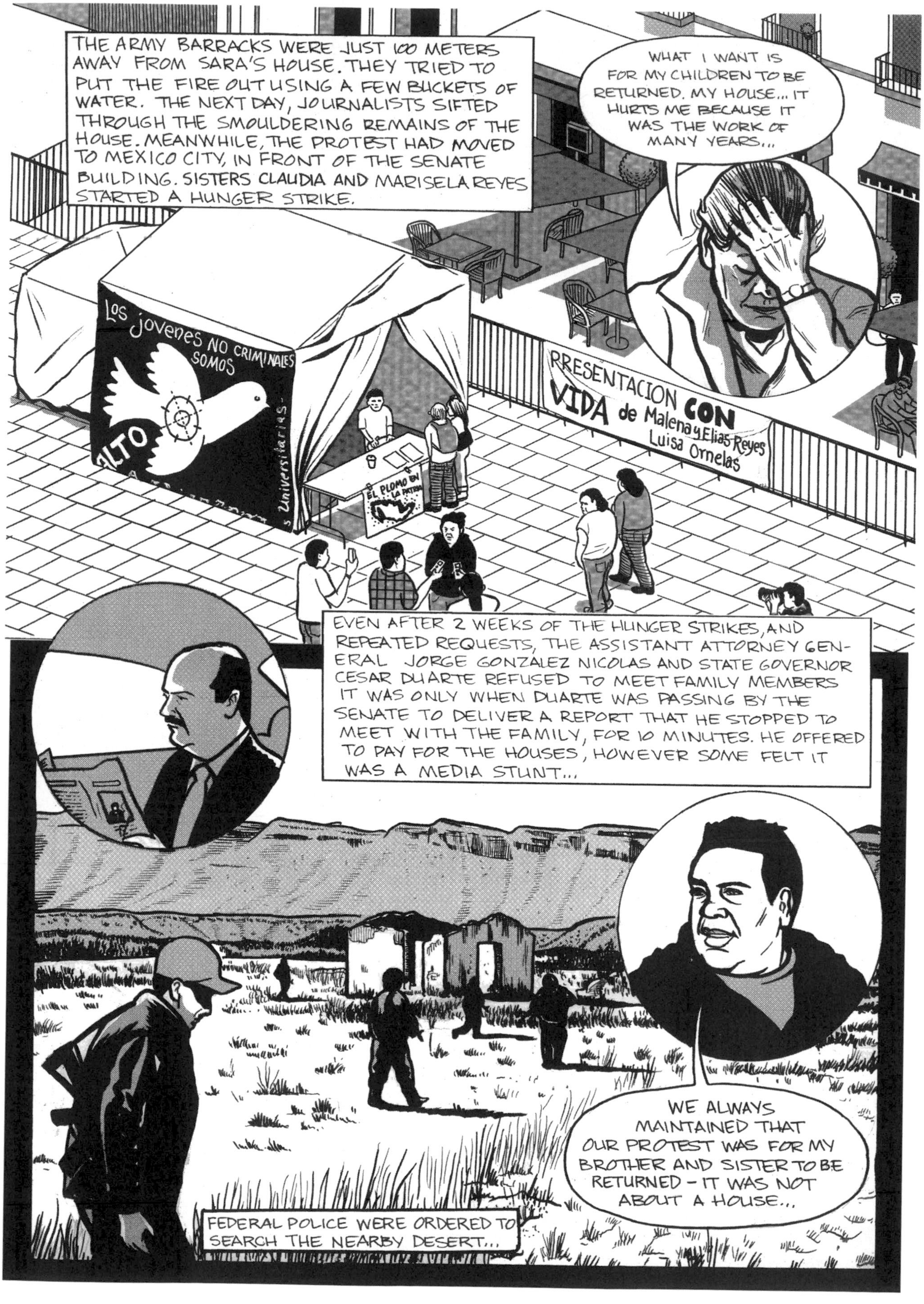
THE ARMY BARRACKS WERE JUST 100 METERS AWAY FROM SARA'S HOUSE. THEY TRIED TO PUT THE FIRE OUT USING A FEW BUCKETS OF WATER. THE NEXT DAY, JOURNALISTS SIFTED THROUGH THE SMOULDERING REMAINS OF THE HOUSE. MEANWHILE, THE PROTEST HAD MOVED TO MEXICO CITY, IN FRONT OF THE SENATE BUILDING. SISTERS CLAUDIA AND MARISELA REYES STARTED A HUNGER STRIKE.
WHAT I WANT IS FOR MY CHILDREN TO BE RETURNED. MY HOUSE... IT HURTS ME BECAUSE IT WAS THE WORK OF MANY YEARS...
Los jovenes NO CRIMINALES SOMOS
Universitarias
PRESENTACION CON VIDA de Malena y Elias Reyes Luisa Ornelas
EL PLOMO EN LA PATRIA
EVEN AFTER 2 WEEKS OF THE HUNGER STRIKES, AND REPEATED REQUESTS, THE ASSISTANT ATTORNEY GENERAL JORGE GONZALEZ NICOLAS AND STATE GOVERNOR CESAR DUARTE REFUSED TO MEET FAMILY MEMBERS. IT WAS ONLY WHEN DUARTE WAS PASSING BY THE SENATE TO DELIVER A REPORT THAT HE STOPPED TO MEET WITH THE FAMILY, FOR 10 MINUTES. HE OFFERED TO PAY FOR THE HOUSES, HOWEVER SOME FELT IT WAS A MEDIA STUNT...
WE ALWAYS MAINTAINED THAT OUR PROTEST WAS FOR MY BROTHER AND SISTER TO BE RETURNED - IT WAS NOT ABOUT A HOUSE...
FEDERAL POLICE WERE ORDERED TO SEARCH THE NEARBY DESERT...

"THAT WAS WHEN THE BODIES OF MY BROTHER, SISTER AND SISTER-IN-LAW APPEARED. A NEPHEW OF MINE FOUND THE BODIES ON THE WAY TO SCHOOL...

BY THEN THE TONE OF OUR PROTEST HAD INTENSIFIED AND WAS ATTRACTING MORE AND MORE ATTENTION FROM THE INTERNATION-AL PRESS...IT WAS A POLITICAL SCANDAL"

THEY WERE APPARENTLY FOUND NUDE, AND ONE REPORT SAYS THERE WAS A MESSAGE ON THE BODIES...

Diario tv

"...MY NEPHEW SPOKE TO THE POLICE AND THE ARMY WHO CORDONED OFF THE AREA..."

"... THIS MESSAGE WAS SOMETHING MY NEPHEW HADN'T SEEN WHEN HE DISCOVERED THE BODIES ...SO IT WAS PLANTED ON THEM AFTERWARDS"

DEL ESTADO DE CHIHUAHUA ZONA NORTE

PRIMERO JUSTI

ERNO INO

THEIR HOMES BURNT DOWN AND RANSACKED, THE ONLY PLACE THE FAMILY COULD HOLD A WAKE THAT NIGHT... WAS IN FRONT OF THE ATTORNEY GENERAL'S OFFICE

"THEY GAVE US THE BODIES TO SHUT US UP..."

"THERE WERE MORE THAN 40 PATROL CARS PRO-
TECTING US AS WE BURIED THEM..."

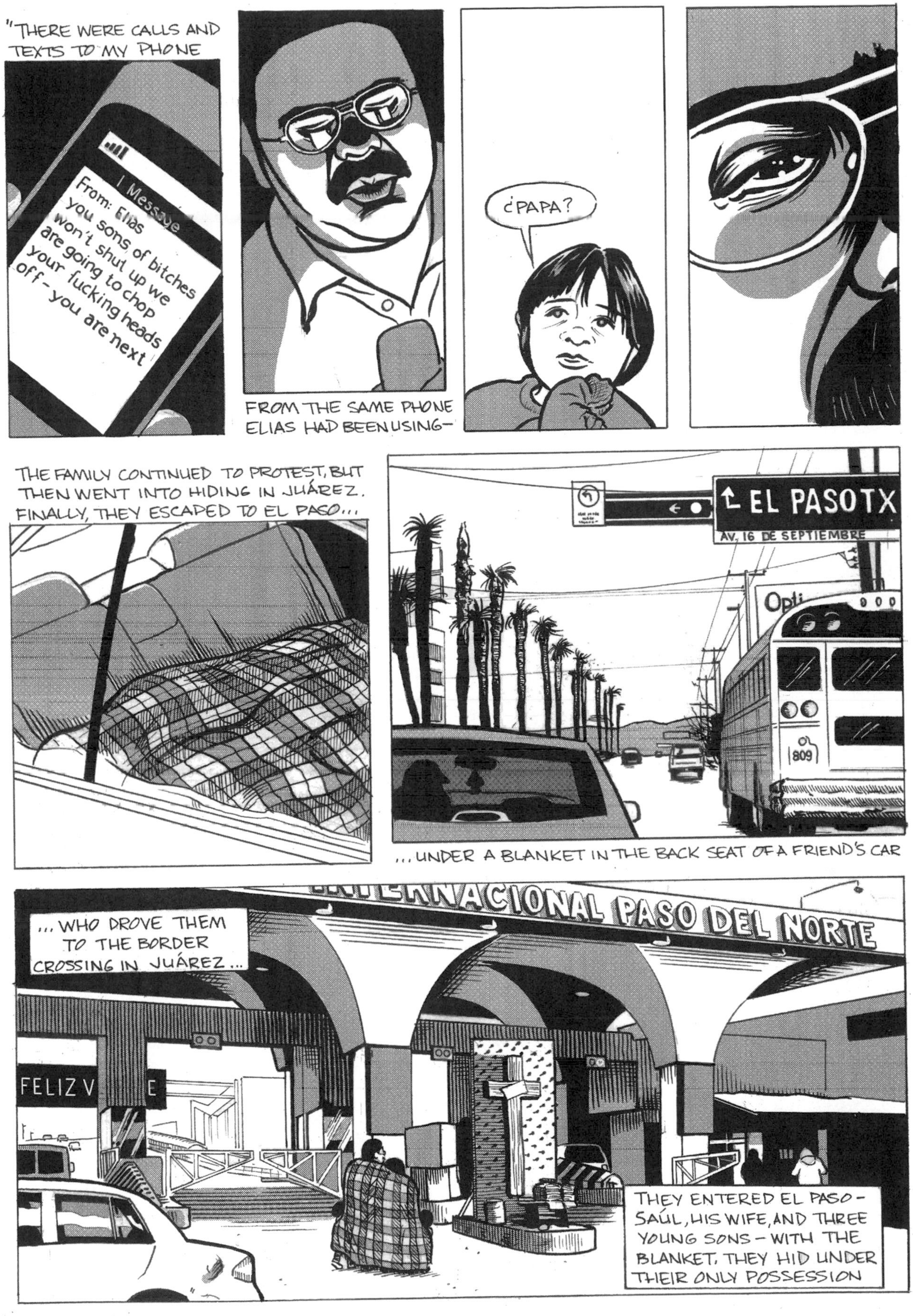
"THERE WERE CALLS AND TEXTS TO MY PHONE
1 Message
From: Elias
you sons of bitches won't shut up we are going to chop your fucking heads off - you are next
FROM THE SAME PHONE ELIAS HAD BEEN USING—
¿PAPA?
THE FAMILY CONTINUED TO PROTEST, BUT THEN WENT INTO HIDING IN JUÁREZ. FINALLY, THEY ESCAPED TO EL PASO...
EL PASO TX
AV. 16 DE SEPTIEMBRE
...UNDER A BLANKET IN THE BACK SEAT OF A FRIEND'S CAR
INTERNACIONAL PASO DEL NORTE
...WHO DROVE THEM TO THE BORDER CROSSING IN JUÁREZ...
FELIZ V E
THEY ENTERED EL PASO - SAÚL, HIS WIFE, AND THREE YOUNG SONS - WITH THE BLANKET. THEY HID UNDER THEIR ONLY POSSESSION"

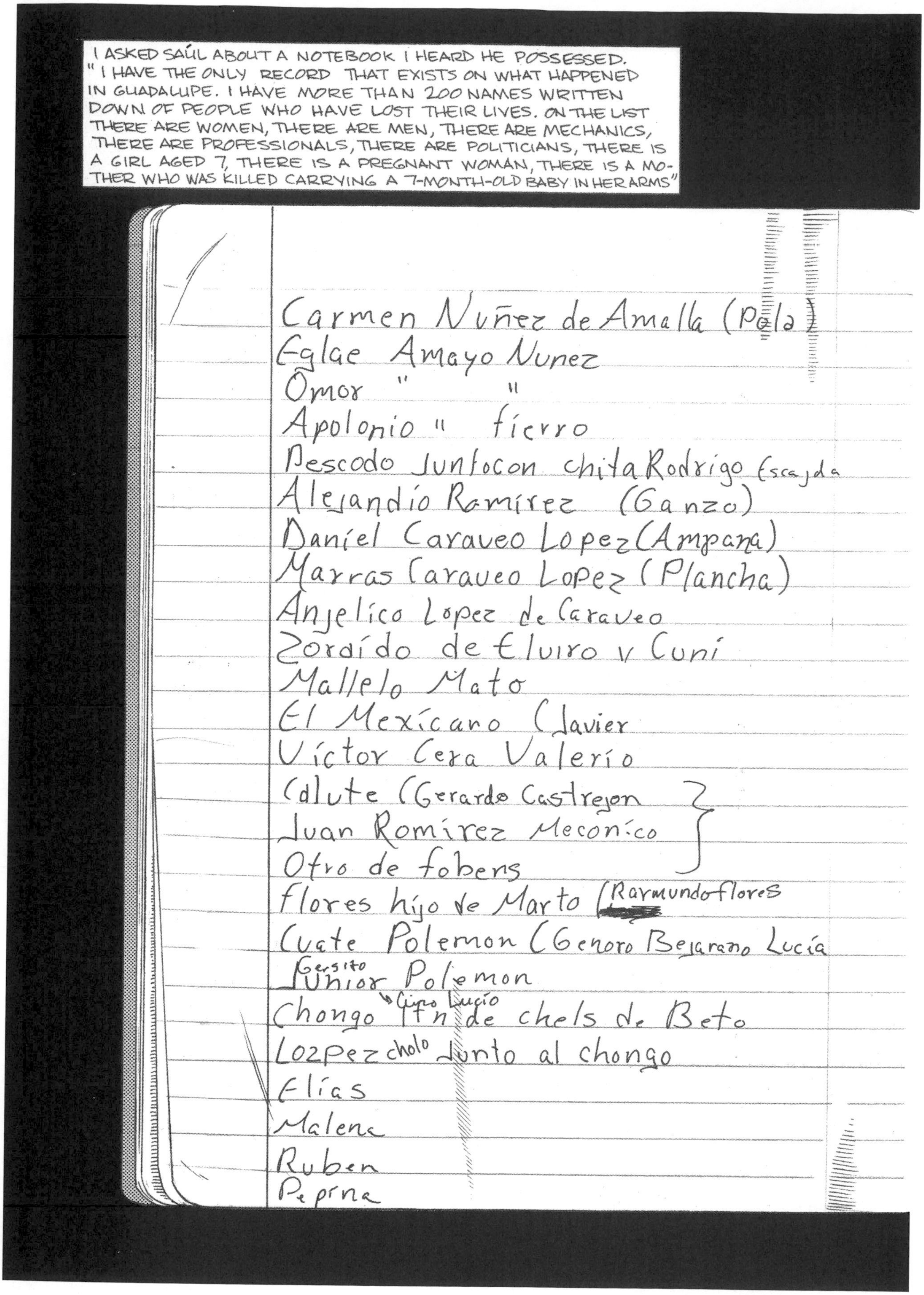
I ASKED SAÚL ABOUT A NOTEBOOK I HEARD HE POSSESSED. "I HAVE THE ONLY RECORD THAT EXISTS ON WHAT HAPPENED IN GUADALUPE. I HAVE MORE THAN 200 NAMES WRITTEN DOWN OF PEOPLE WHO HAVE LOST THEIR LIVES. ON THE LIST THERE ARE WOMEN, THERE ARE MEN, THERE ARE MECHANICS, THERE ARE PROFESSIONALS, THERE ARE POLITICIANS, THERE IS A GIRL AGED 7, THERE IS A PREGNANT WOMAN, THERE IS A MOTHER WHO WAS KILLED CARRYING A 7-MONTH-OLD BABY IN HER ARMS"
Carmen Nuñez de Amalla (Pela)
Eglae Amayo Nunez
Omor " "
Apolonio " fierro
Descodo Juntocon chita Rodrigo Escajda
Alejandio Ramirez (Ganzo)
Daniel Caraveo Lopez (Ampana)
Marras Caraveo Lopez (Plancha)
Anjelico Lopez de Caraveo
Zoraido de Eluiro y Cuni
Mallelo Mato
El Mexicano (Javier
Víctor Cera Valerio
Calute (Gerardo Castrejon
Juan Romirez Meconico
Otro de fobens
flores hijo de Marto (Rarmundoflores
Cuate Polemon (Genoro Bejarano Lucía
Gersito Junior Polemon
Chongo Giro Lucio Ifn de chels de Beto
Lozpez cholo Junto al chongo
Elías
Malena
Ruben
Pepina

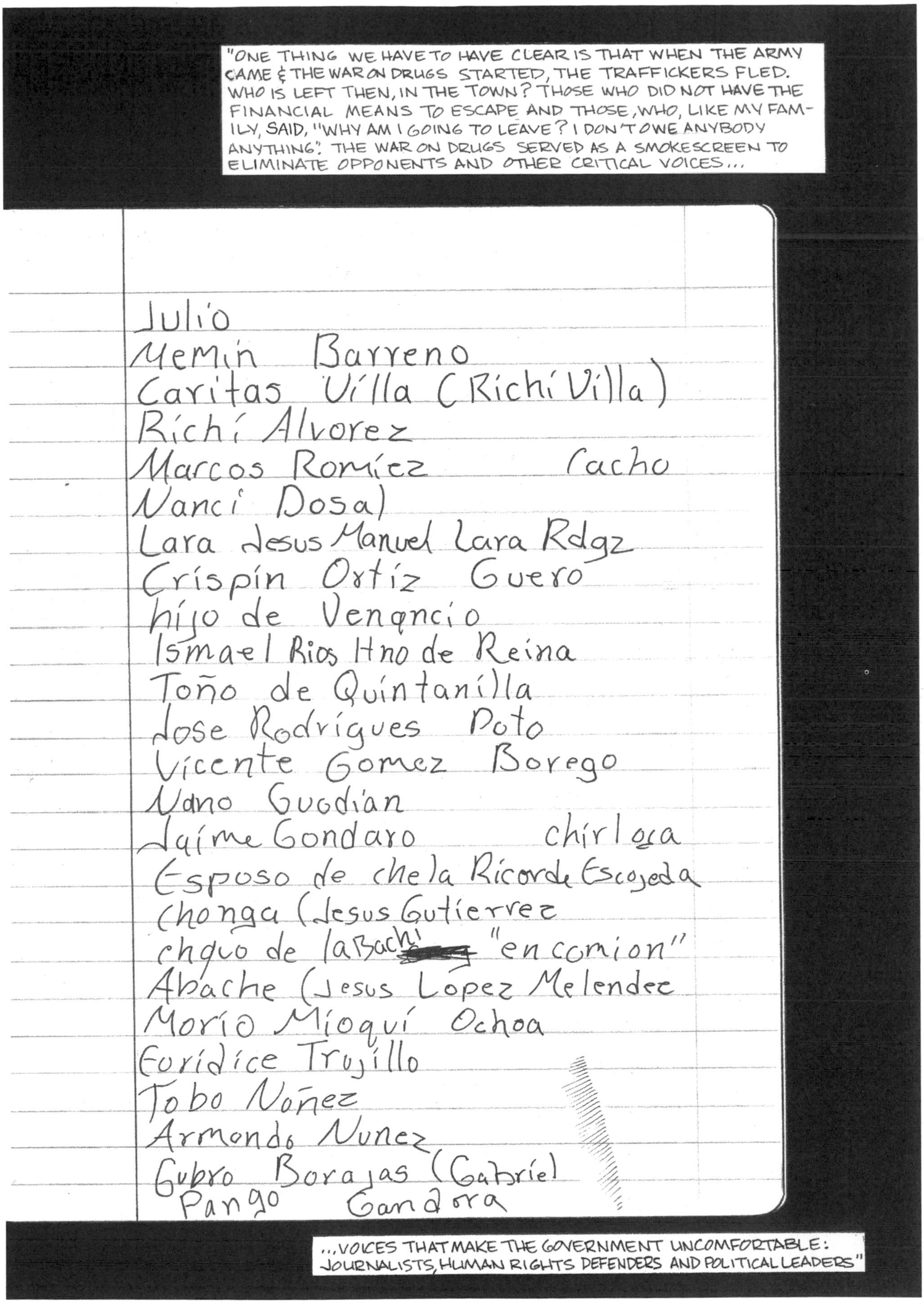
"ONE THING WE HAVE TO HAVE CLEAR IS THAT WHEN THE ARMY CAME & THE WAR ON DRUGS STARTED, THE TRAFFICKERS FLED. WHO IS LEFT THEN, IN THE TOWN? THOSE WHO DID NOT HAVE THE FINANCIAL MEANS TO ESCAPE AND THOSE, WHO, LIKE MY FAMILY, SAID, "WHY AM I GOING TO LEAVE? I DON'T OWE ANYBODY ANYTHING". THE WAR ON DRUGS SERVED AS A SMOKESCREEN TO ELIMINATE OPPONENTS AND OTHER CRITICAL VOICES...
Julio
Memin Barreno
Caritas Villa (Richi Villa)
Richi Alvorez
Marcos Romiez Cacho
Nanci Dosal
Lara Jesus Manuel Lara Rdgz
Crispin Ortiz Guero
hijo de Venancio
Ismael Rios Hno de Reina
Toño de Quintanilla
Jose Rodrigues Poto
Vicente Gomez Borego
Nano Guodian
Jaime Gondaro chirloca
Esposo de chela Ricorde Escojeda
chonga (Jesus Gutierrez
chqvo de laBachi "en comion"
Abache (Jesus Lopez Melendee
Morio Mioqui Ochoa
Euridice Trujillo
Tobo Noñez
Armondo Nunez
Gubro Borajas (Gabriel
Pango Gandora
...VOICES THAT MAKE THE GOVERNMENT UNCOMFORTABLE: JOURNALISTS, HUMAN RIGHTS DEFENDERS AND POLITICAL LEADERS"

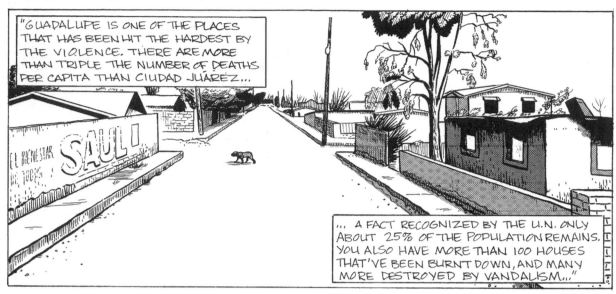

"GUADALUPE IS ONE OF THE PLACES THAT HAS BEEN HIT THE HARDEST BY THE VIOLENCE. THERE ARE MORE THAN TRIPLE THE NUMBER OF DEATHS PER CAPITA THAN CIUDAD JUÁREZ...
SAUL
... A FACT RECOGNIZED BY THE U.N. ONLY ABOUT 25% OF THE POPULATION REMAINS. YOU ALSO HAVE MORE THAN 100 HOUSES THAT'VE BEEN BURNT DOWN, AND MANY MORE DESTROYED BY VANDALISM..."
JUNE 2009
RESTAURANT TACOS TINA
TACOS TINA
Corona
APRIL 2011
RESTAURANT TACOS TINA
"GUADALUPE IS PRACTICALLY A RUIN..."
"I BELIEVE THAT FOR ALL THESE DEAD THERE WILL NEVER BE JUSTICE... NO ONE WILL BE DETAINED...
... NO ONE JAILED...
... NO ONE CONDEMNED..."
(ABOVE) MARCH 2011: 3 DEAD CITY EMPLOYEES AT THE SAME KIOSK WHERE SAÚL'S FAMILY PROTESTED IN 1998

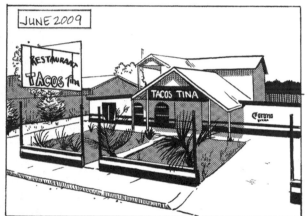

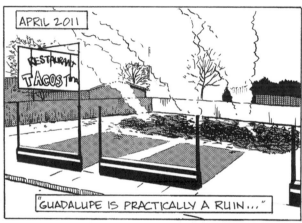

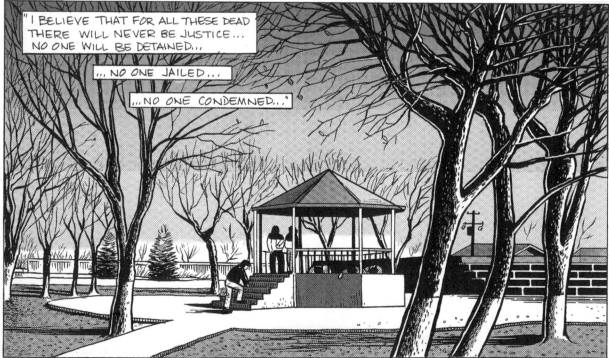

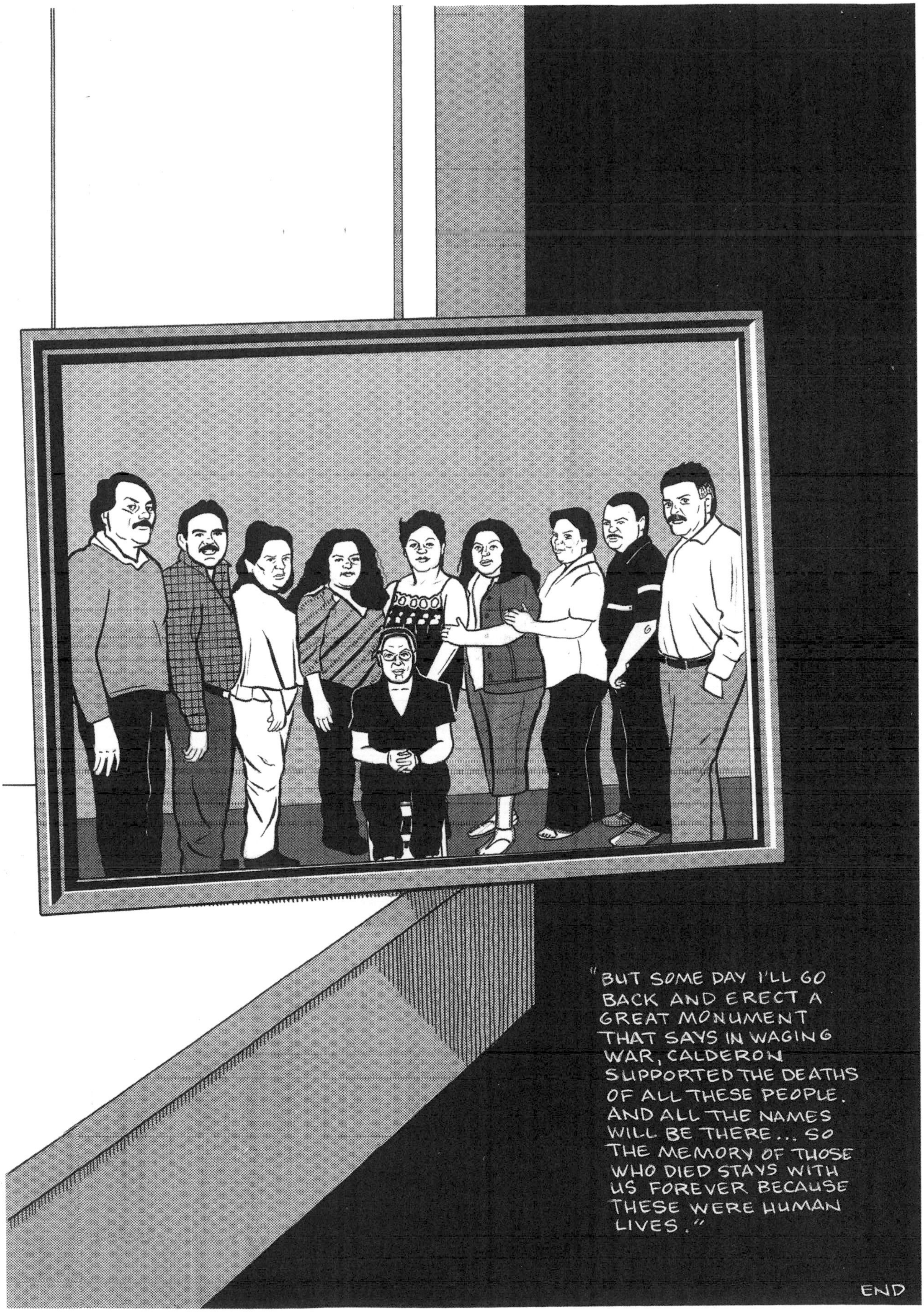
"BUT SOME DAY I'LL GO BACK AND ERECT A GREAT MONUMENT THAT SAYS IN WAGING WAR, CALDERON SUPPORTED THE DEATHS OF ALL THESE PEOPLE. AND ALL THE NAMES WILL BE THERE... SO THE MEMORY OF THOSE WHO DIED STAYS WITH US FOREVER BECAUSE THESE WERE HUMAN LIVES."
END

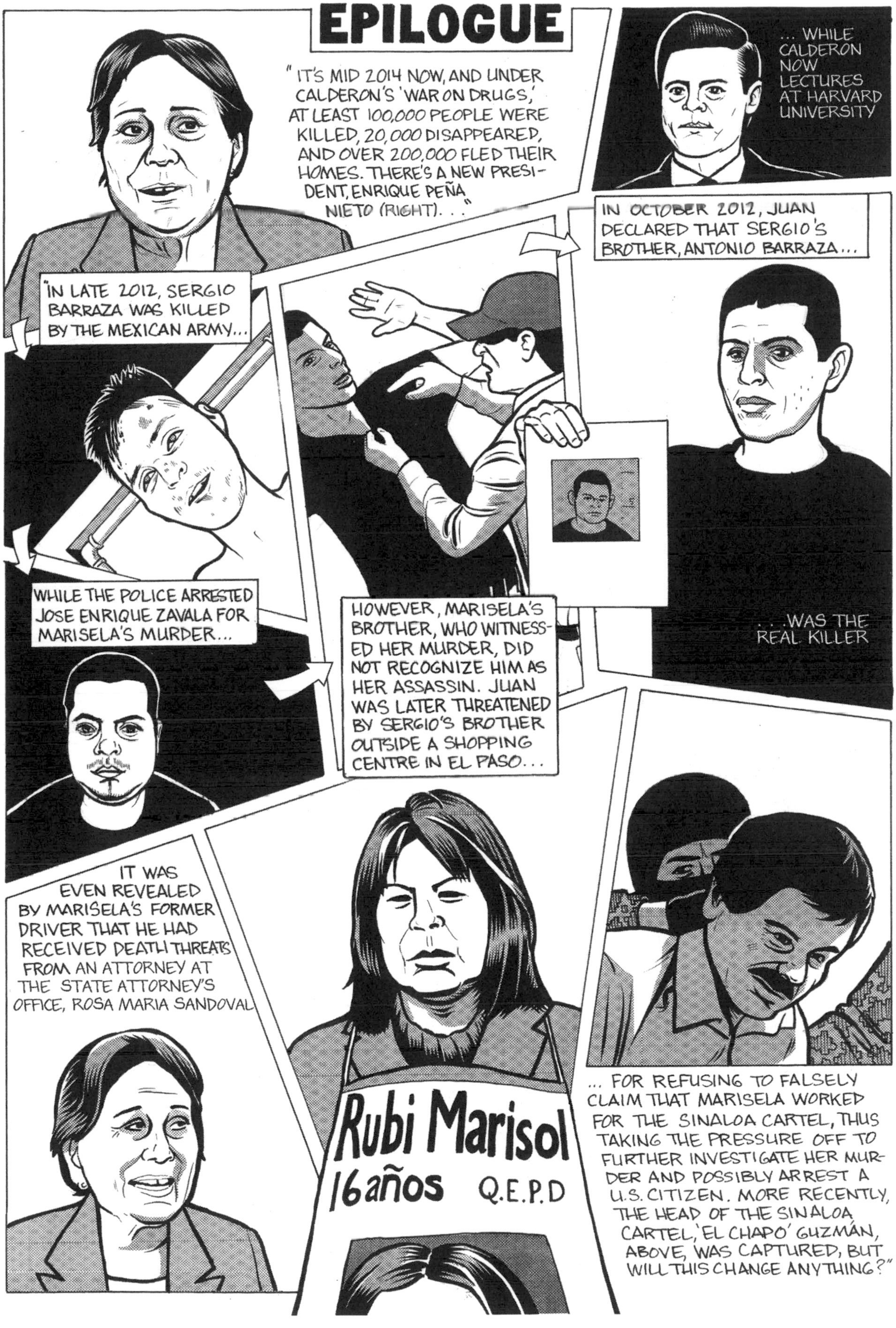
EPILOGUE
" IT'S MID 2014 NOW, AND UNDER CALDERON'S 'WAR ON DRUGS,' AT LEAST 100,000 PEOPLE WERE KILLED, 20,000 DISAPPEARED, AND OVER 200,000 FLED THEIR HOMES. THERE'S A NEW PRESIDENT, ENRIQUE PEÑA NIETO (RIGHT)..."
... WHILE CALDERON NOW LECTURES AT HARVARD UNIVERSITY
"IN LATE 2012, SERGIO BARRAZA WAS KILLED BY THE MEXICAN ARMY...
WHILE THE POLICE ARRESTED JOSE ENRIQUE ZAVALA FOR MARISELA'S MURDER...
HOWEVER, MARISELA'S BROTHER, WHO WITNESSED HER MURDER, DID NOT RECOGNIZE HIM AS HER ASSASSIN. JUAN WAS LATER THREATENED BY SERGIO'S BROTHER OUTSIDE A SHOPPING CENTRE IN EL PASO...
IN OCTOBER 2012, JUAN DECLARED THAT SERGIO'S BROTHER, ANTONIO BARRAZA...
...WAS THE REAL KILLER
IT WAS EVEN REVEALED BY MARISELA'S FORMER DRIVER THAT HE HAD RECEIVED DEATH THREATS FROM AN ATTORNEY AT THE STATE ATTORNEY'S OFFICE, ROSA MARIA SANDOVAL
Rubi Marisol
16 años Q.E.P.D
... FOR REFUSING TO FALSELY CLAIM THAT MARISELA WORKED FOR THE SINALOA CARTEL, THUS TAKING THE PRESSURE OFF TO FURTHER INVESTIGATE HER MURDER AND POSSIBLY ARREST A U.S. CITIZEN. MORE RECENTLY, THE HEAD OF THE SINALOA CARTEL, 'EL CHAPO' GUZMÁN, ABOVE, WAS CAPTURED, BUT WILL THIS CHANGE ANYTHING?"

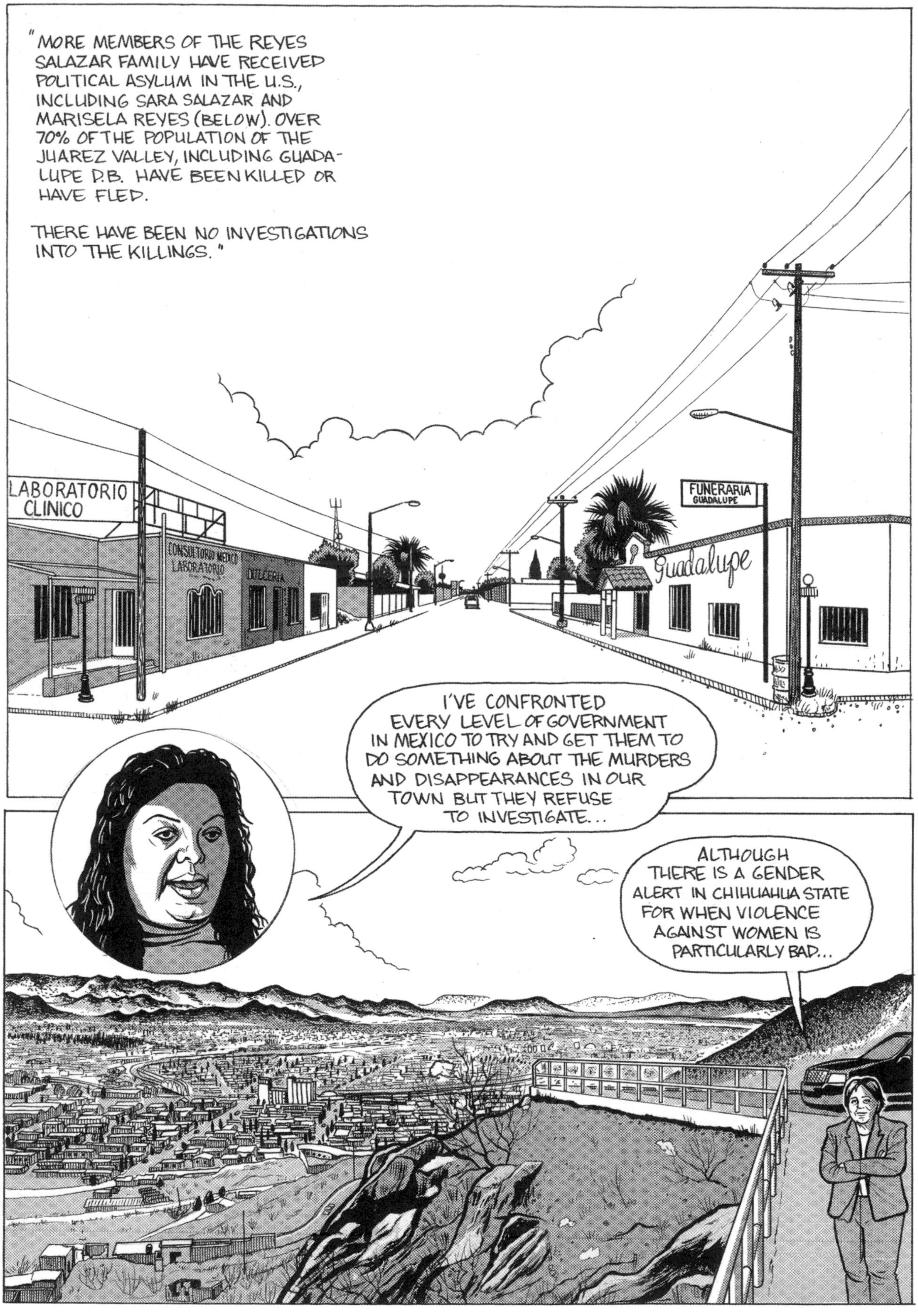
"MORE MEMBERS OF THE REYES SALAZAR FAMILY HAVE RECEIVED POLITICAL ASYLUM IN THE U.S., INCLUDING SARA SALAZAR AND MARISELA REYES (BELOW). OVER 70% OF THE POPULATION OF THE JUAREZ VALLEY, INCLUDING GUADALUPE D.B. HAVE BEEN KILLED OR HAVE FLED.
THERE HAVE BEEN NO INVESTIGATIONS INTO THE KILLINGS."
LABORATORIO CLINICO
CONSULTORIO MEDICO LABORATORIO
FUNERARIA GUADALUPE
Guadalupe
I'VE CONFRONTED EVERY LEVEL OF GOVERNMENT IN MEXICO TO TRY AND GET THEM TO DO SOMETHING ABOUT THE MURDERS AND DISAPPEARANCES IN OUR TOWN BUT THEY REFUSE TO INVESTIGATE...
ALTHOUGH THERE IS A GENDER ALERT IN CHIHUAHUA STATE FOR WHEN VIOLENCE AGAINST WOMEN IS PARTICULARLY BAD...

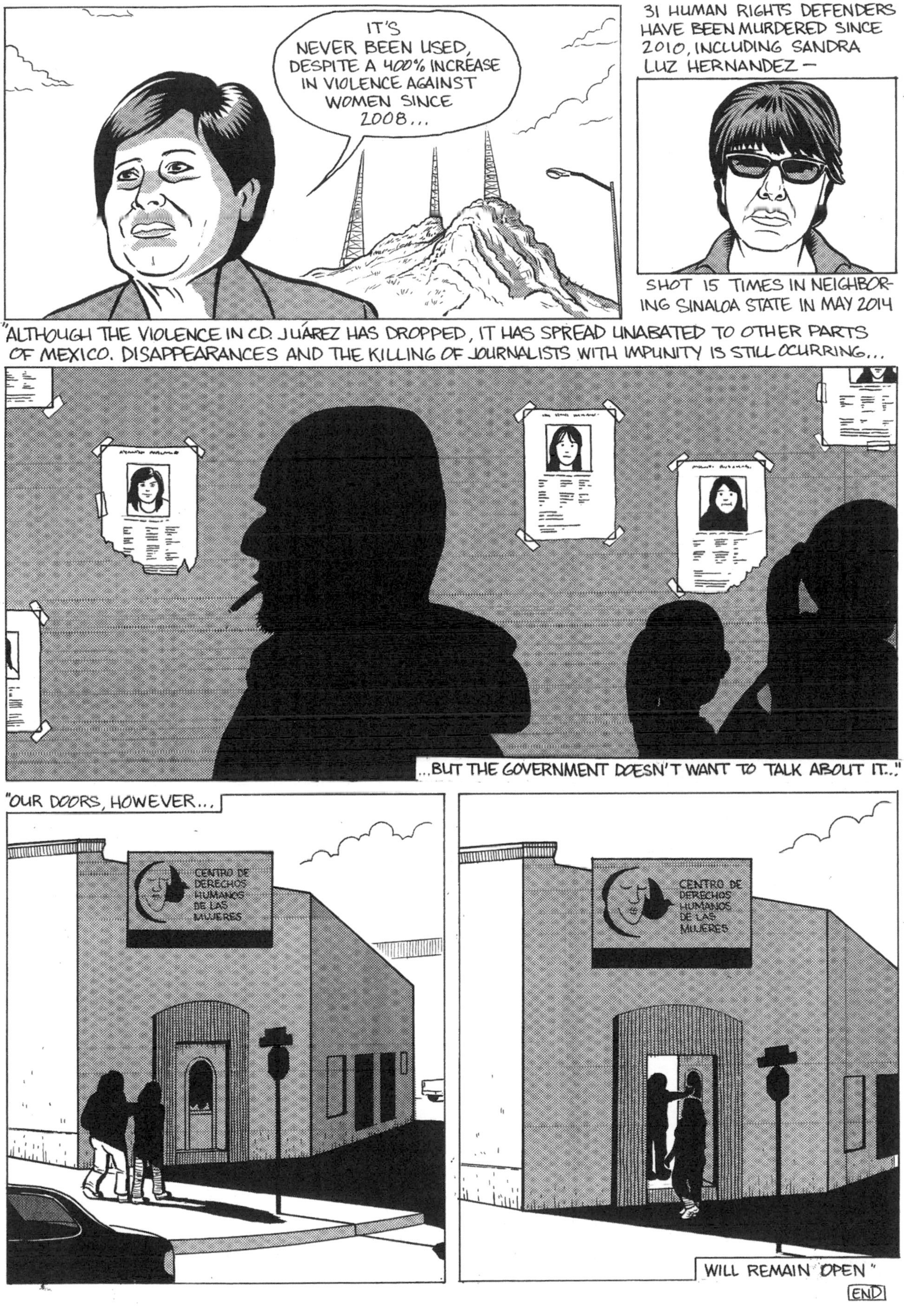
IT'S NEVER BEEN USED, DESPITE A 400% INCREASE IN VIOLENCE AGAINST WOMEN SINCE 2008...
31 HUMAN RIGHTS DEFENDERS HAVE BEEN MURDERED SINCE 2010, INCLUDING SANDRA LUZ HERNANDEZ –
SHOT 15 TIMES IN NEIGHBORING SINALOA STATE IN MAY 2014
"ALTHOUGH THE VIOLENCE IN CD. JUÁREZ HAS DROPPED, IT HAS SPREAD UNABATED TO OTHER PARTS OF MEXICO. DISAPPEARANCES AND THE KILLING OF JOURNALISTS WITH IMPUNITY IS STILL OCURRING...
...BUT THE GOVERNMENT DOESN'T WANT TO TALK ABOUT IT..."
"OUR DOORS, HOWEVER...
CENTRO DE DERECHOS HUMANOS DE LAS MUJERES
CENTRO DE DERECHOS HUMANOS DE LAS MUJERES
WILL REMAIN OPEN"
END

ABOUT LUCHA CASTRO

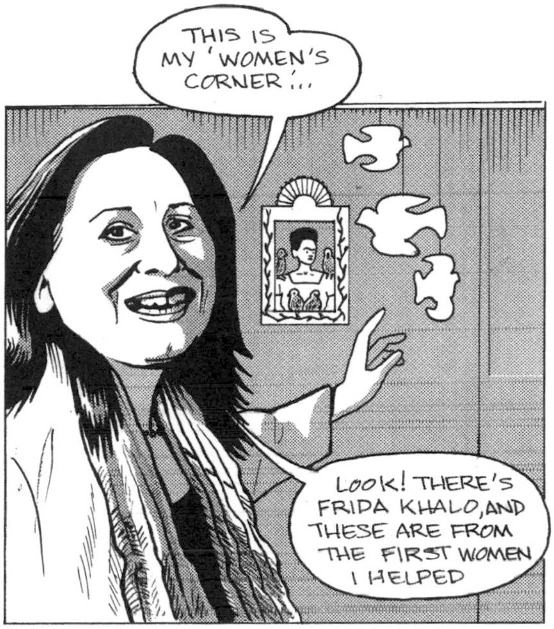
THIS IS MY 'WOMEN'S CORNER'...
LOOK! THERE'S FRIDA KHALO, AND THESE ARE FROM THE FIRST WOMEN I HELPED

Luz (Lucha) Estela Castro Rodríguez is a Mexican woman human rights defender. She has spent the last eighteen years working on cases of torture victims, femicide, enforced disappearances, trafficking, and domestic and sexual violence.

Her work focuses on strategic litigation, advocacy and the promotion of comprehensive support for women in situations of gender violence, including building their capacity to exercise their rights in court. As a lawyer, she has provided free legal representation to hundreds of women. She has also promoted change in other forms of discrimination and violence faced by women in Mexico, in particular regarding property and housing rights.

Lucha has founded several social organizations, tirelessly defended women's and human rights, and promoted women's leadership in her community and her country.

In 1994, she pioneered peaceful civil resistance in her home state in defense of families and particularly women whose heritage was at risk because of the economic crisis in Mexico. She managed to renegotiate debts with hundreds of banking institutions, thereby ensuring the housing rights of women and families. In the early 2000s, she founded—along with mothers of missing and killed women and girls in Ciudad-Juárez and Chihuahua—the organization Justice for Our Daughters, which she directed and for which, to date, she remains as the main legal adviser, providing free legal assistance to these mothers, and serving as their representative at local and international levels.

In 2005, she founded the organization Centro de Derechos Humanos de las Mujeres (Center for Human Rights of Women) in Chihuahua, which she currently directs. She is also a cofounder of the Women in Black Network in Mexico, and in 2010 cofounded the Network of Human Rights Defenders and Families of Missing People in northern Mexico.

She has been nominated for several awards, including in 2003 of the Woman of the Year award in Ciudad-Juárez, was a finalist for the Front Line Defenders Award for Human Rights Defenders at Risk in 2010, and in 2011 was distinguished by one of the most influential media outlets in Mexico as one of the one hundred women leaders in the country. In 2011 she won the International Prize for Human Rights from the Pro–Human Rights Association of Spain.

ABOUT
FRONT LINE DEFENDERS

FRONT LINE DEFENDERS

Front Line Defenders was founded in Dublin in 2001 with the specific aim of protecting human rights defenders, people who work, non-violently, for any or all of the rights enshrined in the Universal Declaration of Human Rights.

Front Line Defenders aims to address some of the security needs identified by defenders themselves, including protection, networking, training in physical and digital security, access to international bodies that can take action on their behalf, and campaigning to enhance their visibility and recognition.

Front Line Defenders provides rapid and practical support to at-risk human rights defenders, including a twenty-four-hour emergency response phone line and a rapid response grants program.

Additionally, the organization conducts research and publishes reports on the situation of human rights defenders in specific countries, contributes to the mandate of the UN Special Rapporteur on the Situation of Human Rights Defenders, and submits to the Universal Periodic Review process at the UN Human Rights Council.

Human Rights Defenders are most at risk when their work as key agents of social change threatens the positions of the rich and powerful who have vested interests in maintaining the status quo. Ranging from legal action and harassment from governments to physical violence from state and non-state actors, human rights defenders find themselves at risk often without many resources for their protection or recourse for accountability and justice.

MEXICO

For many years, Mexico has ranked among the most dangerous countries in the world in which to work as a human rights defender. Gender-based violence has claimed an astounding number of female victims, and women who seek justice and accountability or who advocate for women's rights find themselves targets of powerful forces in the country. The cities of Juárez and Chihuahua have become known around the world for the phenomenon of femicide—the killing of women because they are women. And yet, for decades, women human rights defenders have been at the forefront of the struggle for human rights in Mexico.

In Chihuahua state, corruption and criminality among the security forces has contributed to an environment of total risk. In 2013, Chihuahua was once again Mexico's most violent state, with a murder rate of almost one every hour. According to the Mesoamerican Initiative of Women Human Rights Defenders, between 2010 and 2012 twenty-five women were killed in Mexico because of their work as human rights defenders. Simply gathering data about violence can be dangerous. The Mesoamerican Initiative also notes:

"Violence against women human rights defenders is indicative of how violence against women works to maintain unequal power relations, perpetuate privilege, and prevent or discourage the political participation of more than half of humanity."

THE CENTRO DE DERECHOS HUMANOS DE LAS MUJERES

The Centro de Derechos Humanos de las Mujeres (Center for the Human Rights of Women) was established in 2005 in response to the violence against women in Chihuahua. At the time, the "war on drugs" was at its height, yet violence against civilians, notably women, had reached unprecedented proportions—not just in Mexico, but the world. Luz Estrela (Lucha)

Castro, a lawyer, and her friends and colleagues Gabino and Alma Gomez, established the Center to seek justice and accountability for the victims of the violence, and to put the rights of women on the agenda of the authorities by challenging them—not just in cases of violence, but also in terms of property and housing rights, domestic issues, virtually all forms of discrimination and violence faced by women.

Front Line Defenders has conducted advocacy for Lucha and her colleagues, who have faced a break-in at their offices, death threats and attempts to discredit them and their work. As leading women human rights defenders in the dangerous environment of northern Mexico, they are exposed to risks from numerous sources, including corrupt military and police, armed groups, narcotraffickers and criminal elements.

THIS BOOK

This graphic novel is the first in a series featuring human rights defenders at risk around the world. It is the hope of Front Line Defenders that this book will help generate a greater awareness of the risks faced not only by women human rights defenders in northern Mexico, but human rights defenders in general.

ABOUT THE CREATORS

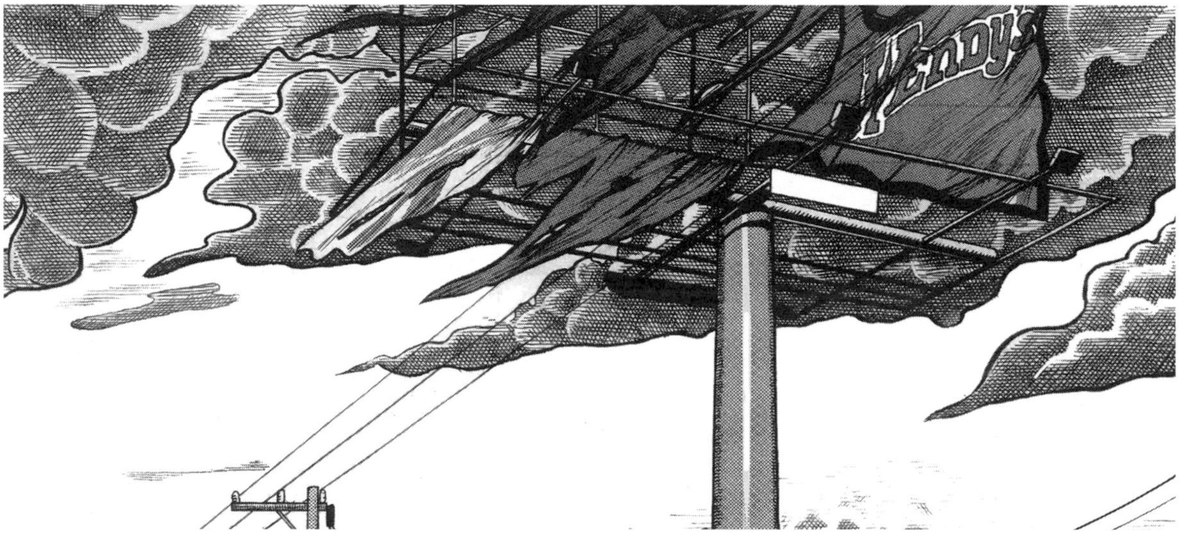
Wendy's

JON SACK is an artist, writer and activist based in the US and UK. He completed an MFA at Goldsmiths College in 2006 and has exhibited in the US and UK. He has published comics about the history of oil in Iraq, the blockade of Gaza and the plight of Syrian refugees in Turkey. His work has appeared in the Daily Star (Lebanon), the Mail and Guardian (South Africa), Red Pepper magazine (UK), and Beyond Borders (Pavement Books, 2012, edited by John Hutnyk).

ADAM SHAPIRO is Head of Campaigns at Front Line Defenders, an Irish international human rights organization. At Front Line Defenders, his work involves innovative campaigns to raise the profiles of human rights defenders at risk, including the development of a monthly web-based video documentary series, Multiple Exposure. Adam is also a documentary filmmaker and human rights activist.